PARTNERING WITH *Nature* IN EARLY CHILDHOOD

A GUIDE TO *Outdoor Experiences*

PATTI ENSEL BAILIE, PhD, AND CATHERINE KOONS-HUBBARD, MEd

COPYRIGHT

© 2022 Patti Ensel Bailie and Catherine Koons Hubbard

Published by Gryphon House, Inc.
P. O. Box 10, Lewisville, NC 27023
800.638.0928; 877.638.7576 [fax]
Visit us on the web at www.gryphonhouse.com.

All rights reserved. No part of this publication may be reproduced or transmitted in any form or by any means, electronic or technical, including photocopy, recording, or any information storage or retrieval system, without prior written permission of the publisher. Printed in the United States. Every effort has been made to locate copyright and permission information.

Cover images and interior images used under license from Shutterstock.com and courtesy of the authors.

Library of Congress Control Number: 2022934214

BULK PURCHASE

Gryphon House books are available for special premiums and sales promotions as well as for fund-raising use. Special editions or book excerpts also can be created to specifications. For details, call 800.638.0928.

DISCLAIMER

Gryphon House, Inc., cannot be held responsible for damage, mishap, or injury incurred during the use of or because of activities in this book. Appropriate and reasonable caution and adult supervision of children involved in activities and corresponding to the age and capability of each child involved are recommended at all times. Do not leave children unattended at any time. Observe safety and caution at all times.

PARTNERING WITH *Nature* IN EARLY CHILDHOOD EDUCATION

DEDICATION

To Anya and Rowen,
our spirited nature child and grandchild,
may you find peace and joy in nature always.

Table of Contents

Acknowledgments vii

Introduction ix

CHAPTER ONE: Making the Case for Nature and Play in an Early Childhood Curriculum 1

CHAPTER TWO: Creating a Nature-Based Classroom 19

CHAPTER THREE: Teaching with Intention 43

CHAPTER FOUR: Putting Intention into Practice 85

CHAPTER FIVE: The Nature-Based Curriculum in Autumn 107

CHAPTER SIX: The Nature-Based Curriculum in Winter 149

CHAPTER SEVEN: The Nature-Based Curriculum in Spring 185

CHAPTER EIGHT: Challenges and Inspiration 237

Epilogue: Partnering with Nature 273

Appendix A: Recommended Books to Share with Children 275

Appendix B: Assessment Tool for a Nature-Based Early Childhood Curriculum 279

References 301

Index 307

ACKNOWLEDGMENTS

Foremost, thank you to all of the preschool teachers, past and present, at Schlitz Audubon Nature Center for your inspiration, your ideas, and your insight. Our nature-based curriculum was literally developed in the field (and forest) under your care and guidance. Thank you for the creativity, compassion, and joy that you carry with you into the classroom, for the depths of your dedication (even on days that require waterproof gear and an extra set of mittens), and for making it your mission to teach in partnership with nature.

Particular gratitude goes to Lorna Hilyard, who developed many of the original chapters in this book when it was an internal document used solely by our teachers. Without her initial framework and content, the book in its current form would never have existed. Thank you for preparing the soil, Lorna, and for planting those first spring bulbs!

Deep appreciation as well to the many wonderful photographers who contributed to this book, and to the generous families who gave permission for their child's image to be included. Thanks in particular to Collette Jarvela-Kuhnen, who took so many of the photographs we used and who once explained that she wanted the pictures she took of all her classes "to tell a story."

Thank you to the preschool's founding executive director, Elizabeth Cheek, who, in 2002, announced to the board of directors that Schlitz Audubon Nature Center needed its own nature preschool. Thank you to our executive director, Helen Boomsma, who has been an avid supporter of this book and who continues to champion the nature preschool as we prepare to enter our twentieth year.

Thank you to Laurie Lukaszieweicz, who makes every child feel they are the most important and best part of her day. Thank you, Laurie, for sharing with us the Irish word *tenalach*, which means "to connect to the land, air, and water so deeply that you can hear the Earth sing."

Thank you to Deborah Schein for reviewing the intentions and sharing her ideas, and to Heather Bowen for providing feedback as she piloted some of the initial drafts of the curriculum.

A special nod to our friends and colleagues at Natural Start Alliance, WiNBECA, WiNACC, Inside-Outside, and the growing regional organizations across the country devoted to the mission of nature-based early childhood education. We are so honored to do this work alongside you.

Thank you to Bob Bailie and John Hubbard, loving and supportive husbands, who would probably agree that writing a book about nature preschool is a whole lot calmer and far more solitary than actually running a nature preschool—but that there are also fewer funny stories to recount at the end of each day.

Thank you to Stephanie Roselli for saying yes to this project and for guiding us with grace and patience through this entire process.

Thank you to the incredibly thoughtful, detail-oriented Marcella Fecteau Weiner, who took four hundred pages of our ideas and helped unify them into one voice.

And finally, an enormous thank you to the many hundreds of children and families who, since 2003, have filled our nature preschool with stories, laughter, tears, and mud pies: without you, the halls in the preschool would be spotless, but the pages in this book would be blank.

INTRODUCTION

Partnering with Nature in Early Childhood Education is a practical guide to creating a nature-based curriculum for young children. It draws its ideas from nearly twenty years of nature-based early childhood programming at the Schlitz Audubon Nature Preschool in Milwaukee, Wisconsin. This book is created as a resource for anyone interested in a high-quality nature-based preschool curriculum. It can support new programs that are just starting up and those hoping to infuse more nature into already existing classrooms. It is written for educators, by educators, and it turns theoretical ideas about the benefits of nature in childhood into achievable results.

The Schlitz Audubon Nature Center is located just north of downtown Milwaukee on a bluff overlooking Lake Michigan. It features 185 acres of forest, prairie, wetland, and ponds. Our mission is to provide a high-quality early childhood environment that will meet young children's developmental needs while initiating them into a lifelong, meaningful relationship with the natural world. Although many of our nature activities seem place-specific, we recognize that most early childhood programs may not have equal access to nature. For this reason, we make a point of including ways to explore nature in a variety of settings, including neighborhoods that seem at first glance to have no natural spaces. We believe that for very young children, a single tree can be as meaningful as an entire forest. A dandelion growing through a crack in the sidewalk is as worthy of attention as a field of flowers. We have collaborated for more than a decade now with two urban preschools in central Milwaukee that serve families whose incomes are below the federal poverty level, and we know firsthand that, with the right mix of understanding and communication, it is possible to create meaningful nature experiences for children everywhere.

For those programs that do have access to a natural area—a city park, a school playground with a small patch of green space—we discuss how to safely and effectively take children outdoors to explore the world beyond the four-walled classroom. We include a list of essential items to carry and discuss challenging weather and bathroom concerns. Our goal is to make *Partnering with Nature in Early Childhood Education* a useful guide while trusting in the creativity and capability of educators to adjust for their specific programs as needed.

Our decision to publish this book comes from a growing national interest in nature-based education in the preschool years. Teachers and directors from across the country regularly contact our school requesting our curriculum. As new nature preschools and forest kindergartens continue to open each year, it is clear that this practical, inclusive curriculum is needed, as it not only talks through daily activities but also shows teachers how nature can support state-mandated standards. We include an assessment tool designed with these standards in mind.

We have organized this book into eight chapters, as follows:

- **Chapter One: Making the Case for Nature and Play in an Early Childhood Curriculum**
  In this opening chapter, we make the case that nature-based play is an essential part of early childhood development. Playing in nature provides children with opportunities to create and problem solve in a stimulating, ever-changing environment. Nature play strengthens social skills and communication. It exercises fine motor skills. And it allows children to develop confidence and self-efficacy, enabling them to encounter new experiences and potential challenges knowing they have the skills to succeed.

- **Chapter Two: Creating a Nature-Based Classroom**
  This chapter demonstrates simple approaches to creating a classroom infused with nature, such as adding potted plants, photographs, and pine cones; constructing campfire circles; and setting up a terrarium or toad habitat. We look at ways to add natural materials to already existing art areas, sensory tables, blocks, and dramatic play zones. We also discuss the purpose of each area and the role of the teacher as children move from space to space, exploring and experimenting. We describe the outdoor classrooms and how these spaces evolve and change over time. The chapter ends with a discussion on licensing and meeting state-mandated regulations.

- **Chapter Three: Teaching with Intention**
  This chapter covers what we consider the most fundamental and important part of our nature-based curriculum: our teaching intentions. We consider these to be the foundation of our program and our approach to assessment. Teaching intentions differ from activities or lesson plans. Our intentions include creating a sense of community in the classroom, developing environmental awareness, encouraging independence, learning to value the ideas of others, developing empathy, and building an awareness of other cultures, all while developing a sense of responsibility and compassion toward nature. We see these as the underlying themes that inform our entire program.

- **Chapter Four: Putting Intention into Practice**
  For early childhood teachers who are new to nature-based education, this chapter is a helpful guide that will allow them to venture forward with confidence. It includes a sample class schedule, advice on the fundamentals of hiking with children, a list of what to include in a backpack, an outline of seasonal topics, and seasonal activities at a glance.

- **Chapters Five-Seven: Nature-Based Curricula in Autumn, Winter, and Spring**
  These chapters provide examples of seasonal topics and activities that link our intentions to our daily practice. Each section includes general concepts about the seasonal topic; a discussion of how to explore that topic outdoors; and ideas for art and science activities, sensory and discovery tables, and group-time opportunities.

A NOTE ABOUT SEASONAL TOPICS AND ACTIVITIES

> At our nature preschool, the four seasons are the backbone of our curriculum, and we observe certain calendar events, such as the winter solstice, with gatherings and celebrations. Because Wisconsin is in the temperate zone, we experience spring, summer, autumn, and winter with noticeable differences in light, temperature, flora, and fauna.
>
> We recognize that not everyone lives in the northern United States. We tend to experience our coldest days in January and February, but we understand that in other parts of the world the coldest days may fall in July. We also understand that some programs may never experience winter the way we understand it and have no use for our snow activities. While you may not have snow where you live, you most likely have a season of rest. Likewise, you may not have sugar maple trees, but you almost certainly have edible plants and local flora with a rich cultural history. You may not have your mud season in March and April, but you almost certainly have a mud season. We know that educators are adaptable enough to transpose these activities to work with their own seasons and climates, just as they take other teaching ideas and reconfigure them to their individual classrooms.

- **Chapter Eight: Challenges and Inspiration**
  This chapter addresses some of the ongoing challenges that come with teaching outdoors, including how to hike with children who walk and explore at different paces (the "runners" versus the "seed counters"); managing bathroom needs when far from a building (one of our most common questions); handling inadequate clothing, threatening weather, and safety; dealing with emergencies; and balancing free play with more focused learning. We also address COVID-19, which introduced a new set of challenges. In an interesting twist, this health crisis pushed us to move outdoors even more and to replace some of our most beloved preschool traditions with new ones. With each new decision, rather than feeling only the loss we expected, we have gained. We end the chapter with a hard look inward, noting that there is still a lot of work to do when it comes to providing nature-based programs for children of diverse needs and backgrounds. We highlight a number of outstanding programs across the country that are leading the way toward greater inclusion, and we discuss our a long-running partnership with two urban preschools in Milwaukee.
- **Appendix A** offers a list of recommended books about nature to share with children. **Appendix B** features our Nature-Based Early Childhood Assessment Tool.

INTRODUCTION

We conclude the book with this seemingly simple but often misunderstood idea: Nature is not simply *what* we teach. Nature is *how* we teach. It is our mentor. Nature reminds us to slow down, embrace the quiet in-between moments, and focus on our deeper intentions. It inspires us to find the courage and the strength we need in difficult moments. Nature, if we let it, can encourage us to become better educators by allowing us to feel more fulfilled and more at peace as human beings. That, we believe, is the greatest gift that comes from partnering with nature—and what *Partnering with Nature in Early Childhood Education* is all about.

INTRODUCTION

- CHAPTER ONE -

Making the Case for Nature and Play in an Early Childhood Curriculum

Play is often talked about as if it were a relief from serious learning. But for children, play is serious learning. Play is really the work of childhood.

— Fred Rogers

Imagine a classroom where there is moss on the floor, sky for a ceiling, and walls made out of towering pines. Imagine a room that is always changing, perhaps cool and sunny one day and warm and rainy the next. In place of indoor art time, the children take watercolor paints to a spot near the edge of a shallow pond. Instead of a sheet of math problems, they measure eight-foot-high sunflowers or subtract water from sap as they cook down maple syrup.

With nature as our teaching partner, the classroom expands beyond its usual four walls to include the natural world, whether it be shoreline, prairie, or the neighborhood sidewalk. Partnering with nature provides teachers with almost endless opportunities to educate and fascinate. Whether we're exploring amphibian life cycles, bird migration, autumn leaves, or the hidden world beneath a rotting log, nature allows us to explore and engage with our students in a classroom that is always in flux. Taking a group of children outdoors does not come risk-free, but, despite the risks (or perhaps because of them), the benefits of outdoor exploration are powerful and lasting.

In this first chapter, we make the case for an early childhood education that's based on nature and play. First, we briefly describe the history of nature in early childhood education. We then look at the skills and dispositions young children develop by being in nature. Finally, we discuss how high-quality nature programs support children's play and learning, prepare them for later schooling, positively affect their brain development, and foster a sense of spirituality and wonder.

THE HISTORY OF NATURE IN EARLY CHILDHOOD EDUCATION

Although there has been a rapid rise in the number of nature-based early childhood programs throughout North America in the past decade, taking children outdoors to learn is hardly a new idea. In the early 1800s, Friedrich Fröbel, the father of kindergarten, provided garden plots for young children to cultivate (Morrison, 2001). Maria Montessori, in the early 1900s, also provided opportunities for children to cultivate gardens, and she connected nature education with the natural development of the child (Montessori, 1912). Rudolf Steiner, who started the Waldorf School in 1919, created classrooms that included natural materials and celebrated the seasons. The time spent playing with these materials formed a foundation for scientific understanding, engendering a sense of responsibility for the natural world (Schwartz, 2009). Following World War II, the schools of Reggio Emilia emphasized the importance of environments as the third teacher (after the parent and the classroom teacher) and pushed for classrooms with natural light and ready access to nature (Edwards, Gandini, and Forman, 1998). Historically, nature education has been a key part of preschool and kindergarten curricula, providing authentic experiences for young children, especially for learning through the senses (Bailie, 2016).

Although nature education has been a fundamental part of early childhood education, following the World Wars and the launch of Sputnik, academic instruction took on more importance in the primary grades. Early childhood programs often sacrificed nature education to prepare children for this higher level of academics (Elkind, 1986). Although children who are encouraged to read at an early age often outperform their peers—at least in terms of test scores—they rarely maintain this advantage beyond kindergarten or first grade. As the years go by, these same children tend to express frustration with school, having never learned to enjoy the actual process of learning, which should have begun with play (Gray, 2013).

In recent years, kindergarten teachers have noted that, for the first time in memory, children are entering elementary school lacking the necessary hand strength and fine motor skills to hold a pencil properly, use scissors, or control a bottle of glue. While these children can cut and paste on a screen easily enough, they lack the coordination to do so in real life. Researchers attribute this decline in fine motor skills at least in part to a dramatic decrease in simple, unstructured outdoor play (Marselas, 2015).

Research backs up what many early childhood educators have known for years—there is a direct link between physical activity and early childhood brain development (Jensen, 2013; Medina, 2014). When you restrict a child's access to movement, you create a developmental delay that should not exist. Early childhood educators often find themselves at odds with a system that emphasizes unrealistic standards, such as reading before children complete kindergarten, and worksheets in place of real experiences. We are left with children who are being asked to perform tasks for which they are physically and mentally unequipped, a reality that many families are starting to resist.

Those of us fortunate enough to teach in schools that support and encourage nature-based play see firsthand the powerful and lasting developmental strides that our students make when allowed to run, climb, touch, and learn in an outdoor setting. At the Schlitz Audubon Nature Center Preschool, we simply do not believe that a worksheet is as valuable as following a stream of water through the woods, down a ravine, over a waterfall, and into a lake. The former is a sedentary and often abstract exercise that holds little meaning for the child. In contrast, the latter incorporates adventure and discovery, large motor skills, curiosity, a sense of place, and scientific concepts such as gravity and the water cycle.

Of course, we understand that most preschool programs do not have access to hills, rivers, forests, or ravines. Yet, authentic experiences can be had with a single tree, dandelion, or patch of sky. And the impact that exploration and play have on children's development is enormous.

NATURE AND THE DEVELOPMENT OF SKILLS AND DISPOSITIONS

A growing body of research supports the benefits of nature-based education on the developmental domains of early childhood for developing motor skills (Fjørtoft, 2001), decreasing symptoms of attention deficit disorder (Di Carmine and Berto, 2021; Faber Taylor and Kuo, 2011), and increasing resilience (Ernst, Juckett, Sobel, 2021). However, we do not intend to repeat the full extent of that research in this book. Much of what we know about the benefits comes from our twenty years of experience working with young children in the natural world. Therefore, we know that a high-quality nature-based program can—and should—support the following skills and dispositions:

Curiosity: Spending time in nature encourages children to notice their surroundings. The natural world is filled with things to pick up, lift, catch, hold, and release. There are animal tracks to follow, storm clouds to monitor, puddles to jump in, and new discoveries around every bend. Teachers provide opportunities for their students to collect and display objects from nature (always taking care to differentiate between what is appropriate to collect, such as a pine cone or an empty shell, and what is not, such as bird eggs or a shell that houses a living creature). When children have opportunities to share what they find with others, to ask questions, and to celebrate their discoveries, their curiosity grows.

Observation skills: In a nature-based program, children spend time exploring sensory-rich natural environments that are constantly changing. They develop observation skills by noticing changing details in the environment and ignoring those that remain constant. We provide them with tools to support their observations, such as magnifying glasses and binoculars, which help children notice changes such as birds flying or plants sprouting. Observation helps a child develop *ecoliteracy*, the understanding of natural systems that support life on Earth. An observant child will soon be able to identify a red-winged blackbird, a swallowtail butterfly, and even poison

CHAPTER ONE: MAKING THE CASE FOR NATURE AND PLAY IN AN EARLY CHILDHOOD CURRICULUM

ivy and will begin to understand the connections among all forms of life in an ecosystem. Such knowledge helps develop confidence, sustainable practices, and a foundation for future academic learning.

Sensory experiences: Young children derive nearly all of their information through sensorimotor experiences. The more comfortable children are in using their senses to make discoveries, the more they will gain from each new experience. Teachers support sensory-based experiences by encouraging children to touch a worm or hold a frog (and by being willing to do so themselves). Using positive language when describing sensory experiences such as walking in mud or going out in the rain encourages nature-based investigation through observing, handling, listening, smelling, and even tasting (when appropriate). Activities that encourage the senses include touching trees, moss, and water; taking color hikes or listening walks; and growing herb gardens and smelling the plants and soil in different seasons. Stepping outside is a sensory experience.

Ecological identity and understanding of self: Teachers encourage a child's understanding of self and of the natural world by visiting the same tree or pond in several seasons, comparing each visit with the one before. Repeat visits help children draw on their memories of past experiences of a place. Opportunities to walk the local landscape, learn the names of the flora and fauna in the area, and grasp the local environment through the senses help children to determine their own place in the natural world. These activities can support children's development of an ecological identity (Pelo, 2013).

Experimentation and critical-thinking skills: Children develop confidence in their ability to make predictions and strengthen their understanding of cause and effect as they experience natural phenomena. Teachers encourage experimentation by bringing attention to children's actions and the resulting effects. They also provide activities specifically designed to promote predictions, experiments, and conclusions. For example, at our preschool, we often try to predict the size of the waves on Lake Michigan. We listen for the sound of the water from a distance, observe the strength and speed of wind, and even note the air temperature. The children may start the year not understanding that these factors are connected, but over time they recognize the links. After several months, the children have an excellent sense, even before they arrive at the beach, of how loud, high, quiet, or still the waves will be. They are learning critical-thinking skills, and they are learning to make guesses based on evidence rather than waiting for the answer.

Communication skills: Language includes reading, writing, talking, and listening. Because young children are in the process of learning to communicate orally, it is important that teachers speak with children, individually and in both small- and large-group settings, every day about their experiences in nature. They should use scientific language in these discussions (for example, saying *cardinal* rather than "red bird" and *migration* rather than "flying away"). Reading stories with nature themes encourages children to look for books about nature on their own. Teachers encourage children to take photographs and to draw pictures of their experiences in nature. Meanwhile, the teachers use a camera to document children playing and exploring, later sharing the images with the children to spark further conversations.

Beginning attempts to communicate about nature in writing and drawing are also valuable. Teachers can introduce children to the concept of writing by allowing them to handle and experiment with different writing tools such as feathers in paint, sticks in sand, and pieces of charcoal on wood. Young children can then simply play with different writing implements and designs before gradually learning to form letters.

Several of our teachers have documented the words and phrases children use on the trails while in the midst of an observation. While watching a controlled prairie burn, for example, a teacher recorded children saying *smoke, crackle, fireplace,* "sounds like popcorn popping," *stinging eyes, white smoke,* and "black ash in the air like snowflakes falling." Later, she transcribed these words and phrases onto paper and showed the parents these wonderful examples of child communication, which is often far more astute and poetic than we may realize in the moment. Communication is a part of literacy. We sometimes prioritize learning to read and write while failing to honor and appreciate the importance of children sharing their own stories aloud.

Large motor skills: Large motor activities in a natural environment include hiking and walking on uneven surfaces, running, climbing, jumping, digging, boot-skating on ice, lifting, pulling, raking, and heavy work such as hauling water and rocks. These types of activities challenge children to take manageable risks and help them learn self-regulation and ways to be safe with their bodies. Activities such as sweeping tall grasses with insect nets involve crossing the body's midline, which promotes brain development. Playing actively in nature also helps children build stamina throughout the year, provides a noncompetitive atmosphere in which to develop physical skills and eye-hand coordination, and gives children a sense of accomplishment.

Fine motor skills: Fine motor activities are abundant in nature play. When children shuck corn, pry caps off acorns, take apart pine cones, and pick up shells, rocks, and beach glass, they are developing fine motor skills. As they pick up sticks and draw designs in dirt or sand, plant seeds, open the pods of a wild indigo plant, and stack rocks, they are using fine motor skills as well as honing their ability to focus. These skills encourage patience and self-regulation, which are necessary before learning to read.

LEARNING THROUGH PLAY AND DIRECT EXPERIENCES WITH NATURE

The National Association for the Education of Young Children (NAEYC) reminds us that "play is the central teaching practice that facilitates young children's development and learning. Play develops young children's symbolic and imaginative thinking, peer relationships, language, physical development, and problem-solving skills. All young children need daily, sustained opportunities for play, both indoors and outdoors . . . Through play, children explore and make sense of their world" (Friedman et al., 2022).

Play is an essential part of childhood and is fundamental to the way children grow and make sense of their experiences. Playing in nature allows children to interact with diverse habitats, identify different plants and animals, and build and experiment with natural materials. Nature affords opportunities for children to overcome physical challenges, work in cooperation with others, and develop empathy for other living organisms.

Outdoor learning experiences help turn children from passive learners into active ones. The teachers act as facilitators, helping to guide experiences while encouraging the children to listen, observe, think, and make connections. In doing so, the children are eagerly involved in their own education. Nature has become their laboratory, a place where they may experiment.

At the Schlitz Audubon Nature Preschool, the children may spend hours looking under leaves and logs. They will regularly uncover pill bugs, worms, millipedes, and beetles. By studying these secretive creatures and learning how to touch, hold, and place them gently back in the soil, children express care and respect for even the smallest living things. In the process, they also discover hidden worlds. They learn about the unique body parts of the worm, so unlike our own, and the importance of healthy soil. They learn about exoskeletons, food chains, and camouflage. They learn through observation, by asking questions, and with the guidance of their teachers. Curiosity lies at the heart of the entire experience.

In the winter, our preschool students might wish to venture across a frozen pond. Before doing so, they must first stop and wait while the adults test the thickness of the ice. They need to learn caution and risk assessment. Once on the ice, they test their balance and quickly discover that they must move

in new ways to manage the slippery surface. Water freezes, they realize, and later it melts, and this melting and freezing is connected to temperature. They may look through the ice and recall the turtles and frogs, now sleeping, that they saw swimming just a few months earlier. The children discover that animals also must change their behavior when the temperature changes. They learn about animal adaptations along with the physical properties of water in a way that is both appropriate and meaningful for their age.

Stephen Kellert (2005), Professor Emeritus of Social Ecology at the Yale University School of Forestry and Environmental Studies, describes three ways children experience contact with nature: direct, indirect, and vicarious. Direct contact with nature is often spontaneous and unsupervised and occurs in spaces such as forests, creeks, parks, or even a child's backyard. Children might, for example, look under logs in the woods, catch frogs in a pond, or chase butterflies in a field. Indirect contact with nature is more structured and organized and occurs in more controlled environments under the supervision of adults, such as during a visit to a park, zoo, garden, or nature center. Vicarious contact with nature involves no actual contact with living organisms. Instead, children are presented with images or representations of nature. Reading a nature book or watching a television show about animals is vicarious contact. All three types of contact with nature are important for children, but Kellert (2005) asserts that "both theory and evidence support the view that direct, ongoing experience of nature in relatively familiar settings remains a vital source for children's physical, emotional, and intellectual development."

In our nature preschool, we do provide vicarious experiences by reading books and looking at pictures. We also provide indirect experiences when we plan a specific structured indoor or outdoor activity.

CHAPTER ONE: MAKING THE CASE FOR NATURE AND PLAY IN AN EARLY CHILDHOOD CURRICULUM

Our primary aim, however, has always been to offer children direct experiences. Such experiences include time for the children to play and explore outside without the perception of adult supervision. There is nothing wrong with vicarious and indirect experiences overall, unless they entirely take the place of direct experiences. Reading a picture book about exploring a forest is hardly the same as actually hiking in a park with a naturalist. And a structured hike in the park isn't the same as unstructured play in a forest where children make discoveries on their own.

SUPPORT FOR INDIVIDUAL SUCCESS

It is worth pausing for a moment to note that while it is important for children to have direct experiences outdoors if they are to develop any lasting relationship with nature, we need to provide these experiences in ways that respect each child's temperament and personal needs. Children with mobility issues or vision impairment, for example, can enjoy nature just as much as children without these specific challenges, but the space may need to be adapted. Children who are just expanding their horizons, venturing for the first time away from the familiar bond of their family into the unknown, need to feel safe as they explore wild areas.

Creating an outdoor play space with clear boundaries will often encourage free play among preschool children in a way that an open, boundless space will not. Providing tools such as watering cans, shovels, and wheelbarrows can help younger children feel more assured as they play outdoors. These tools encourage active movement as well.

We do not advocate taking very young children into the woods and letting them play without limits. Some boundaries, some sense of caution, and some guidelines are important. If children are throwing rocks, breaking branches, or hurting other living things, adults should intervene. If children are climbing logs and testing their balance or are busy building forts and fairy houses, it is best to stand back and let their creativity flourish. Children deserve the freedom to explore and to assess for themselves the limits of their own abilities. Teachers and parents need only step in when children fail to meet expectations for safety or when their explorations are, perhaps accidentally, harming other living things.

Having said this, adults should not remain silent and invisible while children play and explore in nature. While children should not feel overly controlled by adults as they play, our nature preschool teachers regularly demonstrate their interest in and enjoyment of the natural world. They model respect by showing the children how to handle living creatures and when to leave them alone. They are present when children wish to climb trees or logs, supporting them with either hands or words. They are willing to get wet or muddy and are dressed as the children are, in rain pants and waterproof boots, ready to play.

We have found that the more teachers and children interact together within the natural world, the stronger the bond between them. We regularly work to find the balance between joyful adult-and-child interactions and giving children time and space without the perceived presence of adults to experience nature on their own terms.

NATURE AND ACADEMIC READINESS

One question prospective parents ask us most frequently is how a nature-based curriculum will help their child become ready for school. Although several parents in our community agree that young children learn best through play, they also know that kindergarten "is the new first grade," and they do not want their children heading off to grade school without the tools to succeed. "But do you also teach reading and math?" is one of our most common questions.

The answer we give to parents is yes, we do teach early reading and math, but not necessarily using the approach they expect. We do not push writing to children who are not ready to hold a pencil. We do not have a designated letter of the day. Rather, when we learn about life cycles and seasonal changes, we are learning about patterns. When we identify and mimic the springtime calls of chickadees and red-winged blackbirds, we are gaining a deeper understanding of how language works. We use literacy tools and play with numbers in ways that are organic and correspond to how preschool-aged children learn.

Joshua Sneideman, the Albert Einstein Distinguished Educator Fellow at the Office of Energy Efficiency and Renewable Energy, notes that teaching mathematical and science concepts as stand-alone topics with no connection to the wider world not only leaves the subjects devoid of meaning but also fails to consider how younger children learn best. Children need to be at the center of the learning experience. They need opportunities to approach the same topic through a multitude of experiences and lenses.

CHAPTER ONE: MAKING THE CASE FOR NATURE AND PLAY IN AN EARLY CHILDHOOD CURRICULUM

The research is quite clear that the best practice in early childhood education is to break away from passive instruction and allow for more play and investigation, and this kind of learning early in life builds skills and interests that serve children throughout their school years ... Long-term research also indicates that being allowed opportunities to take initiative in your own learning is not only good for STEM learning, but for overall long-term academic success (Sneideman, 2013).

We must not forget to communicate this information to parents. We often see busy parents dressing and feeding their children to save time while simultaneously asking us, "What are you doing to get them ready for school?" As educators, we understand that teaching the children to put on and take off their own boots, hats, mittens, and jackets also teaches independence, self-efficacy, memory, sequencing, and fine motor dexterity. We do not always remember to translate this information to parents, however, which is a necessary part of the process.

At the Schlitz Audubon Nature Center, our preschool children from our inaugural year, 2003, are now out of college. Many of our former students have returned over the years to volunteer in our classrooms. Year after year we have seen firsthand that as children age out of our program, they have had no difficulty transitioning from preschool to grade school. Kindergarten teachers often tell us that they know the children from our preschool are more inquisitive, confident, and willing to take risks. Parents report that their children are well adapted and successful in kindergarten and elementary classes.

Several studies have compared children in nature preschool to those in traditional programs. Researchers have found that children in a nature preschool are at least as ready for kindergarten as their peers in other programs (Skibbe et al., 2017; Ernst and Burcak, 2019). One study looked at the effect of nature on children's resilience, initiative, self-regulation, and attachment, important qualities for children moving from preschool to kindergarten. The authors of that study found that attending a nature preschool was more likely to support these skills (Ernst, Juckett, and Sobel, 2021).

Research shows that "nature preschools positively impact two components of school readiness, peer play interactions and learning behaviors" (Burgess and Ernst, 2020). The independence, curiosity, coordination, ability to get along socially with others, and ability to control one's emotions that our nature-preschool students exhibit contribute not only to future academic success but also to greater overall happiness.

NATURE AND EARLY BRAIN DEVELOPMENT

The staff at Schlitz Audubon Nature Preschool have been especially interested in the effect that positive nature experiences have on early brain development. In 2009, we teamed up with BrainInsights to provide families and teachers with simple activities that help support brain development.

We used this experience to look closely at our own curriculum, using scientific evidence to support our anecdotal observations that engaging with nature at a very young age enhances cognitive development.

HOW WE PREPARE YOUNG CHILDREN FOR SCHOOL

When parents ask, "What are you doing to get my child ready for school?" we offer these replies:

We read to children.

We sing songs together.

We speak to children using complex language and science words.

We encourage book handling.

We keep journals.

We model writing.

We provide writing areas in our classroom.

We identify words and letters, indoors and out.

We learn to use maps.

We look for letter shapes in nature.

We draw shapes, lines, squiggles, and letters using sticks in sand, snow, or soil.

We write children's names.

We take pencils, chalk, and paper outdoors.

We count rocks, branches, leaves, snowflakes, sticks, turkeys, and people.

We measure sunflowers and other tall prairie plants.

We weigh pumpkins.

We sort things by color, shape, length, smell, season, or behavior, such as nocturnal and diurnal.

We make patterns.

We identify shapes, especially circles, stars, and hearts, in nature.

We sing counting songs.

We play adding and subtracting games.

We cook.

We count at snack time.

We count and sing songs in Spanish, French, German, Chinese, and other languages.

We study the changing seasons.

We learn about migration, hibernation, and activation.

We explore puddles, snow, and ice.

We learn about evaporation.

We strengthen children's hands and fingers through fine and large motor play.

We give children time and space to develop friendships and social skills.

We provide opportunities for children to learn patience and empathy.

We provide children time and space to develop confidence and independence.

We encourage curiosity and a desire to learn by allowing the children to explore their own interests.

We explored the relationship between nature-based exploration and early childhood brain development. Current research suggests there are several principles at play: exercise, what children attend to, integration of multiple senses, and exploration (Medina, 2014). In addition, enriching environments are the cornerstones of a brain-based classroom (Jensen, 2013). What could be more enriching than the natural world?

We have condensed much of that information into Ten Simple Ways Nature Supports Early Childhood Brain Development (see pages 14-15). We often use this document as a handout for families; we encourage you to share this information with the families you work with.

THE NATURE-SPIRIT CONNECTION

On a summer afternoon, several five-year-old boys were having fun playing in one of our preschool play spaces. These boys were not graduates of our preschool but had come to the center to hike with their families. As often happens, the families made their way to one of our fenced-in play areas, where presumably the parents could relax and talk while the boys played within the provided boundaries.

Their play was a little rowdy but not particularly concerning, until it shifted into a game called Smash the Bug. The boys were having great fun tipping logs, looking for bugs, and crushing them. Watching them from a distance, one student who was also visiting the center that day grew alarmed. As the boys smashed bug after bug, this young girl spoke up. Despite being two years younger and considerably smaller, she approached them with determination. "You need to stop that," she said. "Bugs live here. You shouldn't hurt them." The boys stared at the younger girl in confusion. This was news to them. Not sure what else to do, they stopped. The teacher who observed this moment could not have been prouder. Not only had this small girl felt keenly that bugs deserved protection, but she had also taken action to intervene on their behalf.

We do not fool ourselves into thinking all young children start out instinctively knowing how to play in nature. Nor are they born knowing how to share or take turns. If a child sees a flower, often their first instinct is to pick it. When they see a bug, they often stomp it. It takes patience, repetition, and modeling for some children to see nature as worthy of protection, just as it takes time to develop any new skill.

Conservation may not be a word they know. Nevertheless, we teach the principles of conservation every day. Over many months at nature preschool, this sense of stewardship for the land becomes a part of each child's experience. By making sure that nature is a part of everything we do, children come to see it as a part of their community, deserving respect, protection, and empathy.

PARTNERING WITH *Nature* IN EARLY CHILDHOOD EDUCATION

There is another, often overlooked, component of nature and early childhood—the place that spirituality plays in a child's relationship with nature. To be clear, we are not talking about religious beliefs, although children will often mention God when discussing natural phenomena. Rather, we are exploring a child's ability to seek nature as a source of comfort and to feel peaceful and calm in the natural world, connected to other living things, and less stressed and anxious. Spending time in nature increases a child's awareness and empathy for others and builds a deeper sense of self. Again, this kind of connection takes time. It requires repetition, as well as trust, comfort, and space to contemplate the mysteries of the world. When children spend time in natural environments, there is the potential to experience what biologist, author, and conservationist Rachel Carson called a sense of wonder. Spirituality has a lot to do with experiencing something grander and greater than oneself.

Deborah Schein (2018) has spent considerable time researching theories of spirituality for young children and suggests, "When we provide time and space for children to explore their relationship with nature, we afford them moments to wonder, room to explore their questions and nurture their own innate dispositions. This also allows us to observe children's engagement with their own learning and support them on their journeys."

Spirituality has many elements and is open to interpretation. Some teachers place an emphasis on mindfulness in their classrooms, encouraging children to slow down, breathe deeply, and be present in the moment. Other teachers may incorporate yoga, music, and dance into their nature play, exploring the connection between mind and body.

When we consider spirituality in children, we are referring to the private, personal relationship that a child has with the natural world. We are referring to those quiet moments spent watching the clouds move and the thoughts that belong to those moments.

> **"A kid today can likely tell you about the Amazon rainforest—but not about the last time he or she explored the woods in solitude or lay in a field listening to the wind and watching the clouds move"** (Louv, 2005).

We are also interested in how nature influences a child's understanding of death. It is common to find dead trees or animals while outside, and so it is important not to avoid the topic but rather frame it as a part of the cycle of life. At our nature preschool, we look at dying trees and decaying logs and discuss how the bark will slowly break down and eventually turn into soil, making it possible for new seeds to take root. We talk about how an animal might have died and about scavengers and decomposers, key players in the food chain. Most important, we allow the children time and space to feel sorrow, if that is what they need in that moment. We also try to invite parents into these conversations, as a child's changing understanding of death is not just a part of their own spirituality but of family culture and outlook.

CHAPTER ONE: MAKING THE CASE FOR NATURE AND PLAY IN AN EARLY CHILDHOOD CURRICULUM

TEN SIMPLE WAYS NATURE SUPPORTS EARLY CHILDHOOD BRAIN DEVELOPMENT

In his book *Brain Rules: 12 Principles for Surviving and Thriving at Work, Home, and School*, John Medina (2014) describes key components of how the human brain works and what influences brain development. Eric Jensen (2008, 2013) provides guiding principles for brain-based education. The following list is derived from the research compiled by both authors.

1. **Nature provides an enriched environment.** Enriched environments are the cornerstones of a brain-based classroom. This includes experiences that are challenging and novel in environments that provide contrast. When children are exposed to enriched environments, such as nature, their brains can actually grow larger neurons and increase neural connections. You can support positive brain development by providing children with hands-on nature experiences as often as possible. Encourage trial-and-error play in an outdoor landscape. Give children opportunities for challenge and feedback, and let children work through problems both alone and in groups.

2. **Nature stimulates the memory.** When children pay attention to something, their brain cells form connections. This is how learning takes place and how memories are made. Meaningful things, such as nature, get our attention. Meaningful learning increases brain-cell survival and functionality, helping us to remember the learning later. Make memories with children through new and interesting experiences in nature. You can help capture their attention with scavenger hunts, memory games, and revisiting the same places in nature throughout the year. Encourage children to recall their memories of earlier nature experiences, compare different seasons, and study the growth of a plant or the life cycle of a frog or butterfly. Provide opportunities for meaningful experiences such as gardening, raking, digging, and planting trees and flowers. Go outside when it rains. Build a snowman. Play together.

3. **Nature allows us to cross the midline.** Activities that cross the body's midline (an imaginary line that divides a person's body into left and right sides) can increase a child's attention and concentration skills. Crossing the midline is important for activities that use both sides of the body together, such as putting on shoes, writing, and cutting. It promotes communication and coordination between both sides of the brain (Child Development Centre, 2018; Evans, 2018). Tracking things visually across the midline makes it easier for children to learn to read, and tracking things physically across the midline makes it easier for children to learn to write. Nature-based activities that involve crossing the midline include catching insects with butterfly nets, catching frogs or small crabs with nets, climbing trees, snowshoeing, building forts, raking leaves, gardening, playing with bubbles, and building sandcastles.

4. **Nature offers a multisensory experience.** All learning starts with sensory input. We learn best when multiple senses are stimulated, either individually or all at once. Provide opportunities for children to play with sand and water, feel different textures, smell plants and flowers, and taste food from the garden. Use magnifying glasses and binoculars to help focus attention. Lay back, close your eyes, and listen to the wind and the birdcalls. Remember the words of one

nature preschooler who, when told she would need to bring earbuds to kindergarten to listen to technology, noted, "At my old school, we listened to nature."

5. **Nature stimulates language development.** Language involves a huge amount of cranial space, including both the right and left hemispheres. The more words a young child hears, the better. Communication between the right and left hemispheres of the brain is key to language development (Norris, 2016). Talk about what you experience, and encourage children to use descriptive words. Play language games such as I Spy while hiking. Sing songs in nature. Have children mimic birdcalls and other nature sounds. Do not be afraid to use challenging science terms. (Children enjoy mastering difficult words.) Give children time to chat with each other, in pairs and in groups, while outdoors.

6. **Nature encourages large motor activity.** Exercise helps increase oxygen levels in the blood and brain and supports the release of brain-derived neurotrophic factor (BDNF). BDNF supports learning and memory function as well as the repair and maintenance of neural circuits. Provide opportunities for large motor activities such as running, jumping, climbing, lifting, balancing, and hiking.

7. **Nature encourages fine motor activity.** Repetitive exercise of fine motor skills strengthens the pincer grip and muscles in the hand and contributes to the brain's development by making connections between neurons. Allow children to pick up pebbles or shells, take seeds from the seedpods of Mexican bird of paradise or a sunflower head, or use small tools such as tweezers and eyedroppers.

8. **Nature provides opportunities for free play.** Play promotes neural development in those brain areas involved in emotional reactions and social learning. Unstructured free play in nature allows children to connect with their peers to explore the natural world. Encourage children to use their imaginations in nature, make up stories with friends, participate in parallel or cooperative play, and build with natural materials.

9. **Nature is calming and reduces stress.** Excessive stress produces a chemical called *cortisol* that reduces the growth of new neurons and the number of dendrites (appendages that receive synaptic inputs) on existing neurons in the brain. Lowering stress reduces the level of cortisol in the brain, allowing for the growth of new neurons and increased synaptic inputs. Take time to look at the clouds, sit near water, or stare up at a tree. Give children opportunities to play in the sand or dirt. Watch the sunset. Dip your feet in a puddle. Make a snow angel. Paint outside. Be intentional about helping children find peace and comfort in nature.

10. **Nature is fun!** Experiences that are joyful are remembered. Memories that contain emotional content help stimulate the amygdala, the center of our brains responsible for emotional behavior. Time spent in the natural world can have a positive effect on children's emotional development.

By creating positive, happy experiences, children will be more successful at controlling their moods, remaining calm, and expressing joy. Encourage a sense of wonder in nature by being a loving and supportive partner to children as you explore the natural world together.

IN SUPPORT OF A NEW EDUCATION LANDSCAPE

Over the past thirty years, the American education system has not had a close relationship with nature. We have seen recess time decrease (Ginsburg et al., 2006; Associated Press, 2006) as the call for test preparation takes precedence over play. We have seen inquiry-based approaches to learning replaced by direct instruction. We have seen a rise in large and fine motor delays, increased stress, and young children struggling with depression.

There have always been educators willing to push back against the system, creating spaces for nature and play even in the face of resistance. We know of outdoor STEM labs, gross motor challenge courses, teaching gardens, and *en plein air* art studios designed and championed by determined teachers. Here in Wisconsin, our colleague Peter Dargatz created a forest kindergarten program at his local public elementary school by adopting and transforming the unused green space beyond the asphalt playground. The Tomorrow River Community Charter School in Amherst Junction was founded by parents who wanted a nature-based, Waldorf-inspired program for their children. Fox River Academy in Appleton is a public charter school that uses weekly field experiences along the Fox River to inform its curriculum. In short, there are many innovative educators who take children outdoors and who provide authentic, hands-on learning and nature-based play for their students.

But we know of just as many, if not more, who have been limited in their efforts. They have been stopped short by standardized testing, rigid curricula, and a lack of support from their administration. There may also be resistance from fellow teachers. Often, this resistance comes from those who simply do not understand what a nature-based experience looks like. The assumption is that nature is a parenthesis; it is a nice enrichment option for those programs that don't rely on test scores for funding but not worth the insurance risk or the time away from test preparation to be worthwhile.

But it is worth pushing back. Sometimes, it is a simple matter of educating the doubters. Policymakers need to see and understand the many ways academics (and test scores) are supported and even enhanced by nature-based education. Those who are alarmed by the risks need to understand the specifics of safety. Teachers who feel uneasy in nature need to be given well-thought-out plans for managing clothing and gear, handling bathroom issues, and coping with challenging weather.

We know from personal experience that a nature-based curriculum can only succeed and thrive when there's a supportive infrastructure holding it up. This requires more than a safe outdoor space. It requires teachers who are trained in how to take children outdoors. It requires parents who are supportive of a nature-based approach to teaching. It also requires politicians and policymakers who are willing to prioritize the emotional well-being of students. It means no longer assuming all learning is quantitative or that good test scores make the most thoughtful citizens. It means taking a bold leap of faith and seeing how outdoor learning can actually improve critical-thinking skills while also supporting empathy, curiosity, and a sense of place and community. It means having the energy, imagination, and—most of all—the resources to make nature a priority as we reconsider and reinvent the traditional American classroom.

In developing a nature-based curriculum for young children, we are not simply strengthening a child's early development or laying a foundation for future learning. We are helping to set children on a path to becoming the people we hope they will one day be. Building meaningful relationships with nature occurs when time spent outdoors is frequent, when children are allowed to climb a tree without help, or when they drop a leaf into a creek and follow its journey downstream. We are helping them develop a relationship with nature that will stay with them throughout their lives, a relationship that includes caring for, connecting with, and finding solace in nature.

CHAPTER ONE: MAKING THE CASE FOR NATURE AND PLAY IN AN EARLY CHILDHOOD CURRICULUM

- CHAPTER TWO -

Creating a Nature-Based Classroom

Come forth into the light of things,
Let nature be your teacher.

—William Wordsworth | **"THE TABLES TURNED"**

In chapter 1, we made the case for nature-based education in an early childhood classroom. In this chapter, we explore what a nature-based classroom looks like and how you can begin to create one.

When developing a nature-based classroom, one of our goals is to merge best practices in early childhood education with best practices in environmental education. (We recognize that the term *best practices* is problematic to some and that perhaps a better phrase would be *evidence-based practices*, but for now we use the more common expression, understanding that best practices should always be evidence based.)

Many early childhood educators do not feel qualified to teach natural science programs. Likewise, many environmental educators do not know what to say when faced with a group of wiggly preschoolers. It is, therefore, useful to remember that what works best in one approach—hands-on, inquiry-based learning—also works best in the other. Paying due attention to developmentally appropriate nature-based education results in a program and physical space in which early childhood education and environmental education seamlessly weave together.

In the remainder of this chapter, we explore strategies to get your nature-based classroom started, examples of how to bring nature *inside* your classroom areas, ideas for bringing your classroom *outside*, and tips for handling licensing regulations.

CHAPTER TWO: CREATING A NATURE-BASED CLASSROOM

GETTING STARTED

ADD NATURAL MATERIALS

Begin by setting up the classroom with learning centers that contain nature-related materials.

Your classroom could be indoors, but it might also be in an outdoor area where regular teaching and learning occur. In either case, be intentional about adding nature to your existing space. Consider large motor play and fine motor work, and then think about how you might use nature to support these activities in different learning areas. Consider a few quick examples, such as adding acorn caps, pine cones, pebbles, and sea glass to your math and manipulatives center; large logs, branches, stones, and shells to the block center; and tree stumps, fossils, leaves, seeds, and flower petals to the dramatic play area. These items can be used for sorting, counting, weighing, building, designing, and creative play, often all within the same hour. It is neither complicated nor expensive to supplement traditional (plastic) early learning materials with natural materials. For example, in the building area, you might add an assortment of tree cookies, sticks, and rocks alongside classroom blocks. (See pages 25–33 for additional information about materials to add to classroom areas.)

We are not advocating that nature replace existing classroom materials. Nor are we suggesting that teaching materials made of wood and sold in catalogs of high-priced goods are the way to go. (We have seen tree cookies selling for twenty dollars a round through some companies. Our tree cookies are made on site from branches, using a chainsaw.) We are big fans of reusing materials. Paper-towel tubes make wonderful telescopes, for example, and cast-off wrapping paper and ribbons are always a popular addition to an art area. Adding nature, along with recycled materials, into the classroom should be neither cost prohibitive nor difficult.

ENCOURAGE SENSORY EXPERIENCES

Provide daily opportunities for the children to interact with sensory-rich materials. Even when it is not possible to take children outdoors, it is possible to provide them with sensory-rich natural materials in the classroom (see pages 25–33 for suggestions). Sensory tables or smaller sensory tubs are a fun and creative way to experience different textures, liquids, and even tiny habitats.

Provide items such as buckets, scoops, plastic insects, rubber frogs, watering cans, and eyedroppers to these sensory tables or tubs to encourage imaginative play and strengthen fine motor skills. Some children find water particularly soothing. They will happily spend an entire hour scooping and pouring water, transfixed and in the moment. Providing smocks and towels is always a good idea, and making sure there is room for more than one child to play with water—and enough time to do so—is essential.

CHAPTER TWO: CREATING A NATURE-BASED CLASSROOM

INVITE NATURE EXPLORATION AND ENGAGEMENT

Give children time and space outdoors in various habitats that are diverse, safe, and enjoyable.

Introduce children to natural habitats rich in diversity. Provide outdoor environments that are safe (free of poison ivy, thorns, and other hazards), and give children uninterrupted blocks of time to explore and interact with nature through free and creative play. For some, this may mean leaving school and walking to a nearby park; visiting a part of the school grounds seldom seen; or walking around the block, counting trees, or looking for birds' nests. What is important is to make the natural world a part of a child's everyday experience and to give children time to interact, play, and forge connections with nature in their own way.

Enable each child to engage physically, cognitively, socially, emotionally, and spiritually with the natural world. Provide opportunities for climbing and balancing on logs. Give children opportunities to roll down hills and jump off rocks or tree stumps. Provide sensory-stimulating experiences such as smelling the soil after a rainstorm, touching rough bark, listening for birds, and looking for insects under the leaf litter. Include moments for stillness, such as taking time to lie back and look at the sky. Remember, these experiences can take place anywhere. Many preschools in urban areas have gardens or trees with leaves that come down in the fall or include ancient fossils in their limestone walls. And everyone, no matter their space, has a sky overhead.

FOSTER COMMUNITY

Foster a sense of community through cooperative exploration, experimentation, and problem solving. Build a snow fort or a log bridge as a group. Plant and care for a community garden. Allow children to help take care of animals and plants in the classroom. Give children opportunities to hug trees, listen to birds, and water plants. Consider reading, doing yoga, or playing musical instruments together. Give children opportunities, such as experimenting with what sinks and what floats, to discover cause-and-effect relationships with objects from nature. Your community is both your classroom and the natural world beyond.

CHAPTER TWO: CREATING A NATURE-BASED CLASSROOM

INVOLVE FAMILIES

Respect the diversity of families and involve them in the nature-focused preschool program.

Invite families to participate in special nature-related activities and field trips. Provide ideas for nature-related activities and hikes they can do at home or in the community. Work on developing an understanding of each family's cultural relationship to the environment. Invite parents to share ideas of nature-related activities, games, songs, and stories from their cultures. Ask for donations of recyclable materials, and take advantage of any special skills parents want to share.

An example of a cultural relationship to the environment that one family shared is the Hindu celebration of Holi, which marks the beginning of spring. This celebration, also known as the festival of colors, usually falls in February or March. For our celebration of this event, as with other celebrations, we opted to downplay the religious elements of Holi and focused instead on the cultural. The parent who shared this cultural tradition read *Festival of Colors* by Surishtha Sehgal to the children. Then everyone, including parents and teachers who chose to participate, donned white T-shirts (over their raincoats). Children and teachers mixed powdered paints together with lots of water and transferred the paints to small spray bottles. Children were given the spray bottles with instructions to aim at each other's torsos, covering both the front and back of their white t-shirts, while avoiding spraying paint in faces. Several teachers, a few parents, and every child began spraying one another with diluted paints, creating beautiful designs on one another's shirts while also laughing, shrieking, and otherwise enjoying this deeply celebratory experience.

PLAY TO LEARN

Emphasize play as the most appropriate way that young children learn. Model, facilitate, and guide children through conceptual learning rather than rote learning. Children learn by constructing their own knowledge about the natural world, not by memorizing facts. In everything you do, model ecologically appropriate behavior such as recycling, caring for local animals and plants, and conserving resources. Encourage children to search for answers in field guides and by experimenting, instead of

providing the correct answer immediately. Spend time in the natural world to increase your own understanding of habitats, plants, and animals. Facilitate divergent thinking, critical thinking, curiosity, and creativity. In the end, children's experiences *in* nature are more important than teaching them *about* nature.

TIPS FOR ADDING NATURE TO YOUR CLASSROOM

Part of offering a predictable classroom for children includes offering ongoing activity centers, arranged in such a way as to provide children free and ready access to different materials. When children can make their own choices during free play, they are able to further their own interests, vary their approach to play, and learn how to share and socialize with others.

Activities in the classroom should address the children's general development: physical (motion, active games), emotional (curiosity, delight), social (collective games, problem solving), and intellectual (reading, constructing, observing). Over time, the materials in the centers can change based on children's needs and interests. This section discusses different activity areas of the classroom in more detail, with suggestions on ways to infuse nature into each area.

ART AREA

The art area usually includes materials for painting, drawing, collaging, and so on. Offer both natural and human-made materials in this space. Markers and tape may not grow on trees, but they are appropriate materials for an early childhood art center! Natural materials to add might include clay, dried leaves, branches, twigs, pine cones, pebbles, shells, seeds, feathers, and flowers. Change art

CHAPTER TWO: CREATING A NATURE-BASED CLASSROOM

25

materials often, providing new items regularly—especially natural materials, which tend to disintegrate quickly—and arrange them in such a way that children have the freedom to choose what they like. There should be no limitations on how much they can take or how they want to combine the materials. You can offer materials in baskets or bins or put them on an art cart on wheels that can be moved outside or to a covered porch. Introduce new art activities related to specific seasons in small groups, and then place those materials in the art area for future use. Occasionally, an idea that began in the art area may inspire a larger project.

SENSORY TABLE

Natural materials in a sensory table might include sand, water, leaves, dried corn, sunflower seeds, soil, snow, pine cones, shells, feathers, natural cotton, pine needles, and pebbles of various sizes, shapes, and colors. Tools and other items to use with the sensory table include containers and scoops, small shovels, animal figures, funnels, sieves, sponges, tongs, and molds.

Children can use water, sand, and soil to fill and empty containers and for sink-and-float experiments. They can also plant seeds or hide rubber worms and plastic insects in soil; sunflower seeds can be measured, weighed, manipulated with tweezers and tongs, or used to fill and empty containers.

PARTNERING WITH *Nature* IN EARLY CHILDHOOD EDUCATION

26

Children can even play with snow, sculpting and working with tools to create mini slopes or to form shapes with different containers. Spray bottles of colored water add another dimension to their exploration. (We often add mittens to this area if we are playing with snow.)

While observing the children and playing beside them, teachers may discover other tools and materials they want to add to expand on the experience.

BLOCKS AND BUILDING AREA

Wooden blocks, hollow blocks, blocks made of recycled cardboard boxes, branch blocks, clipboards with paper and pencils, pictures of buildings and other structures, and children's books are tools that children can use to deepen their block-building experiences. Natural materials such as rocks, small stones and sticks, and tree cookies can complement typical block accessories such as toy vehicles and rubber, plastic, or wooden figures of people and animals.

Children will use the blocks in various ways, depending on their experience and developmental level. They may build habitats for the toy

CHAPTER TWO: CREATING A NATURE-BASED CLASSROOM

animals, especially with branch blocks that look more like a natural habitat. This gives the children and teachers opportunities to talk about the animals that would live in a particular habitat and the needs they might have.

Children should have opportunities to work cooperatively or alone, depending on their goals. Teachers can increase STEM learning by asking informal questions such as, "Can you redirect the water in the river you just built? Can you make it go up hill?" Observing how the children use the materials enables teachers to add other items to enhance the experience.

MATH AND MANIPULATIVE AREA

Materials in this area typically include puzzles, construction toys, board games, and objects for counting and sorting, including plastic animals and natural objects such as feathers, acorns, pebbles, coral, and seashells. Consider adding small bowls and mancala boards to the area to encourage the children to sort and to create sets.

PARTNERING WITH *Nature* IN EARLY CHILDHOOD EDUCATION

28

Homemade puzzles made from photos of the outdoor environment around the school can provide ways for children to connect to their surroundings and can support a sense of place. Homemade games such as placing acorns from a bowl on a strip of laminated squirrel pictures, making sure each squirrel receives an acorn, encourage practicing one-to-one correspondence.

Begin the year with simple materials and add complexity as children's skills develop. Be sure to also offer a developmental range so that both the most competent and least competent children in the class can find manipulative activities that are challenging without being frustrating. Children can choose games and toys to play with individually or in groups with other children, which gives them the opportunity to work out social issues. Ask open-ended questions such as, "What would happen if you took two pebbles out of this group?" and "How could you sort these differently?" while observing their play, to assist children in discovering new ways to play with these hands-on materials.

CHAPTER TWO: CREATING A NATURE-BASED CLASSROOM

BOOK AREA

Supplement the book area with brightly colored books about nature for individual exploration and class reading. These books should provide a positive outlook on the natural world and feature animals and plants that are real and relevant to the children's experience. Try to offer an assortment of topics and styles, including board books, hardback and paperback books, big books, fictional picture books, and nonfiction books. Field guides on various topics with high-quality photos of plants and animals are particularly relevant. There are several "first guides" that work well for young children. These guides usually include beautiful photos or drawings that appeal to young children. They are often smaller in size or printed as children's books. (See appendix A for a list of recommended books.) Some of these nature guides can also be found in Spanish. To further enhance the book area, consider creating a writing area nearby, so that children can create their own books and stories.

As you read to children, interact with them, letting them respond to the book and interrupt as needed. Listen to children narrate their own stories of their activities outdoors, and write their words down. Then read the stories back to the children to help them connect the written words to their speech.

DRAMATIC PLAY AREA

Each classroom should maintain a basic home-living center with play props such as a kitchen set with dishes, dolls, and dress-up clothes, even when special dramatic play centers are available. Provide animal costumes and puppets as well, so children can imitate the behavior of the animals.

Extensions of dramatic play can include a fruit and vegetable farmer's market in the classroom during the autumn months, a pumpkin patch, a garden center, a firewood store, a fishing pond, a ranch, a farm, a tree house, a veterinarian office, a science lab, a campfire circle, and even a nature center!

This area provides an opportunity for teachers to use imaginary play with children. Ask questions about the type of play to better understand the theories the children are developing. This information will assist you in providing ideas for future projects and support for children's development.

ANIMALS AND PLANTS

Animals and plants may not be in a particular center or learning area; you might have plants throughout your classroom. Wherever they are located in your classroom, living things provide lots of opportunities for the children to develop a caring attitude toward something other than themselves as they help feed the animals and care for the plants. Animals can be as simple as live earthworms in a classroom worm bin or more complex creatures such as salamanders, tree frogs, turtles, and toads. The care and comfort of the animal should be at the forefront of any planning, from the size and condition of its indoor habitat to its ongoing health care, diet, and handling.

CHAPTER TWO: CREATING A NATURE-BASED CLASSROOM

Be sure to consider licensing rules about animals in the classroom. At our nature preschool, we have an exemption written into our license that allows animals in the classroom as long as they are seen regularly by a vet and are kept in properly maintained habitats away from bathrooms and eating areas. We do not place animal containers on top of cabinets or shelves containing toys, art supplies, or other materials used by children. Rather, the animals are kept in their own containers on individual stands. We keep careful health and feeding records and make the feeding, handling, and care of our classroom animals an important part of our curriculum.

Plants in the classroom must be nontoxic and should be located where they can be enjoyed but are not a tripping or watering hazard.

SCIENCE AREA AND DISCOVERY TABLE

The science area and discovery table encourage children's observation and experimentation.

Include items such as binoculars, magnifying lenses, small scales, tape measures, field guides, and felt circles or baskets for displaying objects that children have collected. Items for observation may include

birds' nests and feathers, animal pelts and bones, shells, tree parts, snakeskins, turtle shells, cocoons, insects, and so on. Experimental activities may include working with inclines, growing plants, exploring with magnets, and using scales and tape measures to determine weight and size.

Items in the science area and discovery table are there for children to touch and explore. Children can look up information in the field guides to make identifications, experiment with different materials, and begin to develop a greater understanding of cause and effect. Encourage children to add interesting items that they discover outside, and facilitate and model ways to explore the items.

MUSIC AND MOVEMENT AREA

The music and movement area usually includes simple instruments, such as shakers, as well as instruments that require instruction, such as rhythm sticks. Add instruments made from natural materials, such as rain sticks, wooden frog scrapers with sticks, and various drums (including some made from bamboo). Natural materials such as stones and sticks can be brought in and used to make rhythmic sounds. Play recorded music with sounds from nature, such as bird calls, waterfalls, and so on.

Movement activities in the classroom can include dance; yoga; stretching; opportunities to balance, twist, or contort; limbo games; and even puppetry. Some schools are introducing gross motor labs to encourage enough physical activity throughout the day. Although we fully support these activities and are happy to see them in classrooms where children do not get to spend time outdoors, we prefer the option of taking children outside every day.

Provide opportunities for children to use the instruments individually or in planned group experiences. Initiate songs and allow children to make up their own words and accompanying movements. Lead yoga, dance, or other controlled movement opportunities.

CHAPTER TWO: CREATING A NATURE-BASED CLASSROOM

CREATING AN OUTDOOR CLASSROOM

In the previous section, we talked about bringing the natural world *inside* your classroom. In this section, we'll talk about taking the classroom and bringing it *outside*.

The goal of an outdoor play space is to provide a natural area that is safe yet challenging for young children, allowing them to interact with nature through play and encouraging a range of different activities, types of movement, and social interactions. This should be a place where children can dig in soil, play with water, build habitats, plant flowers, climb on logs, roll down hills, catch insects, watch birds, listen to stories, stomp in puddles, and relax in the sunshine. It should be a safe place for children to feel excited, inspired, and comfortable, no matter the season or temperature.

THE BASICS

The outdoor play space or classroom should have plenty of loose parts, hiding spots, and, if possible, a shelter or two (for example, a tree house, lean-to, tipi, wigwam, or log cabin). Add a variety of free or inexpensive materials to the area, such as watering cans and containers for flowers; a pile of rocks and logs; a sandbox and a designated digging spot; and baskets, tree stumps, tin dishes, shovels, buckets, and tree cookies. Gather natural items such as pine cones, acorns, twigs, dried grasses, and leaves, and place them in buckets for the children to carry around, dump, or bury. Magnifying glasses, small spray bottles filled with water, and tools for digging encourage children to interact with the environment. On a seasonal basis, bring out musical instruments, colored chalk, twine, stepping stones, sorting tables, and rain barrels filled with water.

You may wish to add outdoor looms, water tables, a mud kitchen, or perhaps an all-natural climbing structure. These are wonderful additions to a play area. Be aware, however, that they can quickly become expensive. It may take time to acquire or build such structures. For children, a bucket of mud, a small scoop, and a place to sit will often provide just as much delight. A few uneven stumps

can give children a platform from which they can jump or where they can balance. While there are many companies out there selling magazine-worthy natural play space equipment, children have been playing outdoors for generations with little more than what nature provides, equipped with their own imaginations. Do not fear simplicity.

Children grow to care about nature by connecting with it in an intimate way. Provide opportunities for children to forge their own trails and paths, give them hiding spots in nature, and give them growing plants to care for. Let children take off their shoes now and then to walk in shallow water.

Remember that an outdoor play space is not without risk, nor should risk be eliminated. Keep in mind what is and is not age-appropriate when designing an outdoor play space. Areas for children ages three and four may include water, rocks, logs, loose materials, and uneven terrain. This same space may not be appropriate for toddlers, or even for older, elementary-aged children, who may be too tall or too heavy for certain structures. Consider risk an opportunity to further the children's confidence and skills in an outdoor setting, but be aware of hazards and adjust the space based on the age and developmental levels of each group that will use it.

CHAPTER TWO: CREATING A NATURE-BASED CLASSROOM

ADDITIONS TO THE OUTDOOR CLASSROOM

Commercially manufactured outdoor play structures or mud kitchens are certainly not necessary for the outdoor classroom. However, for teachers and program administrators who want to add them—and have the resources to do so—we have found a few bonus items useful.

All-terrain wagons: Wagons make it easy to rotate teaching materials and to bring more perishable items, such as blankets, books, and art supplies, outside. Our teachers regularly fill our wagons with children's journals, paints and markers, book baskets, science tools, and extra gear such as spare mittens.

An outside seating area of logs and stumps: We have deliberately cut some of our outdoor seats to be taller, for the benefit of our older volunteers and pregnant mothers who find it difficult to rise from and settle on seats too close to the ground. If the ground is fairly even, tree stumps make good seats. However, Lincoln Log–style benches make it easier to provide more balanced seating. Assume that over time the bark will peel away (often with the help of small hands), the wood will decay, and your outdoor seating area will need to be replaced.

Outdoor sinks: Not only do outdoor sinks invite handwashing (always good for overall health), they can also be used if a child gets dirt or sand in their eyes or to wash a minor cut. Outdoor sinks make it easier to do art activities, such as painting and watercoloring. Sinks that include water filters allow children to fill and refill water bottles. Our sinks are attached to hoses that connect to our building. Another option is to acquire a portable, hands-free sanitation station, which usually includes a foot pump. These can be useful for more distant locations where hoses aren't an option.

Outdoor patio heaters: When the weather gets particularly cold, we use outdoor patio heaters to create warming stations. These are placed and mounted in such a way as to ensure maximum safety. It is important that the heaters can withstand strong winds, that they are far from branches and debris, and that children cannot crash into them as they run and play. The patio heaters are bolted to concrete blocks so they won't tip over, and the heaters are never left unsupervised.

 **A wood-burning stove:** For those interested in outdoor cooking with children, we like using a portable tabletop wood-burning stove. Often referred to as a rocket stove, this small, fuel-efficient device can sit atop a table (we use a metal folding table), away from the reach of small children. While it still requires constant monitoring, the stove contains the fire far better than an open-flame campfire, is much more compact, and allows us to share cooking experiences with children in a way that is both meaningful and safe.

THE OUTDOOR CLASSROOM OVER TIME

Although it may seem obvious, one often overlooked side effect of the nature-based outdoor play space is that it is built from nature. And nature is not constant. Climbing logs will eventually break down and decay. A lush green hillside may become trampled and muddy. Trees may become infected with fungal diseases or invasive insects and have to be removed. It is important not to despair when lightning brings down your favorite tree or flooding washes away a resting spot. Instead, incorporate these losses and the changes they offer into your curriculum.

At Schlitz Audubon Nature Preschool in 2017, we lost sixty-eight ash trees from two of our play spaces because of the emerald ash borer beetle. While many children were upset by the loss of these trees, we still preferred this reaction to one of unconcern, as it demonstrated a gratifying empathy and connection to nature. It also meant we could work with the children on deepening their understanding of death and renewal in the natural world. By spring, we had harvested and dried much of the ash wood and had turned it into plate-sized tree cookies. We then distributed these to our families, asking each to take one home and create an art piece.

Once the tree cookies were returned, we held an all-school art fair called Ash to Art. In addition to the children's pieces, local artists donated more than ninety pieces of artwork made from our fallen ash wood as part of a silent auction. Money raised from the auction went back into our play spaces to help fund new trees and new climbing structures that made further use of the fallen ash wood. In this way, we turned our

  loss into something positive, while providing the children and their families with a yearlong lesson on ecology and land management.

Because so many of our materials come from nature, our play spaces are never fixed.

CHAPTER TWO: CREATING A NATURE-BASED CLASSROOM

Wood rots, trees fall, and mud dries up in the hotter months. Different children use the spaces in different ways, and teachers have their own ideas about the spaces they feel work best for their class. Some teachers may feel a space is too cluttered or should remain free of indoor materials, while others may add blankets and books to help ease children into outdoor play. Like nature itself, outdoor spaces change and evolve, due in equal doses to time, the elements, and the interests and needs of the many people who use them.

Do not underestimate just how valuable your spaces are to your curriculum. This is true whether your program takes place largely indoors, entirely outdoors, or in a little of both. If an outdoor play area feels overgrown, closed in, or neglected, a nervous three-year-old will enter that space with added trepidation. If an outdoor play area is too large, too manicured, or was designed to be seen but not touched, a child will feel unsure of where and how to play. We find that colorful, cheerful, and just-a-little-bit-messy spaces that include sticks and mud puddles and rocks to upend will invite a child in. Our goal is to create outdoor spaces that can be used by children, not spaces deserving of a photo spread. A lovely botanical garden with neat little fairy houses placed among the flowers may look charming to a parent, but when the child is told, "Look with your eyes but do not touch," the space no longer belongs to the child.

Our own fairy gardens contain plastic dinosaurs, upended flowerpots, gemstones, seedlings, a hodgepodge of flowers, and a plethora of homemade gnome homes in various states of decomposition. The children move things around, look for worms, taste-test chives, add things, subtract things, and otherwise engage in and with our classroom gardens daily between March and December. The end result is

MOVING ENTIRELY OUTDOORS

Throughout the COVID-19 pandemic, a great many nature-based programs moved entirely outdoors. This was certainly true at Schlitz Audubon, where the indoor classrooms were used primarily as staging areas or as temporary shelters during extremely cold weather. Within just a few weeks, it became apparent to our teachers that even the indoor play and exploration centers translated easily to the outdoor spaces. In some instances, teachers established art, writing, or journaling spaces using the features of the landscape. An art area can be easily recreated outside under the trees. The teachers strung clotheslines between tree limbs and used clips to hang paintings from pine boughs. Later, during the warm, dry season, the teachers sometimes opted for ease and simply rolled their indoor easels and art carts outdoors. Teachers created reading areas by laying large, soft picnic blankets with waterproof backings in designated spots on the ground and carrying out baskets of books. We used this same method to bring out manipulatives and puzzles. Once, during a quick visit to the classroom bathroom, a few children spotted the multicultural baby dolls that were a part of our indoor dramatic play center. The next day, these too were brought outdoors. It was a warm day, and the teachers filled a plastic play pool with soapy water so that children could wash and bathe the dolls while sitting on the ground. Very few centers were unsuitable for transporting to an outdoor setting.

While there are some who may advocate for keeping outdoor play entirely free of baby dolls, sensory tables, and art carts, during COVID-19 we were operating under highly unusual circumstances. But we will likely continue some version of this practice even as the pandemic subsides. We did not feel that bringing these traditional "indoor" activities outside was a violation of our nature-based principles. In some ways, it was the logical continuation of our goal to bring more of the outdoors in. Part of our objective has always been to break down the wall between indoors and out. Setting up easels, paints, or blankets full of books in our outdoor spaces allowed us to eliminate that wall entirely. There is a purpose to every center, as well as a role for the teacher and a method of implementation; these aspects remained unchanged, even as we took them outside.

hardly magazine worthy. But our garden beds, whether blooming, empty, or filled with weeds, provide opportunities for creativity, play, and fine motor movement that are far more valuable and lasting.

A nature-based classroom, whether that classroom is indoors or out, should provide opportunities for play, discovery, social interaction, experimentation, and independence. When everything is working just as it should, the teacher can stand back, observe, and simply enjoy being in the moment with children.

A SPECIAL NOTE ABOUT LICENSING

When nature preschool teachers get together, they often bemoan that state licensors have no idea what to do with us. Licensing rules exist to protect the children in our care, and we support any regulation designed to keep children safe. Being licensed forces us to maintain our already high standards. It can reassure some families to know that our innovative, nature-based program is also state approved. We do not dismiss the value of being licensed, and we encourage all nature preschools to know and adhere to their own state licensing guidelines for child care.

At the same time, our own licensors are often left baffled when faced with their regular checklists. They are trying to inspect a program that takes place largely outdoors and are frequently the first to tell us that we do not look like most traditional preschools. They are trying to check boxes, they say, that do not apply to us.

When dealing with licensing, there is a learning curve on both sides. We strive to meet the strict licensing requirements of our state because they exist for a reason. We keep knives and cleaning products away from children. We make sure EpiPens and medications come with the mandatory authorization forms. We regularly review our paperwork to make sure our forms are up to date and that teaching certifications, including CPR, have not expired.

But we are not afraid to state our position when we feel strongly about something. We have made the case that, as a nature-based program, going outdoors in cold weather is a crucial part of our curriculum. We have pushed to take children outside on very cold days by demonstrating that the children will always be dressed appropriately. In fact, we make dressing for the weather a part of our curriculum and take the time to teach parents and children how to dress for the Wisconsin winters. While many schools have a cutoff of 20 degrees Fahrenheit or thereabouts, we have been able to keep our cutoff at −1 degree Fahrenheit. Several nature schools have even colder temperature cutoffs, which means there is more room for conversation and compromise than many people realize. We also argue for wood chips, climbing logs, sticks, and plants in our play spaces. We make the case that these materials are far more appropriate for a child's play area than asphalt and pop-up tents.

Licensors often want to work with individual programs, especially unique ones. As a nature-based program housed at a nature center, from the beginning we planned to have animals in the classrooms. To allow this, our licensor suggested that we apply for an exemption from the rules that do not allow certain animals, such as turtles, snakes, salamanders, and other reptiles and amphibians, in the classroom. We provided a list of animals we would like to have and our protocol for ensuring that the children would be safe when interacting with the animals. This included having properly locking lids on the animal cases so children could not open them without an adult and ensuring that animals would be kept away from eating areas and hands-on teaching materials. We also created a written policy for proper animal-handling techniques. This exemption was so successful that our licensor came back to us years later to ask us to provide information to other programs on how they could apply for exemptions.

PARTNERING WITH *Nature* IN EARLY CHILDHOOD EDUCATION

Eventually, we would love to see a child-care license designed specifically for a nature-based program. But our goal in pushing for this is not to get around the rules. It is to make sure that the evaluation process corresponds more accurately to our program. This may mean more flexibility on environmentally sustainable practices, such as allowing for greener cleaning products. It may mean no longer having to write exemption requests to have live animals in the classroom. It does not mean we would abandon the exacting standards required to maintain a high-quality program. It does not mean we would be negligent in how we care for other living creatures. We strive to work with, not against, our state licensors.

A couple of states have looked into licensing specifically for outdoor programs. Washington was the first state in the country to pass an outdoor preschool pilot to develop state licensing requirements for outdoor preschool programs. "Through the licensing process, programs began implementing more consistent practices, particularly around benefit-risk assessment and supporting children's safe and educational explorations of natural environments" (Washington State Department of Children, Youth, and Families, 2020). Differences between existing licensing and outdoor program licensing were in areas such as ratio and group size, benefit-risk assessments, teacher qualification in environmental or outdoor education, curriculum requirements, weather-related policies and emergency procedures, hygiene, and outdoor/nature-based–specific standards for toileting and campfires. Other states are interested in developing similar licensing for outdoor programs, which we see as a way to establish best practices for nature-based preschools.

Over the years, we have gotten our hands dirty, both literally and figuratively, as we develop spaces that reflect our curriculum. And while we do our best to comply with all state licensing requirements, we are not afraid to begin a conversation when we feel that it's important to do so.

CHAPTER TWO: CREATING A NATURE-BASED CLASSROOM

- CHAPTER THREE -

Teaching with Intention

Interest is the master teacher... We try to develop in the child the spirit of exploration, so he may enjoy the search for facts, both in books and in the outdoors.

— *Enos Mills* | **NATURALIST AND FATHER OF ROCKY MOUNTAIN NATIONAL PARK**

In chapter 2, we looked at how to add nature to your physical classroom and how to bring your classroom areas outside. In this chapter, we explore how nature supports the deeper intentions of your early childhood program.

WHY TEACHING INTENTIONALLY MATTERS

A cohesive nature-based curriculum is more than a collection of lesson plans. Its purpose is to meet the developmental needs of each child while providing time and space for children to develop meaningful, lasting relationships with nature. To achieve this, we have placed a series of intentions at the center of our curriculum that are less about our weekly activities and more about the deeper goals within the activities. Our intentions could range from self-regulation and emotional development to full-body movement, critical-thinking skills, literacy, or social justice. Some activities might address multiple intentions. Some may be born from a need, such as discussions about peace and equity, while others are born from a desire to infuse more fun and silliness into our program, such as The Adventures of Captain Rainbowbeard, which used to be called simply *mapping*.

CHAPTER THREE: TEACHING WITH INTENTION

Because ours is a nature-based program, we include environmental awareness in all that we teach. This means developing empathy toward living things, nurturing respect for wild spaces, and building personal connections to nature. We also strive to include environmental literacy—which we define as an understanding of fundamental natural science concepts such as the water cycle, migration, and camouflage—whenever possible and appropriate.

We have also made a conscious choice to place peace, community, and spirituality within our curriculum. Contrary to what many may think, this does not mean including religion or even religious conversation. It does mean creating a classroom where children have the freedom to be themselves, without judgement, while they learn to make room for others so that they too are free to be themselves. It means seeking resolutions to conflict. It means taking comfort in and deriving solace from the natural world around us. It also means pondering natural phenomena and grappling with concepts of death and renewal. Such concepts are a part of the human experience as much as they are embedded in nature.

Spirituality for us simply means recognizing that part of being human includes looking inward as we ponder our relationship with the world. If we encounter a frozen shrew in the winter, the children will likely have a dozen questions about how it died. Rather than dismiss it, a gifted educator will seize the moment, encouraging guesses and helping the children read the landscape for more information. The class may also need to decide whether to leave the shrew as they found it or perhaps to cover it with sticks and leaves. What is the best way to show respect at this moment? We strive to create a classroom that acknowledges every child's innate spirituality and provides space to ask big questions and think ethically, without dictating the answers.

By leading with intention, we also have the freedom to pivot when something unexpected occurs. We may spend hours developing carefully thought-out activities on, for example, the monarch butterfly. We may map migratory routes from Minnesota to Mexico. We may come to school with a bilingual mariposa lullaby that we are eager to share with the children. Yet when the anticipated week arrives, we may step outside only to find that the temperature has dropped and there is not a single monarch to be seen. Or, just as likely, we may instead find the ground awash in slugs following a late summer rain. The children may be fascinated by these washed-up *Mollusca* and soon become interested in prying sticky slugs from the pavement and less concerned with whatever the teacher had planned on her lesson sheet.

It would be simple enough to indulge the children for a moment or two and then get back on track, proceeding to the prairie in search of monarchs. This is a common approach; most of us, as educators, are unwilling to give up on something that we have worked hard to create. On the other hand, when we look at our curriculum in terms of intention, what are our deeper goals? Are we hoping to encourage fascination and respect for other living things? Do we want to spark curiosity? Do we want to build on the children's initial sense of wonder by following up with deeper exploration? In the pulled-from-real-life scenario above, the class spent the entire week celebrating slugs. They wrote songs about them. They built a classroom terrarium in which they could keep their slugs temporarily to study them more closely. They created artwork using silver paint that mimicked glistening slug trails. They read several books about snails and slugs that included their biology and behavior. Rather than viewing their monarch lesson as a failure, the teachers realized that replacing butterflies with slugs did not diminish their objective. Nor did the teachers abandon all those beautiful lesson plans; they simply saved them for another time. The week's activities may have changed. The week's intentions did not.

Another benefit to teaching with intention is that it gives teachers many opportunities to consider the needs of the children. When we see children struggling on hikes because they have not yet adjusted to their new environment or do not yet know how to hike safely, we are reminded to reconsider our intentions. Developing environmental literacy, while an admirable goal, might need to come later. First, the children need to learn how to walk on uneven terrain, how to stay with their group, and how to follow simple directions. They need to know that their parents will return to school to pick them up. They need to know that their teachers care for them and will keep them safe. Studying food webs at the pond, as interesting as that is, can wait until these more pressing needs are addressed.

Older, returning students may be ready much earlier to venture out. They may have already mastered hiking on difficult terrain or feeling comfortable in the beyond. (Coined by Scottish nature pedagogist Clare Warden, *the beyond* is an increasingly common term in nature-based education. It suggests spaces farther afield, deeper in nature, that are "beyond the fence.") Teachers may wish to challenge these more experienced children in new ways, perhaps by adding reading and writing to their outdoor experiences or by exploring issues of conservation and discussing how our own actions can harm or benefit natural environments. It is possible to set individual intentions for one or more groups of children alongside broader goals that affect the whole group.

While we hope to meet all our intentions over a nine-month school year, it may happen that we emphasize some intentions over others, depending on the children and the culture of the class. If the

CHAPTER THREE: TEACHING WITH INTENTION

children are struggling to show respect to nature, if they are destroying plants and crushing insects, the teacher needs to make respect for the environment a core intention for that class. If, in contrast, a class already shows a kind and caring attitude toward other living things, perhaps the children are ready to help feed and care for living animals in their classrooms. Perhaps they are ready to learn more about life cycles, habitats, and what different living species need to survive. Our intentions are not a checklist. We do not achieve one and then move on to the next. Where we place our focus will be largely guided by the children.

After the COVID-19 stay-at-home orders, several teachers in our program decided they should emphasize more social and emotional development and less emerging literacy and math. They felt that children who had been at home for six months needed more help learning how to play with others upon their initial return to school. They needed more support feeling safe and comfortable in this strange new world of facemasks and hand sanitizer. Other skills could wait, they concluded, until children learned how to make friends.

As it turned out, the majority of children were quick to jump in and make friends. Math and literacy ultimately remained a part of our daily play—not because the teachers missed the mark, but because it was clear the children were eager to explore these concepts. Children who wanted to count were given every opportunity to count. Books were a natural extension of play and community building. This experience reaffirmed to many of us that while we may distinguish between various skills and intentions for assessment purposes, they are part of an integrated whole. It often happens that as we are focusing on social and emotional behaviors, we are simultaneously helping children develop empathy, comfort in nature, or emerging academics. We cannot encourage a single area of development without encouraging multiple areas, try as we might to separate them into distinct boxes. Just as we announce our intention to learn about monarchs and end up with slugs, we may decide our goal is kindness and respect yet still end up addressing scientific thinking and environmental connection.

ESSENTIAL TEACHING INTENTIONS IN A NATURE-BASED EARLY CHILDHOOD CLASSROOM

On the following pages, we highlight our intentions while also providing some context so that the reader can see how they apply to real-life situations. We then provide a sample assessment tool, which can easily be adapted to correspond to your own curriculum and teaching intentions.

ENVIRONMENTAL CONNECTION

Introducing young children to the natural world is the first step to developing a lifelong, caring attitude toward the environment. Our immediate hope is that during their time in our program, children will begin to develop meaningful relationships with nature. Our long-term hope is that this connection flourishes in the years that follow our program. Happily, we do not have to work particularly hard

to create environmental connections in our classrooms. Mostly, we can simply let children explore, play, touch, wonder, and spend their days in nature. This is where connection is born. However, positive connections are not guaranteed. Teachers and parents do have a role to play. Here, again, we can draw from a real-life example.

> A few years ago, we worked with a group of children who were visiting the nature center from a nearby school. They were invited to play in a little wooded clearing off-trail, filled with stumps and climbing logs. The visiting teacher, although well-meaning, was not in her comfort zone. "That log doesn't want you climbing on it!" she exclaimed as children prepared to summit a decaying oak lying on its side. "I want to see everyone's feet on the ground at all times." The nature preschool teacher overseeing their visit ventured a gentle rebuttal. "Actually, I think that log would *love* to have children climbing on it."
>
> The nature preschool teacher did her best to explain to the visiting teacher that climbing on logs was a part of our curriculum at our nature preschool. She explained that we feel strongly that nature should never become a place where you can look but not touch. The visiting teacher, however, had assumed that a visit to a nature center meant learning facts about nature. She had not anticipated play, let alone risky play, and she was not convinced that climbing on logs equaled learning.

Now, besides the obvious lesson here, which is that the adults in this scenario went into this partnership with very different understandings and expectations regarding nature and play (something we learned we should discuss in advance), we also see that adults have a lot of power to either encourage or discourage outdoor play. Instructing children to step around puddles, keep their feet on the ground, and halt their nature investigations because such explorations are too messy, loud, or unstructured stifles curiosity. It stifles joy. It prohibits meaningful connections with nature.

CHAPTER THREE: TEACHING WITH INTENTION

On the other hand, we want to be careful about judging other parents or teachers too harshly, especially when they demand that children in their care avoid mess or risk. Allowing children to get messy assumes that cleaning them up is a simple and inexpensive process, which may not necessarily be the case. We also know that at some schools, teachers will face a barrage of complaints from parents and administrators if children go home with cuts and scratches, let alone sprained ligaments or broken bones. This makes a lot of teachers (and administrators) loath to allow any risk.

We also want to acknowledge that setting limits to nature play is important. We have seen one or two nature-based programs that we felt bordered on chaos, if not outright recklessness. In those programs, children could climb trees as high as they liked without adult supervision. There were no safety provisions in place to prevent children from wandering away from the group, often toward open water. Children were free to destroy nests, break branches, and cause harm to other living things. Nature is our classroom, but we are also its guests and its guardians. We need to behave accordingly. Fostering environmental connection includes setting respectful boundaries.

Yet, children can create their own fun in nature if only we let them. Activities need not be complex nor destructive or dangerous. Often, the simpler and more joyful, the better. Jumping in a pile of fresh autumn leaves inspires connection. Climbing a frozen mound of snow and sliding to the bottom inspires connection. Chasing waves on the shoreline, making messy mud pies, building forts or fairy houses—they all help to inspire connection. The less we interfere and the more we step back and allow the children to engage with nature and with each other, the more we are allowing connection to thrive.

One activity our teachers do take the lead in is something we call Nature's Theater. This is a rather grand name for a simple experience: it just means that we stop whatever we are doing and are temporarily silent. (We take the lead on this because it is unlikely a group of sixteen children will simultaneously choose silence without prompting.) We then sit as a class and watch the "performance" taking place around us. We may watch a line of treetops blowing in the wind. We may watch a hawk perched on a branch. We may watch the drifting clouds overhead. We also listen. We listen to the shuffle of leaves as a single chipmunk scurries by. We listen to birds calling out overhead. We listen to the muffled sounds of our own snow pants or our mittens patting the soft ground around us. We may sit for as little as two minutes or remain in place for ten minutes or more, depending on the group, the temperature, and the show itself. The purpose is not to see who can sit still and listen the longest. Our intention is simply connection.

HOW A YOUNG CHILD DEMONSTRATES ENVIRONMENTAL CONNECTION

- Taking an interest in the natural world and the living things in it
- Expressing a growing respect and empathy for the natural world
- Demonstrating actions that reflect this empathy and respect
- Developing a deeper connection to nature and taking action to protect it

ENVIRONMENTAL LITERACY

For a long time, we placed environmental connection and environmental literacy under the common banner of environmental awareness. In recent years, however, we have separated the two. Very young children may not yet understand environmental concepts such as adaptation and conservation, yet they can still have an emotional response to nature. It is important to acknowledge their response. There are also others in our program who are beginning to ask science-oriented questions and seek thoughtful, scientific answers. These children have observed that the land around them changes and that animals may exhibit behaviors specific to the season. We do not want to dismiss their questions just because other children may not be ready for them.

When children leave our program, we want them to have a deeper understanding of why things are the way they are. We want them to know where the water goes after it rains. We want them to know why they do not see turtles basking on logs during a Wisconsin winter. From our perspective, environmental literacy is something that may stem from environmental connection, but it addresses a different skill set, as illustrated in the following story.

For the past several years at Schlitz Audubon, we have had "our own" eastern screech owl, who has taken up residence from November to March in one of our outdoor

classrooms. She peers out of her chosen tree with seeming interest whenever the children are outside playing. We have theorized that she may feel safer from predators when the play space is filled with noisy children, but perhaps she simply enjoys the activity. Because the owl returns year after year, we have taken to celebrating her arrival. Everything stops when she makes her appearance. Word spreads over the walkie-talkies. Each class takes a special trip to the woods to see her, as do parents and staff. The owl is not always easy to spot. She sits in a high cavity, and her feathers blend in almost perfectly with the surrounding ash bark. It takes a practiced eye to spot her. A few years ago, a young boy walked away after viewing her, looking positively dazed. "All this time we talked about camouflage," he said, "and I finally get it. I mean, I really get it."

This is where environmental literacy begins. It starts with an authentic experience and takes something that was once a vague concept, such as camouflage, and provides a meaningful context. Nature adds richness and depth to concepts and experiences, and it makes the things we have read about, or perhaps only heard about, come alive.

Here is another example:

Every year when the sap runs (usually in early March), we tap our sugar maple trees. The children learn to identify the trees by the structure of the branches. They learn about the different layers, including the heartwood and the sapwood. For several weeks, they visit their tree to collect the sap, holding out their tongues (or spoons) to taste the liquid as it drips from the spouts, which are called *spiles*. Next, the children watch as we cook the sap down over our wood-burning stove. They see the steam the sap produces, which evaporates into soft maple clouds. They look in the pot and spy amber liquid while we discuss how we are subtracting water and leaving the sugar behind. They also learn that woodpeckers, squirrels, and insects enjoy the taste of the sap as much as preschool children do. They learn about the history of maple sugaring, about the Potawatomi and Ho-Chunk peoples who once lived along the shores of Lake Michigan and tapped sugar maple trees by the hundreds each spring. They learn about contemporary maple-sugar farmers and quickly come to understand that maple syrup does not just appear, ready-made, in the grocery store.

Finally, they enjoy warm cups of maple tea as they sit communally around a fire. They can enjoy the sweet, smoky flavor knowing how hard it was to create it. At the end of the season, they return to their maple trees to remove the spiles. They know that the tree now needs its sap to create food for growing leaves. They take time to circle their trees, to thank them for the gifts they give.

Children who have participated in the four-to-six-week maple-sugaring process end up with incredible knowledge. They know the layers of the tree, the feel of the bark, and the taste of the sap. They have a deeper understanding of the tree's cultural history. They can recognize their "own" maple tree in an instant, and they can take a walk through the woods and identify almost any maple they see without pause.

In the first example, when an owl transformed the notion of camouflage into something real, an experience in nature brought a scientific concept to life. In the second, an in-depth study and hands-on investigation added far greater meaning and reverence to what had previously been "just a tree." Environmental literacy includes not only moments of awe and wonder but in-depth ecological concepts made relevant by authentic experience.

HOW A YOUNG CHILD DEMONSTRATES ENVIRONMENTAL LITERACY

- Showing an interest in identifying objects in nature by name
- Showing an emerging understanding of environmental concepts such as camouflage or metamorphosis
- Indicating a desire to learn more about the natural world by initiating investigations
- Developing a sense of personal responsibility within the environment

CURIOSITY AND ENGAGEMENT

A few years ago, one of our staff members found an old-fashioned mailbox shaped like a small log cabin. On a whim, we decided to secure it to a tree stump in one of our outdoor classrooms. The teachers placed small provocations in the mailbox, and during our daily circle time, special helpers were invited to open the door and share what was inside. Items might include a wishing rock from the Lake Michigan beach or a piece of charcoal following a prairie burn. It might be a bird feather, a trail map, a shell, or perhaps a special book.

One day while the children were out hiking, they spotted a chipmunk running across the ravine, directly under the bridge we call Chipmunk Bridge. The children named it Chippy, and for the rest of the afternoon, they wanted to know all about Chippy:

CHAPTER THREE: TEACHING WITH INTENTION

Why did he live under Chipmunk Bridge? Did he have a family? Was he looking for acorns to store for the winter? The next day during circle time, the special helper opened the mailbox, and there was a letter from Chippy the Chipmunk. Chippy wrote that he had overheard their questions and wanted to provide some answers. He talked about his underground burrow and its tunnels with different entry holes. He explained that he collects a nice cache of food throughout fall so that when he wakes in the winter, he can eat underground. He talked about having to keep an eye out

for foxes, hawks, minks, and weasels. He thanked the children for all the delicious pumpkins they had been playing with in their outdoor classrooms and the seeds they had scattered on the ground.

He also had questions for the children. What did they do when the winter came? How did they get their food? Where were their homes? Why did they sit in a circle each day, wear such bright colors, and sing songs?

What followed was an eight-month correspondence between the children and the animals of the woods. Chippy introduced the preschoolers to a few of his friends who did not hibernate over the winter, so that the class could keep up their letters even while he napped. Indoors, the teachers set up a writing area with a second mailbox, envelopes, postcards, and stickers that could be used as stamps. During free play, children drew pictures, dictated cards, or even wrote their own letters describing themselves, their class, and their daily activities.

The teachers eventually introduced the children to the book *Snail Mail* by Samantha Berger, and soon the class was imagining a group of snails that delivered their letters back and forth to the animals in the woods. They went outside in search of snails and perched a giant snail puppet on their mailbox.

The teachers were clearly the ones who brought these activities to fruition. But they did so by following the lead of the children. They provided tools to enhance and expand on the children's play, adding their own sense of humor. Several children were wise enough to realize that these experiences were as much about their interactions with their beloved teachers as they were about the animals they saw in the wild.

We have taken to using the phrase "curiosity and engagement" rather than "approaches to learning" when we talk about how children learn. We recognize that children learn through a variety of means, but ultimately they must want to learn. This, far more than memorizing the alphabet, is what creates eager, active thinkers. In the example above, the children were eager to develop their own reading and writing skills to partake in letter writing with Chippy and his friends. They were not only learning

about natural history, they were communicating ideas, sequencing events, strengthening their motor skills, and making connections between things they learned in books and real-life experiences.

Teachers should encourage children to enjoy and participate in their own learning. This means providing space for play. It means offering direct and indirect experiences by balancing indoor time with books and paper with observing, hiking, and playing outdoors. Most of all, it means creating an environment in which a child's curiosity is appreciated, celebrated, and encouraged.

HOW A YOUNG CHILD DEMONSTRATES CURIOSITY AND ENGAGEMENT

- Using a variety of senses to explore the environment
- Demonstrating an eagerness to learn by asking questions and pondering observations
- Sustaining attention and showing flexibility and persistence
- Extending learning through attempting, repeating, experimenting, and refining experiences

EMOTIONAL DEVELOPMENT

For a long time, we placed social and emotional development together, at least in terms of our teaching intentions. This is a fairly traditional practice in early childhood education, as social and emotional development are so closely interwoven. Yet pairing the two never felt quite right, for as integrated as they are, they are two distinct things. *Emotional development* is learning to recognize and eventually express one's own feelings. *Social development* requires the presence of others, as it is the skill of learning to interact with those around us. One could make the case that social development builds on a foundation that begins with emotional development, as the ability to develop relationships with others depends, in part, on learning to manage one's own emotions and having a deeper sense of self. But one skill does not necessarily follow the other, and so we prefer not to scaffold them in this way.

Very young children may not yet have the ability to express their feelings through language. Some children may not have the self-regulation required to reign in their emotional impulses. That does not necessarily mean they cannot make friends. It means that perhaps they are just beginning to develop personal resilience when faced with emotional challenges. Perhaps they are just starting to realize that their peers have their own opinions and feelings, separate from yet as equally valid as their own. This is a fact that can be quite new (and startling) for a three-year-old.

We do not believe in a single activity that promotes emotional development. It is something that happens daily, over time, through ongoing interactions and practice. One of the most important roles that adults can play is to stand back, doing little more than guiding and encouraging children as they undertake this very personal journey.

Having said that, we are here to help them. One of our biggest jobs in the preschool classroom is to be there for the children as they learn to find appropriate outlets for big feelings and to create a space in which children may feel all their feelings in a way that is safe and respectful. We would never announce that today our intention is going to be "emotional regulation." But we may quietly set that as a goal for individual children who are struggling to communicate with words, who can easily feel overwhelmed by their feelings, and who need help finding ways to express themselves. And we use nature to support us as we set about helping the children practice and develop this skill.

> Several years ago, one of our teachers attended a workshop that focused on children with emotional struggles. She returned to school inspired by a particular activity called the turtle technique, developed by Rochelle Lentini, Lindsay Giroux, and Mary Louise Hemmeter (2008; Vaughn et al., 2009) from the National Center for Pyramid Model Innovations. She followed the advice from the activity's authors and modified the Tucker the Turtle book they had created by featuring dozens of photographs of a plush turtle puppet placed in real-life settings on our trails and grounds.
>
> The text describes a turtle with big feelings who does not always know how to express them in ways that do not frighten or upset the other animals at the pond. The middle

of the book introduces something called Tucker's Toolkit, a small box filled with helpful tools that Tucker can use when he needs help finding words or actions that could assist him whenever his feelings feel too big.

The toolkit contains, among other things, a one-minute timer and flash cards with different symbols on them, including an image of a flowing river and another image of children trading toys. The idea behind the toolkit is that Tucker the Turtle uses the contents to help him better express his wants and needs, particularly in moments of stress. The timer, for instance, can help determine when one person's turn with a toy has ended and another person's has begun. The picture of children trading toys offers one possible approach to solving a conflict. The river symbol means "Go with the flow." Tucker can (at least to a point) decide whether to let a particular emotion or moment overwhelm him or to let it go, reminding him that while his feelings are valid no matter what, he also has the power to determine his response.

In the story, Tucker the Turtle uses his toolkit to help him not only express his own feelings to others but also better recognize them when they arise. Is he upset because he is worried he won't get a turn? Is there anything in his toolkit that could help him? At the end of the book, Tucker is far happier, as he has found a way to make himself understood and has greater control over his emotional responses with others. The other animals are also happier, as they are no longer afraid of Tucker's reactions. The final page shows a photo of Tucker the plush turtle happily basking on a log with several real-life painted turtles, who seem to take it in stride that there is a puppet in their midst.

At the time, the teacher modified the book with a few particular children in mind, but we have continued to use it—and the small kit that goes with it—off and on over the years whenever needed. We have found it to be both compassionate and empowering. The latter cannot be overemphasized, as both the book and the accompanying kit do far more than just sympathize with a struggling child. They provide very useful, practical assistance for helping a child express emotions and solve social difficulties.

Tucker's Toolkit is a prop we tend to bring out when we sense a child is having particular struggles that our day-to-day nature experiences may not address. It is not something we use every day or even every year. For children who may need some help with emotional regulation, but who are, mostly, typically developing three- and four-year-olds, we often find that being in nature is truly enough. If a child has strong emotions, being free to run and move in the outdoor wind, rain, or sunshine is exhilarating. Jumping in puddles and getting splashed can be incredibly emotionally satisfying. Challenging oneself to climb a tree or jump from a rock creates a wonderful feeling of pride and purpose. Water play can be wonderfully soothing. Mud play can be mindful.

Other living things also affect the children. If the group encounters a wild deer and the children wish to see what it does, they must quickly learn to be quiet and calm so that it does not run away. If they express an interest in birds or butterflies, then they should also be taught that the birds and butterflies depend on the flowering trees and prairie plants to survive, which means, by extension, that we cannot pick and destroy those flowers. The need to develop restraint and control as we hike helps regulate mood and behavior.

Nature can also be challenging. We are often outside in uncomfortable weather. We may be wet and cold. We may get sand or rocks in our boots. We may brush up against stinging nettle. At Schlitz Audubon, a one-hundred-foot hill leads from the beach to the building. After the children have spent considerable time playing along the shoreline, they have no choice but to hike back up, a feat that can feel overwhelming to a tired three-year-old. A willing parent might pick them up and carry them to the top, but with a one-to-eight ratio of teachers to students, our teachers make it clear the children have no other option but to hike back up the hill themselves. "Try" becomes our mantra. We try even when something is hard. We try even when we're tired and hungry. Nature sometimes makes us work. But oh, the pride in our accomplishment after we reach the top of the hill! Nature allows us to release and express our feelings, to control how we express our feelings, and to even experience feelings that we have never had before.

HOW A YOUNG CHILD DEMONSTRATES EMOTIONAL DEVELOPMENT

- Needing adults to help regulate emotions
- Learning to regulate emotions without adult intervention
- Finding solutions to emotional conflicts most of the time
- Looking to nature for solace and reduction of stress

SOCIAL DEVELOPMENT

Social development is a child's ability to engage with other people and to form meaningful and positive relationships with them. It is generally assumed that by the time a child is three years old, the child will be able to separate from his or her parents (at least for a few hours), show concern for the feelings of others, take turns, and begin to play cooperatively. These things do not happen the instant the calendar turns over, and these skills do not happen without parents and teachers doing what they can to support the child who is learning these skills. Children depend on nurturing adults to model kindness, consideration, turn taking, friendship, and the tacit rules of social interaction. Such behaviors are not automatic.

How does nature support social development? The natural world provides great examples of animal social systems, such as beehives and anthills, and symbiotic relationships between animals and plants. For example, oak apple galls and goldenrod galls are produced by an insect laying an egg in the plant. The sociobiologist E. O. Wilson (PBS, 2015) suggests that we as humans share with insects the mysterious instinct to build complex societies. Social behaviors we have in common with insects such as bees, ants, wasps, and termites include group belonging, cooperation, and altruism. Our survival as a species depends on our instinctive ability to work together.

The outdoor classroom is a wonderful environment in which social development can flourish because it offers an abundance of materials and the freedom to create, experiment, and problem solve in groups. In a well-thought-out outdoor classroom, there are plenty of sticks, rocks, tools, and building materials to go around. There is enough mud and water to be shared by everyone, and enough space to run and feel free. There are spots to hide and feel concealed. There are also items that specifically require group effort: large branches to haul, large boulders to move, sand and water, shovels and scoops.

If providing inspiring materials and opportunities for interaction is the first step, then the next is knowing when a child is best left alone and when to encourage cooperative play, as illustrated in the following story.

Years ago, we had a class that failed to click right away. It was a group made up of many individuals but without the cohesion of other preschool classes. There was a lot of parallel play. The teachers offered the children many opportunities to interact, but the combination of several introverted children and others who struggled to express themselves verbally made free play feel almost challenging. The teachers felt that, while a few nudges now and again were acceptable, for the most part the children needed time to move forward at their own pace.

One afternoon late in the fall, a single child in the class decided that he wanted to build an outdoor fort. He gathered several long poles from the far corners of the play space, dragging them to a cluster of trees. As he built a framework between the supporting branches, his activities sparked the interest of others. Soon, a few more children joined in, and after some time, even more did too.

The teacher filmed the group as they considered the placement of different logs and poles. After realizing the branches were too big to lift alone, they team-lifted the bigger items and went out on smaller group missions to scout out additional materials. For nearly twenty-five minutes, she filmed the children at work and at play, but even after the camera stopped, the fort building carried on. The teachers canceled their hike so the children could continue their project. They felt that the activity the children had created themselves was far more powerful and far more necessary than going on a hike would be.

Later, the teacher showed the video to the rest of the teaching staff. It was interesting to watch, but not, at first glance, remarkable. The children were not engaged in lengthy conversations. Their fort was nothing out of the ordinary. To some, it did not seem that this activity was worth canceling a hike for. Then the teacher explained that this was the first time in almost eight weeks the children had worked together to complete a project of any kind. They had done so entirely unprompted, and the teachers were in no way involved in the process apart from supporting the activity and allowing it to carry on. She pointed out that, among the participants, there were a few children who had never spoken to a classmate before. There was one who had mostly interacted through pushing. There was another who had cried nearly every day at drop off, but who was seen here happily offering advice and ideas. She described the incredible pride she felt as a teacher as she watched her class finally come together in a way that felt natural but pointed out that the outcome had required weeks of nurturing so the children felt comfortable and safe.

That additional information cast the video in a new light. As they watched again, the other teachers saw children learning multiple social skills at once: overcoming personal fears, practicing communication, and learning to lead and follow. The children were taking turns, solving problems, and forming relationships with one another, all because they had a cool project that they wanted to complete. What did it matter if the fort was no better or more impressive than any other created in preschool? For the children, it was spectacular. It quickly became spectacular to the rest of us too.

HOW A YOUNG CHILD DEMONSTRATES SOCIAL DEVELOPMENT

- Engaging in parallel play near other children using similar materials or actions
- Joining a group successfully
- Joining in and sustaining positive cooperative play in small groups
- Initiating cooperative, complex, and imaginative play

SENSE OF COMMUNITY AND PLACE

When we began to examine our curriculum in terms of our teaching intentions, we did not have a category for community or place. One could argue that the ideals of community and place are already covered by environmental connection and peace (described later in this chapter). Yet when we spoke about our curriculum, the phrase "creating a sense of community and place" came up time and again. We decided that there was, ultimately, something about community building and understanding our own place in a much larger story that made these concepts distinct from other domains.

Creating community requires us to focus outward, toward others. Our nature preschool community includes our students' families along with our volunteers, classroom animals, the natural world, wildlife, birdwatchers, and guests on the trails. It also requires an understanding of place, which includes our city and the other towns and cities that share the Lake Michigan shoreline.

Taking this concept even further, developing a sense of place must include a deeper understanding of the past. Who was here before us? How did they shape the land? Where we are on the map dictates what plants and animals live around us, when the sun sets on the winter solstice, how much rain we get in the summer, and whether or not we see monarchs or moose.

CHAPTER THREE: TEACHING WITH INTENTION

Our program includes daily circle time. We gather on outdoor logs, sing our hello songs, read books, and talk. This is how we strengthen our own class community. We acknowledge who is missing from our circle—perhaps a classmate is home sick, or perhaps someone is traveling. We send our love and good thoughts for absent friends out into the universe. Depending on the age of the group and the topics the children themselves bring up, our circle time may touch on more serious subjects, such as what is happening in the wider world or what has happened in the past, including who lived on this land and what they did there years before we arrived.

Circle time became even more important to our program's sense of community in 2020.

> When COVID-19 struck our state and the numbers of positive cases in our immediate community grew alarmingly high, we decided to stop serving snacks because removing our masks to eat suddenly felt unsafe. The teachers were not very concerned about the loss of food, as our classes meet for less than three hours and the children do not depend on us for their meals. However, they did wonder how we would replicate the feeling of unity that accompanies snack time. It turned out we already had the answer. Circle time simply expanded, allowing the children more time to talk. Without daily snacks, we no longer had to rush through our day. Instead, the children could share ideas, tell stories, and participate fully in the group when we gathered on our logs. Those who were shy had the time they needed to grow comfortable before speaking.
>
> In the winter, we introduced fire. Our fire circles were places where we could take literal warming breaks. They also became places where the children talked, sipped

warm cups of tea, and told stories. Soon our fire circles were also places where community was being created. The children and teachers spoke of feeling more connected to one another and to the fire, the land, and the winter itself because of sitting around that daily fire. We wondered if the social component of snack time had always been less about the food and more about the circle.

It is difficult sometimes to know where one's sense of place ends and community begins. We would argue that they form one continuous circle. All of our intentions are a part of a whole. If one of our goals in creating a stronger community is to learn how to treat ourselves, others, and our surrounding environment with kindness and respect, then isn't developing a sense of community really just an extension of social and emotional development and environmental connection? If another goal is developing a relationship with nature by forming a deeper understanding of who was here before us and how they used the land, isn't developing a sense of place just another way of building environmental connection? The answer to both is an emphatic yes. Just as children are whole beings, our intentions are not meant to be sorted into carefully curated drawers and boxes. It is okay and expected that they overlap.

At our school, we are big fans of classroom codes. They may look different from year to year, as they are created with every child's input. Yet stripped to the bones, they ultimately break down into just a few simple ideals:

- We are kind to feelings.
- We are kind to bodies.
- We stay safe.
- We try.
- We are free to be ourselves.
- We have fun.

Almost everything the children come up with when creating their classroom code falls into one of these categories. Don't swat at hornets (We stay safe). Help a friend with their mittens (We are kind to bodies). Don't laugh when someone trips and falls (We are kind to feelings). I like to paint every day (We have fun). I am transgender and that's okay (We are free to be ourselves).

CHAPTER THREE: TEACHING WITH INTENTION

What is especially interesting is when our classroom codes encounter conflict. It may be fun for you to throw water on someone else, but is it fun for the child who gets wet? (It might be.) Is it being kind to feelings if you know your friend wants to stay dry? Where do the rights of one child stop and those of another child begin?

"I am free to be me" is a code that invites fascinating discussions. What makes us *us*? What are our likes and dislikes? What makes us happy? What makes us laugh? Do we like red apples best, or green? What are our favorite colors? Are we who other people say we are, or is that decision up to us? "I am free to be me" provides a safe space for children who are shy, children who are loud, children who speak languages other than English, children who don't speak, children who like to dive into mud, and children who like to stay clean to be themselves, without judgement. When one child tells another what to think or believe, this is when the response "I am free to be me" becomes powerful.

Being kind to feelings includes giving others the freedom to be themselves. Being kind to bodies means that no one will be hurt for being different or for having different ideas. Having fun means every child feels welcomed. Being safe means that we take care of ourselves and each other. These intentions support social and emotional development. But we place them alongside community because, for us, they are not the same as expressing personal emotions or encouraging social interactions. Developing a sense of community and place means doing our part to make the world a safer and more welcoming space for all.

HOW A YOUNG CHILD DEMONSTRATES A SENSE OF COMMUNITY AND PLACE

- Not yet considering the needs of the group or of other living things
- Understanding that different people have different needs and emotions
- Expanding their understanding of community to include local flora and fauna
- Showing respect for the diversity of others

COMMUNICATION AND EMERGING LITERACY

In many early childhood programs, communication and emerging literacy are treated as two distinct developmental domains. *Communication* is described as a child's ability to understand receptive language and to express meaning through words or gestures. *Literacy*, in contrast, is all about the written word. Educators encourage children to engage with books and to recognize and learn to write letters as part of the ongoing path toward literacy.

While there is nothing wrong with this approach, it is also somewhat limiting. Literacy, especially in early childhood, does not always have to mean books. Storytelling is literacy. Singing is literacy. Nonspoken language can also be literacy. Literacy begins when we provide opportunities for children to communicate their thoughts and ideas. Adults can record children's stories in print, and in doing so, children begin to understand that there is meaning in the written word and that words can be transcribed into text. They also begin to associate feelings of love and comfort with reading. The spoken word and the written word are not separate; one grows directly from the other. At our nature preschool, we have made a conscious effort to include verbal and nonverbal communication as a part of our approach to literacy and have found it works wonderfully in a play-based classroom.

If a child creates a painting, we might ask that child to share the story of the painting. It is important to remember that sometimes there is no story. (We always want to be mindful of the fact that not every painting or work of art comes with a narrative, and that's okay too.) Does the painting have a title? What was the child thinking about as they painted? If a child doesn't speak, we may still ask questions about their mood as they painted, which a child can express through facial expressions. Or we can simply record the date, the time of day, and the weather on a sticky note and attach it to the painting like a museum placard.

The purpose of this is to encourage children to become narrators. This not only gives them the chance to explain the meaning of their creations but also gives the teacher and child an opportunity to engage in one-on-one conversation. This can later be repeated when a parent or family member sees the painting and the sticky note and is inspired to engage in a discussion as well.

We embrace the philosophy espoused by the National Council of Teachers of English, who describe *literacy* as "the way that we interact with the world around us, how we shape it and are shaped by it. It is how we communicate with others via reading and writing, but also by speaking, listening, and creating. It is how we articulate our experience in the world and declare, 'We Are Here!'" (Peterson, 2020).

We have spent hours playing in the mud kitchen creating elaborate recipes from wet, sticky mud. Even if the mud dries up, the play continues, easily supplemented by dirt, wood chips, and stones. As the children concoct recipes, teachers write them down and later read them aloud during our circle time. Some teachers have taken this idea even further, creating mud-kitchen menus and cookbooks that the children can take home. The cookbook is not only a fun way to remember our mud recipes; it's also a wonderful form of documentation, recording emerging literacy in a way that is far more fun and engaging than any assessment checklist. Other examples of literacy abound.

> One year, one of our classes was invited by our land managers to observe a controlled prairie burn. The children watched for nearly an hour. The head of the land-management team came by at intervals to explain what was happening, and the children were full of observations and questions. One teacher eventually grabbed her notebook and recorded what she was hearing. Later, she rewrote the children's comments on a large sheet of paper and hung it where both the children and their parents could see it. Their spoken words, transcribed, read like poetry:
>
> - It's hot
> - And orange
> - It smells like a campfire
> - Like marshmallows roasting
> - Like burning leaves
> - I see sparks
> - And flashes of tiny things, burning
> - Floating away
> - I like the smell
> - It makes a loud cackle sound
> - It's a little bit scary
> - It's for the Earth
> - The roots grow deep
> - The fire is to make things grow again

There is a difference between the spoken and written word. It is important when discussing literacy to recognize the two as separate skills. The spoken word depends not just on learning words but also on being able to engage in back-and-forth conversation (Walinga and Stangor, 2021). The ability to read and write means being able to create, interpret, and communicate through written materials. Literacy as a whole may be partially understood as the ability to derive meaning from context or as a tool with which to engage with society.

Adding books and journals to an outdoor classroom is perhaps one of the easiest and most direct ways to incorporate written language into a nature-based program. It is also possible to add these elements to play. We have already mentioned our mud-kitchen cookbooks. Learning to read maps as we hike is also a part of literacy. Reading one's name on one's boots, mittens, and outdoor-gear bag is literacy. Having each child "sign in" each day (we use tree cookies emblazoned with each child's name) is literacy. So too is singing, talking, engaging in one-on-one or group discussions, and giving each child an opportunity to share aloud with the class.

During the school year, teachers might help children write tiny notes for their fairy houses, decode pirate clues leading to buried treasure, or search for hidden messages left by the animals in the woods. We include slabs of slate and chalkboards in our play spaces, along with baskets full of chalk. We mimic songbirds, sing songs, and provide many opportunities for children to sit together in communal conversation. We use maps, read trail signs, provide trail guides, search for letters in the shapes of nature, and trace intricate designs in the dirt. All of this is the beginning of literacy.

HOW A YOUNG CHILD DEMONSTRATES COMMUNICATION AND EMERGING LITERACY

- Listening to and understanding receptive language
- Demonstrating an ability to communicate through conversation and narration
- Understanding that text is meaningful and using strategies to determine written words
- Beginning to use writing to record and represent ideas

MATHEMATICAL THINKING

It should be abundantly clear by now that at nature preschool we do not divide up our days by different areas of study, allotting thirty minutes for reading, thirty minutes for writing, and so on. Our days are play based, and while they follow certain patterns, they unfold in ways that feel organic, responding to the needs and rhythm of each class. It follows that we do not have a designated time reserved just for learning numbers.

Even so, hardly a day goes by when we are not at some point sorting, counting, adding, subtracting, exploring spatial relationships, and noticing shapes and patterns. Teachers encourage mathematical thinking by bringing tape measures into the field. We measure the height of sunflowers, the circumference of tree trunks, and the diameter of fallen logs. We count the legs on insects and the points on snowflake crystals. A few years ago, we deliberately placed the numbers one through ten on wooden posts in one of our outdoor classrooms; now, the children can run around and track the numbers as a part of their play. Because we are lucky enough to tap trees in our Wisconsin winters, we also use measurement when creating maple syrup.

As winter gives way to spring, we spend six weeks gathering maple sap from our sugar bush, slowly cooking it

PARTNERING WITH *Nature* IN EARLY CHILDHOOD EDUCATION

down into maple tea or syrup. In the process, the children begin to understand subtraction. Just consider the mathematical thinking that takes place when learning about evaporation! A "maple sap map" illustrates the water-to-sugar ratios, with bright yellow dots representing the sugar, and bright blue dots representing the water. In a typical gallon of maple sap, there is mostly water with just a few drops of 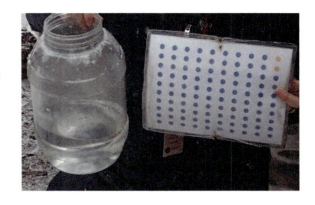 sugar. On a sap map, there will be mostly blue dots interspersed with a few dots of yellow. Once we have boiled the water away, our sap maps will be reversed, meaning mostly yellow (sugar) with a few dots of blue (water). While abstract, the children can visualize a fairly advanced mathematical concept and can connect the dots, as it were, between the meaning of subtraction and a real-life experience.

But math doesn't need to be complex. One of the most delightful ways to make mathematical thinking a part of our daily experiences is to, again, make it a part of play. While hiking, we may look for heart shapes in nature. Basswood leaves, beach pebbles, butterfly wings, flower petals, clouds, or uncurling fiddleheads can all resemble valentines. When we visit the live raptors at our raptor center, we measure and compare our own wingspans to theirs. When we stop to identify poison ivy, we count the leaves of three. Children enjoy counting rocks and pine cones, turtles on logs, Canada geese, and one another. They enjoy counting aloud when they play Hide and Seek. They enjoy counting their steps up a giant hill. Math comes to life when it is a part of real-life experiences. But it is also brought to life when it is allowed to become a part of play.

HOW A YOUNG CHILD DEMONSTRATES MATHEMATICAL THINKING

- Demonstrating counting skills and beginning number concepts
- Demonstrating a growing understanding of the concept of quantity (more, less, fewer)
- Developing an understanding of spatial relationships
- Applying a variety of mathematical strategies to real-world scenarios

SCIENTIFIC THINKING

Young children are scientists by nature. As they play, they are exploring, discovering, asking questions, and using scientific tools to solve problems. At our nature preschool, we have two primary goals when it comes to scientific thinking. One is to provide a range of opportunities for children that promote inquiry and hands-on experimentation. The other is to get out of their way.

It is easy enough to provide the former, particularly in nature. Woods, prairies, ponds, sidewalks, city parks, desert landscapes, sagebrush steppes, decaying tree stumps, and even tiny rain puddles all have the potential to serve as outdoor laboratories. Simply allowing children time and space to investigate these tiny worlds up close encourages scientific discovery. Adults can also help children make predictions by wondering aloud with them. "I wonder what will happen if we take this bucket of snow inside. I wonder how much water will be in the bucket by tomorrow."

So often, teachers new to nature-based early childhood education tell us that their biggest concern is their own limited knowledge of nature. "I don't know the names of the plants" is a common refrain. While we believe it's important for nature-based teachers to have some knowledge of the natural world, we also believe there is value in the reply, "I don't know either. Let's find out." Reading field guides together, conducting experiments, and observing and discussing your observations together are skills that promote scientific thinking.

Sometimes, the teacher actually does know the answer but chooses not to share it, giving the children time to discover it on their own. This is often more challenging than it sounds: getting out of the way while children explore can be difficult. Teachers may find it hard to sit back while the children crack open layers of ice with a stick. Teachers may feel that they are not properly supervising when they allow too much noise on their watch. They may also feel that they are not actively teaching when they fail to provide immediate answers. But scientific thinking is not about memorizing information that someone else has provided. It is about decoding the mysteries of the world on one's own. This is done by asking questions, observing processes, and reaching one's own conclusions. The process matters more than the answer.

HOW A YOUNG CHILD DEMONSTRATES SCIENTIFIC THINKING

- Using senses to explore the natural environment
- Demonstrating an understanding of living things and their habitats
- Demonstrating an understanding of physical properties
- Making predictions and using evidence to determine conclusions

---

LARGE AND FINE MOTOR DEVELOPMENT

Physical movement is a natural part of the outdoor nature-based classroom. Running, jumping, climbing trees, building snow sculptures, raking leaves, and using pond nets support large motor development. Handling insects, playing with sticks, collecting seeds, and prying caps off acorns support fine motor development.

For the most part, we simply provide the space and the tools and then watch as the children play. Most preschool-aged children are more inclined to move than sit still. They are supposed to discover the world through movement. There are times, however, when adults need to be mindful of different needs and abilities and add materials that may be missing. Children with limited mobility may feel left out of many nature-based classrooms, unless there are opportunities for movement and play that consider their specific needs. Our program has benefited from "walk-through" visits with physical therapists, who have been able to suggest ideas for more overhead shoulder mobility, including "dead-hanging" and hand-over-hand swinging and climbing activities. (We address this topic in more detail in chapter 8.) We also recommend reading *Naturally Inclusive: Engaging Children of All Abilities Outdoors* by Ruth Wilson to anyone looking for more information on how to make nature experiences as inclusive of all abilities as possible.

The following are a few simple ways to make outdoor nature-based play spaces more accessible (YoungStar, 2017):

- **Make sure there are plenty of choices and different options for play.** A single activity that only allows for one type of movement will leave out many children, not just those with limited mobility. Make sure there are options for both fine and large motor movement. Include a range of sensory experiences, such as mud, water, sand, and so on. Add dramatic play props that could allow children to turn a wheelchair into a steamroller, tractor, or locomotive. Try to ensure that there are a variety of terrains, including flat ones that could accommodate wheelchairs or walkers. Remember that some children may require quiet, soft places to feel safe, and be sure to provide cozy, calm areas as well as busy, active ones.

- **Break the rules!** You can bring books outside. You can bring art materials outside. You can even bring puzzles, paper, and plush toys outside. Many schools have a "down only" rule on their playground slides. But there are many benefits to going up the slide, especially for a child who may be unable to climb the ladder but can use their arms to pull themselves up the smooth, sloped surface of the slide itself. Remember that rules exist to keep children safe. They should never take precedence over the harm done when a child is left out.

- **Lend a hand.** If possible, have an adult carry a child with limited mobility onto a slide or a swing. Provide structures overhead—perhaps even tree branches—from which children can hang or swing. Develop and lead games that require mental as well as physical problem solving. Design activities that require shutting down one sense in favor of another, such as identifying objects by touch rather than sight. Invite parents, therapists, and even playground designers with experience in creating ADA–compliant play spaces to visit your grounds and share their ideas. Creating accessible experiences outdoors will not only invite children with specific disabilities into play, it will create experiences that are more meaningful for every person in your program.

Play, as much as it is possible to do so, should encourage a range of muscle use. Hiking should aim to involve different types of terrain. Children should have opportunities to test their balance on ice or to walk atop a slippery log, to run, to lie down, or to flap their wings like migrating birds. Allow them to hang from branches or to safely climb higher. Allow them the chance to swing, bounce, slide, and roll. There must be a balance between sitting still in nature and plenty of physical movement.

The curriculum should also include natural loose parts, such as pine cones, acorns, pebbles, sticks, branches, shells, grasses, and even dried corncobs (which can be shucked). Provide twine, scissors, hammers, drills, and pliers. Set out art materials, such as chalk, charcoal, brushes, pencils, paint, and glue. Give children scoops, bug boxes, measuring spoons, and magnifying lenses. Allow them to sort, carry, weigh, tinker, push, pull, and take things apart. These activities strengthen the hand muscles, which are essential for manipulating pencils and paper and learning how to write.

It is an alarming fact that, for nearly a decade now, kindergarten teachers have been reporting an increasing number of children entering elementary school with significant motor delays. In her article "Losing Our Grip: More Students Entering Schools without Fine Motor Skills," journalist Kimberly Marselas reports, "an increasing number of children are showing up for kindergarten without the fine motor skills needed to grip a marker, hold their paper still while coloring or cut and glue shapes . . . in some cases, young students are unable to stay seated for sustained periods because they don't have adequate trunk strength" (Marselas, 2015).

These days we are even seeing young children lacking the vestibular sense—the sense of balance and space—that allows them to sit at their desks, meaning small children are literally falling out of their chairs during class time (Hanscom, 2016). Many are easily exhausted or use all their energy reserves to keep still without any opportunity to do what children do best—to squiggle, wriggle, and play. Lack of physical movement can cause delays that cross over into academic learning.

Angela Hanscom has written on this topic extensively, most notably in her outstanding book *Balanced and Barefoot: How Unrestricted Outdoor Play Makes for Strong, Confident, and Capable Children*. She explains that children who find it hard to focus, who struggle to control their own bodies in space, and who lack balance and coordination often have difficulty managing classroom work. By contrast, children who experience unstructured free play, particularly outside, are exercising their whole bodies, including their brains. They find it easier to concentrate and easier to maintain control over their limbs, and they are less exhausted because they are not required to sit still each day for an unreasonable amount of time. Further, children who know how to manage their skills for daily living, such as getting dressed, washing hands, and managing their own comfort, have greater self-confidence and a greater sense of their own self-efficacy, which are also important ingredients for academic success.

Finally, physical movement promotes better health. Throughout the COVID-19 pandemic, health took center stage in our program, often in ways it never had before. Keeping track of each runny nose and each cough and trying to ensure that every child, teacher, and parent came to school healthy and remained that way became a part of our daily experience. Children learned to wear and handle their own face masks. They learned to give each other space during circle time. To help manage COVID-19, we moved our program entirely outdoors, even during a long Wisconsin winter. We successfully managed the coldest days of the year through a combination of warm drinks, outdoor heaters, good-quality winter gear, and *frequent movement*.

This does not mean we ran relay races or set up daily exercise drills. It does mean we let children sled down hills, slide through tunnels, balance on logs, and skate across ice. We gathered wood for our outdoor fires. We hauled buckets of heavy sap. Moving one's body in nature is a wonderful, easy way to encourage large and fine motor development, physical fitness, endurance, and overall good health.

CHAPTER THREE: TEACHING WITH INTENTION

HOW A YOUNG CHILD DEMONSTRATES LARGE MOTOR DEVELOPMENT

- Maintaining a short hike on flat terrain without falling
- Demonstrating balancing skills, such as walking along a log
- Hiking in a controlled manner along a variety of terrains
- Using large motor manipulations with growing competence and strength

HOW A YOUNG CHILD DEMONSTRATES FINE MOTOR DEVELOPMENT

- Holding objects in fist with limited fine motor coordination
- Exhibiting growing eye-hand coordination in the manipulation of objects
- Using fingers to manipulate tiny objects
- Using writing and drawing tools with control

AESTHETIC DEVELOPMENT

First, a disclaimer. Whenever we gather to discuss our goals for the children, we seldom, if ever, refer to their aesthetic development. As much as we enjoy the arts, we have never forced a child to stop whatever they were doing to come to an easel. As much as we enjoy music, we never discuss a child's love of singing or playing drums in terms of their aesthetics. We often dismiss the term *aesthetic*, if only because it is so unusual to meet a child who does not love to create, whether it be art, music, dance, movement, a mess, or mud pies.

However, art and creative expression are a large part of our daily experiences. Some children are so drawn to art projects that they would happily spend hours each day doing nothing else. Others may need more coaxing or may actively dislike certain types of art, such as fingerpainting, which is also fine. Building block towers is a form of creation. Spinning in circles is a form of creation. Our goal is not to create a class full of artists but to give children opportunities to experience paint, sculpture, music, dance, construction, photography, and so on as means of expression.

It is also important to us that we expand our definition of aesthetics to include the natural world. Throughout the year, we see the leaves on our deciduous trees turn myriad shades of orange and red. We collect delicate snowflakes on squares of frozen black felt. We celebrate the early spring wildflowers and late summer sunflowers. It is easy for children to develop an aesthetic sense when they are surrounded by beauty, and it is easy to surround children with beauty when their classroom takes place in the natural world. It is also possible to find beauty on a much smaller scale. A single dandelion growing proudly in a sidewalk crack can be beautiful. The color of pavement after the rain can be beautiful.

> Over the years, we have collected several inexpensive children's cameras for each classroom. One year, a teacher who was herself an artist made photography a central part of the children's experience. Each day, the special helpers could photograph their experiences in the outdoor play spaces and on their hikes. Over many months, the class had a gallery of more than five hundred photographs, all taken by the children. With parental help, the teacher curated the collection and had sixty-four prints professionally printed and mounted. She then put together an exhibit, to which the entire preschool was invited.
>
> Our first realization was that the children photographed nature differently than the teachers did. They were less concerned about technical perfection and whether the image was in focus or centered. Teachers, thinking in terms of documentation, might photograph the entire class or even just a few students busily engaged in play at the

CHAPTER THREE: TEACHING WITH INTENTION

lakefront. A child, however, photographed peers close-up, nearly nose to nose. When they photographed a fallen tree, it was from their vantage point, showing us just how enormous that hollowed log looked through the eyes of a four-year-old.

The photography project encouraged self-expression, inspiring the children to slow down and spot things they found beautiful or interesting or worthy of capturing. It also reminded us that children see the world differently than we do. They often zoom in on details that we deem unimportant. A single patch of moss might be magical to a child. Children are more likely to take a picture of a single rock or a bubble on the water. They are more intimate with their peers than we are, as their close-up pictures of one another's faces made clear. Their experiments with the camera often resulted in dizzying swirls of leaves, raindrops, and sunlight, creating images we likely could never quite duplicate. The project allowed us to assess the children's relationship with nature in ways we had never fully seen before and allowed the children to give us a glimpse of their world.

Aesthetic development can also be fostered through planting a garden. We invite the children in our class to plant flowers in our garden beds, without dictating where the flowers go or what kind of flowers they can put in the ground (as long as they aren't invasive perennials, which could escape and do harm to the surrounding landscape). By summer, our garden beds are a brilliant hodgepodge of color, texture, and shape, bursting with flowers of all different heights and hues. The effect is marvelous, but again, it is something most adults are unlikely to create, as it is also cluttered and disorganized. But to the children, the gardens are inviting. They are filled with glass gems, tiny fairy houses, and colored trails made from sand or biodegradable glitter, all of which can be moved around to an individual child's preference.

Finally, we are huge fans of painting *en plein air*. Simply translated, this means "in the open air." We use large sheets of cardboard as easels and secure heavy paper to the cardboard with clips. These can easily be transported outside in reusable shopping bags. We also keep bags ready to go, filled with paints, crayons, or oil pastels. On any given day, we may set up outside by the ponds or in a shady grove and just sit together as a group to paint, draw, or play with the effect of the different art materials on paper. We don't care whether the children produce elaborate landscape paintings or opt to draw robots. Aesthetic development, for us, doesn't mean we are actively teaching art class. We are simply using art—whether it be studio art, music, dance, or song—to express our thoughts and experiences. Aesthetic development is never about the product. It is about the process.

HOW A YOUNG CHILD DEMONSTRATES AESTHETIC DEVELOPMENT

- Expressing creativity through the arts
- Showing interest in a range of art forms
- Showing an appreciation for the beauty of nature
- Using imagination and inspiration from nature to create art

RISK ASSESSMENT AND SELF-EFFICACY

Learning to navigate risky situations is a part of our daily experience. This is especially true in a nature-based classroom. Children climb trees, play by water, encounter thorns, and traverse sheets of ice. We must teach them how to manage and assess risk, giving them the space they need to experiment within their own comfort levels while still ensuring their safety. Does that mean we deliberately want to introduce risk into our daily activities? Yes.

To be clear, this does not mean taking a safe environment and making it dangerous. Very young children should never be placed in danger deliberately. We are mindful to keep children safe from anything truly beyond their control. We do not push the children outdoors during a lightning storm. We do accept that on any given day we might need to hand out an adhesive bandage.

We make it a point to walk through our spaces and assess them for hazards, using our own, more experienced eyes. We also stoop down low and consider the space from the view of a child. Are there branches right at their eye level that could cause injury? We meet as a team to discuss our own comfort level with different risks. We have gradually eased our restrictions on going up the slide, coming to embrace slide ascension as a positive activity. But we continue to have rules in place about the ways sticks and rocks may be handled, where to place our bodies at the ponds and lakes, or how high a child may climb a tree. Some programs may look at this and think we're far too restrictive, while others may be aghast at our leniency. Risk is often subjective.

CHAPTER THREE: TEACHING WITH INTENTION

In general, we appreciate and celebrate risk. We do not remove every rock, stick, or branch from our outdoor classrooms, as we want the children to use these materials. We cook over open fires but teach the children about fire safety in the process. We visit the lakefront on stormy days so that we can see the power of the wind and the waves crashing on the shore. Knowing what is within your control and what isn't builds confidence and common sense.

We also understand that not every risk is a physical one. For some, asking another child to play is a risk, requiring the same determination and bravery that it may take to climb a tree. For some, learning to go to the bathroom at school is a risk, especially if toileting itself is a relatively new skill.

We view risks as challenges, difficulties, or obstacles that require determination and courage. They also require assessment: if you try to tackle it one way and it doesn't work, try it again a new way. There is a fair amount of thinking that goes into assessing risk. By taking thoughtful precautions—testing the thickness of the ice, testing the firmness of the branches—it is easier to make an informed decision.

Children who are always told what they can and cannot do are not learning to assess risky situations, nor are they learning to sort through the problem. If they have never learned to consider different outcomes, never made a decision that ended badly, and never developed their own comfort levels in difficult situations, how will they assess risk when they are older? Will they continue to wait for other people to tell them what they can and cannot do? Any parent of a teenager will immediately understand that we want our children to assess risk with a clear head, knowing what situations are beyond their control and what situations they can manage.

> We have a tunnel in one of our play spaces that runs through a tiny hill. In the winter, the tunnel often fills with snow, making it a tight squeeze for anyone who dares to go through. One year, a group of six intrepid preschoolers formed a line, each child determined to navigate the narrow crawl space, while a teacher sat near the exit, ready to assist those who wanted help.
>
> One particular child grew frightened when she found herself in the middle of the tunnel, which was darker and narrower than expected. She started crying. The teacher

coaxed her through, calmed her down, and assumed that the child would now find something else to do. Instead, the child got back in line. When her turn came up again, she immediately started crying. She cried the entire way through the tunnel, but she did not want help. She went back in line again. On her third round, there were no tears. She giggled nonstop, overjoyed at her own ability to do something that she found frightening but with determination had mastered.

There is a direct line between learning to navigate risks and developing self-efficacy. Self-efficacy is not quite the same as self-esteem. Self-esteem is born from the praise and encouragement of others. Self-efficacy is a confidence that can only grow from having mastered a particular skill and knowing—without being told—that one can do it. A child who, having taken risks and learned from them, can walk into elementary school on the first day knowing how to ask questions, make friends, and even use the school bathroom, and understands they have what is needed to succeed. A child who has never had to face down a challenge, try something new, or take a chance on something intimidating is not nearly as prepared. That is why risk is so important. It enables us to grow and learn. We do children such a disservice when, in the name of absolute safety, we try to eliminate risk from their world.

HOW A YOUNG CHILD DEMONSTRATES RISK ASSESSMENT AND SELF-EFFICACY SKILLS

- Expressing an interest in trying new and potentially challenging things
- Showing a willingness to keep trying even when something is difficult
- Demonstrating an ability to assess risk—that branch is too high, that log is too slippery
- Developing an understanding of personal comfort zone and abilities

PEACE

The promotion of peace within a nature preschool curriculum refers to the peacemakers, to those children who offer comfort when someone is upset and strive to resolve conflicts. It refers to the role that peace plays in community, to social justice, and to a sense of fairness. Finally, it refers to a sense of calm and stillness, to ensuring that children have moments during their school day to feel safe, relaxed, and at ease.

It is not always easy to talk about peace in the wider world, but we can talk about the role of peace by asking children what they think *peace* means. Does opting for peace over violence mean acquiescing and letting others have their way, or does it mean standing your ground and speaking up for what is right? Which is easier, peace or anger? Which is more powerful?

CHAPTER THREE: TEACHING WITH INTENTION

We promote peace when we speak of community and when we create our classroom codes. We promote peace when we learn how our actions affect the land and animals around us. We promote peace when we encourage children to speak up for themselves, to take care of each other, and to consider different views and perspectives.

Peace is both a feeling—a sense of solace in nature, a desire to add goodness into the world—and an action. Chances are that when children who experience profound moments of joy, kinship, and connection in the natural world seek comfort later in life, they will find it in nature. When we can present peaceful resolutions to conflicts as powerful, meaningful tools that leave us feeling stronger and more connected to the people around us, we are helping to create future peacemakers.

The role of peace in the preschool curriculum is quiet, mindful, and ever present. Teachers can demonstrate peace through the way they speak. Do they exude a sense of calm, love, patience, and understanding, even when a child is angry? Do they maintain fairness? Do they ensure that every child feels welcomed and valued? Do teachers (and all adults in the program) speak to each other with respect? Do they model compassion?

Peace in the preschool classroom is a mindset, just as it is in the larger society. By providing a classroom that embraces peace as both a feeling and an action, teachers are modeling "positive peace" and character development. The seventeenth-century philosopher Baruch Spinoza (1670) wrote, "Peace is not mere absence of war; it is a virtue, a state of mind, a disposition for benevolence, confidence, justice." The idea that positive peace stems from one's character is also supported by the United Nation's definition of *peace* as written in the Earth Charter: "the wholeness created by right relationships with oneself, other persons, other cultures, other life, Earth, and the larger whole of which we all are a part." One of our goals at our nature preschool is to create a group of future citizens who care about the land and about the well-being of others, which includes developing an understanding of the principles of peace. The Earth Charter provides us with a foundation for such a goal. (To read the Earth Charter, see https://earthcharter.org/read-the-earth-charter/)

HOW A YOUNG CHILD DEMONSTRATES PEACEFULNESS

- Exhibiting a peaceful approach toward life
- Showing empathy and respect for living things
- Engaging in meaningful conversation about what is fair and right
- Showing an interest in resolving conflicts and encouraging peaceful play

SPIRITUAL DEVELOPMENT

Whenever we tell other educators that our intentions include spiritual development, we brace for their hesitation. Spirituality has become so interwoven with religion that even the mention of it can give people pause. Ours is not a religiously affiliated school, and we would never dream of dictating anyone's religious beliefs. For us, the two are not the same. When we speak of spiritual development, we speak not of religion but of each child's individual spirituality: the awe and wonder they experience in response to the natural world; their interpretation of natural phenomena; their reaction to death, life, and renewal; and their own sense of being a part of something greater than they are.

We believe that children have their own spirituality. It is something they are born with, regardless of whether they are raised within a particular culture or set of religious beliefs. We also believe that nature and spirituality are intrinsically linked. How many of us as adults can speak to the experience of feeling calm, comforted, and even enlightened after a quiet walk alone in the woods or to the sense of awe, joy, and wonder we feel when watching a sunset over a still body of water? Some people deliberately seek nature when dealing with stress, loss, or trauma because they find it healing. Some might say this is yet another version of environmental connection or even just a deeper, more enriching form of emotional development. We call it *spiritual development* because we don't want to shy away from the term. Perhaps we want to reclaim it, to bring the idea of spiritual development back to nature, where it can be enjoyed by all.

When a child asks questions about nature such as "What is that flower called?" and "Where does that animal go in winter?" teachers rarely hesitate. They either answer the child's question directly or help the child look into it further, arriving at an answer together. When children wonder about things on a much broader scale—"Who made the world?" "Does God live in the sun?" "What happens to a baby bird's soul when it dies?"—we often freeze. We are afraid, as preschool teachers in a secular school, of giving any answer that could be misinterpreted as religious teaching. Often, the other children are quick to jump in with the answers: "Yes, God lives in the sun, traveling around the world every time it rises and falls." "Earth was created by a giant turtle, rising out of the mist, and we are now all living on the turtle's back." "The baby bird's soul flies up to the sky." For us, nurturing a child's spiritual development means giving children a safe, loving, nonjudgmental space to ask questions and consider answers.

> We are fortunate that our little nature preschool sits on a bluff overlooking Lake Michigan. We are also fortunate that the shape of our shoreline, combined with a specific mix of strong winds and tides, results almost every winter in unique ice formations all along the lakefront. We call them ice volcanoes, or *ice-canoes*, hollow, conical sculptures made of frozen lake water. As fresh lake water splashes inside these cones, they grow taller and thicker until the temperature shifts. Then they vanish,

CHAPTER THREE: TEACHING WITH INTENTION

sometimes within hours. Visitors come to us every year just to spend time alone at the lake, contemplating these powerful, unique formations.

For the children, visiting the ephemeral ice-canoes is a spectacular experience. It is like walking on another planet, and they remember it years later. The familiar sandy beach and blue water are gone, and in their place are hills, cones, caves, and valleys made of ice. Yet the ice isn't stable, which means the children cannot run and shout or slip and slide across it. They must move slowly, cautiously, and be mindful of their own safety. Temperatures often hover just a few degrees above zero, which makes rapid movement more difficult. They speak in whispers, if at all. Most children ultimately just sit and stare, full of awe and wonder. The teachers ensure the children are safe and then sit back in silence, allowing each child to experience the ice on their own.

There is no doubt that for many of us, viewing the ice-canoes touches the spirit. It reminds us of the incredible beauty of the natural world and makes us feel part of something ancient and powerful. From a teaching perspective, particularly in a nonreligious program such as ours, spirituality in nature does not have to mean anything more than this. It is simply the awareness that something is stirring deep within us when we sit in stillness and silence in nature. We are more aware of the interconnectedness of all things and are perhaps a little more aware of our own place in the wider world. Experiences such as these, relationships that result, and the interconnectedness of oneself and the natural world help children to know themselves and others more deeply. This is an important component leading to empathy and kindness, counteracting depression and stress (Schein, 2018).

Developing an individual spirituality in nature requires an environment that allows for spiritual moments in and with nature to happen (Schein, 2018). Perhaps this means touching snow for the first time or seeing one's first sunset. Spiritual moments also occur when children are provided with "significant time, beautiful spaces, authentic relationships, quality time in and with nature, and the opportunity to think, articulate, and explore big questions" (Schein, 2018). We support spiritual development in children by adopting a mindful approach to our days. This includes slowing down. Stillness and reflection are important spiritual components. We do not have to pack every day with activities, answer every question asked, or fill every silence with words. Even if you, as an educator, feel that you would prefer not to embrace *spiritual development* as an official term, it is still possible to nurture and promote spiritual development simply by creating a safe environment in which children can ponder big questions and contemplate answers without ever feeling squashed by adults. Early childhood is all about addressing the development of the whole child. As intangible as it may be, that surely includes the nonphysical, where character and personality are formed.

In her book *The Spiritual Child: The New Science on Parenting for Health and Lifelong Thriving*, Lisa Miller (2015) shares, "natural spirituality is a birthright and can be accessed at any age. Natural spirituality is described as a direct sense of listening to the heartbeat of the

CHAPTER THREE: TEACHING WITH INTENTION

living universe, of being one with the seen and unseen world." She also suggests, "spirituality is a great source of resiliency . . . (possibly) the single most significant factor in children's health and ability to thrive."

HOW A YOUNG CHILD DEMONSTRATES SPIRITUAL DEVELOPMENT

- Expressing awe and wonder in response to the natural world
- Deriving comfort and meaning from nature
- Asking big questions about how things came to be
- Showing awareness of having an individual spirituality

CREATING A NATURE-BASED ASSESSMENT TOOL

Any meaningful assessment tool must include an understanding of both the program curriculum and the deeper teaching intentions. That is one reason we took the time in this chapter to outline our intentions in such detail. Our nature-based assessment tool was created to correspond to these intentions. It is not meant to guide them. We are the first to admit that there is no such thing as an assessment tool that captures the whole child. Like all assessments, ours is limited. However, it is a significant improvement over those that fail to take nature and place into account at all.

Before proceeding, we must acknowledge that *assessment* is a professional term that makes many educators sigh. It often means more paperwork, along with the unpleasant task of checking boxes and sorting students into brackets where they do not always seem to fit. When an assessment tool is not in line with a particular curriculum, it is often an exercise in frustration. But when it works, assessment can serve a valuable purpose. It provides useful feedback about the children under your care and can help identify any significant learning and developmental concerns. It can also help you better evaluate the effectiveness of the curriculum.

Creating this particular assessment tool forced us to consider our intentions in a much more thoughtful and coordinated way. Identifying our intentions allowed us to understand our goals and to recognize what was truly important to us as educators. It granted us the grace to forgive ourselves when our days went awry, to identify the "why" behind our decisions, and to let go of certain habits that continued simply because that we had "always done things that way." We became less concerned about the specific activities in our lesson plans and focused more on the transitions between them. Taking the time to wash hands, to gather at the gate, or to walk safely down a narrow trail were no longer inconveniences in our day but important and relevant parts of our program. Had we not taken the time to identify the skills children learn as they struggle to put their thumb in a mitten hole, we might have raced through this experience to get to our planned activity. By taking the time to explore and understand what our actual teaching intentions were, we began to understand just how integrated learning *about* nature and learning while *in* nature truly are.

One of the goals of assessment should be helping programs better evaluate themselves. This can only happen when the tool itself reflects the intentions of the program. When we explored the idea of creating our own nature-based assessment tool, we felt the following aspects strongly.

- An assessment tool should reflect the things we actually observe: We watch children balance on logs and traverse rocky terrain. We see them manipulate scarves, hats, and mittens. We know that they can distinguish between birdcalls. We do not ask them to stand on one foot while we time them with a stopwatch. The tool should reflect our daily experience.

- An assessment tool should recognize that child development is often nonlinear. One day a child exhibits wonderful self-regulation, and the next day the child might struggle. We should remove the boxes, as much as we can, and recognize that child development is not a straight line on a graph. It is the overall trajectory that matters.

- An assessment tool should indicate exactly what is being evaluated or observed and what is meant by the objective or criteria. That is one reason we work so hard to clarify our definitions. If we conclude that literacy means only the written word, then our assessment of a particular child's emerging literacy skills might look very different than it would if we decide literacy also includes verbal narration.

- An assessment tool should be based on age-appropriate expectations and should include the guidance of professionals in the child-development field to remind us of what these expectations should be. We have based our assessment tool on the *Wisconsin Model Early Learning Standards* (Wisconsin Department of Public Instruction, 2017), which are high-quality benchmarks grounded in research-based practices.

- An assessment tool should be meaningful for all ages served in the program and should be sensitive to family values, cultures, identities, and home languages.

- An assessment tool should be easy to use.

- An assessment tool must be confidential. Records from parent conferences and other written assessment materials should be stored in a space not accessible by the public.

- Finally, an assessment tool must be flexible. This may mean changing a word or two, or it may mean adding new elements (such as peace or spiritual development) as the curriculum changes. Just as nature itself is never stagnant, an assessment tool is only useful if it remains up to date. We want our tool to be relevant, reflecting a curriculum that is always evolving.

Appendix B features our Nature-Based Early Childhood Assessment Tool, which grew directly from our teaching intentions. We believe that, with a few modifications, it can be easily adapted to other programs. We encourage those who would like to use it to adjust it however you must, so that it lines up with your own program. It should reflect your own early learning standards, your own intentions, and your own natural environment.

CHAPTER THREE: TEACHING WITH INTENTION

- CHAPTER FOUR -

Putting Intention into Practice

Let the children be free; encourage them; let them run outside when it is raining; let them remove their shoes when they find a puddle of water; and, when the grass of the meadows is wet with dew, let them run on it and trample it with their bare feet; let them rest peacefully when a tree invites them to sleep beneath its shade; let them shout and laugh when the sun wakes them in the morning...

—Maria Montessori | **THE DISCOVERY OF THE CHILD**

In chapter 3, we explored how nature supports the deeper intentions of the early childhood classroom. We made the case that playing in nature strengthens early social and emotional development, independence, physical coordination, emerging literacy, and scientific thinking. Nature also supports a child's sense of peace and spiritual development, inspiring big questions and personal responses.

Nature serves as a teaching partner, providing the classroom, the learning materials, and the daily provocations. Nature can even influence mood and behavior. We have often observed that a stormy day on Lake Michigan, with its crashing waves and gathering clouds, sparks high energy in children who need to run and jump. On the other hand, a calm day, with warm sun and glasslike water, will often inspire children to relax on the sand, building castles and hunting for beach glass.

But nature is more than a teaching partner. It is also the subject of our investigations. When the monarch butterflies are migrating through our prairies, it doesn't matter what we had originally planned: our focus turns to this orange and black ballet in flight. Monarch migration is fleeting, and we don't want to miss our chance to experience something so magical. At the same time, we want the appearance of the monarchs to mean something to the children. We want them to know *why* the monarchs are migrating through our prairies. We want the children to understand where the butterflies

If you are just getting started, one of the best places to gather relevant information is to visit your state's department of natural resources (DNR). Many state DNR sites offer field guides, wildlife-identification cards, and other educational materials, either free of charge or on loan. If your state has its own association for environmental education, you can almost certainly contact someone there who will connect you to supplies, activities, tool kits, and training events. The North American Association for Environmental Education (NAAEE) is also an outstanding resource. Teachers can use the NAAEE website to search for information related to their particular question, simultaneously joining a global community of educators, conservationists, nonprofits, and foundations committed to the mission of environmental education for everyone.

are going and what physical changes have to occur for the monarchs to undertake this journey and to appreciate the entire life cycle of the monarch, so that when we see them again next summer, their reappearance will have significance.

We know from talking to other early childhood educators that a lack of knowledge about nature can be intimidating. It can even be an impediment, keeping otherwise interested teachers indoors because they do not feel qualified to take children outside. "I don't know the names of the plants," we often hear educators say. "I don't know the macroinvertebrates in the ponds." While we would be the first to say, "Just start small. Try taking an indoor activity outside," we also understand that having some nature knowledge does make a difference.

We certainly don't expect every early childhood teacher to hold an advanced degree in ecology. But having a few useful facts up one's sleeve is important.

This chapter serves as a quick guide for putting your nature-based teaching intentions into practice. It provides a brief overview for those who are new to the field. A far more detailed exploration of the curriculum is provided in the following chapters. The purpose here is to demonstrate a few simple ways to put intention into practice by offering at-a-glance ideas for outdoor exploration, a sample daily schedule, a list of possible topics for an outdoor classroom, and tips on how to hike and explore the outdoors with children.

AT-A-GLANCE IDEAS FOR OUTDOOR EXPLORATION

In this section, we list ideas that teachers can easily incorporate into daily outdoor activities. For teachers more experienced with nature education, these might serve as reminders or perhaps spark additional ideas.

WAYS TO EXPLORE LANGUAGE IN NATURE

- Use sticks, pine cones, brushes, rocks, and other implements to make designs, pictures, shapes, letters, and words in the sand, snow, or dirt.
- Take paper and writing materials outside. These include individual journals, large sheets of paper for group projects, watercolor paper, crayons, markers, pencils, and charcoal.
- Use maps to navigate, paying attention to keys and landmarks. Make your own maps.
- Study field guides to plants, animals, birds, shells, mushrooms, flowers, and trees in your area.
- Create cozy reading and writing spots by water, under trees, in the shade, and so on.
- Take an alphabet hike and identify letter shapes in nature: look at the shapes of tree branches, twigs, shells, plants, and even bent grass.
- Write letters to migrating and hibernating animals.
- Document children's voices in nature; later, read their words back to them.
- Make mud-kitchen recipes.
- Use chalk and slate in nature to write, doodle, and scribble.
- Write your own books with the children about their experiences in nature.

WAYS TO EXPLORE MATH IN NATURE

- Play adding and subtraction games with acorns, pine cones, rocks, wood chips, leaves, shells, feathers, flowers, birds at a feeder, and living creatures under a log.
- Make patterns with rocks, colored leaves, different sized pine cones, acorn caps, and so on.
- Place a large, plastic hoop or an embroidery hoop on the ground; count the number of different plants in the circle, the total number of plants, or both.

- Measure sunflower stalks, a flower's circumference, the width of a tree, the height of grasses, the depth of a rain puddle or a tide pool, and the height of the children's shadows at different times of the day.
- Weigh pumpkins, rocks, wood chips, bark, soil, sunflower heads, birdseed, and pine cones.
- Count the number of needles on a white pine, a red pine, a ponderosa pine, a scotch pine. (Or count the spines on a cactus, provided you can do so safely.)
- Look for stars, hearts, and circles in nature.

- Look at the shapes of spiderwebs, clouds, nests, and animal footprints in the snow, sand, or dirt.
- Compare the amount of water in fresh snow versus snowmelt.
- Compare opposite and alternate branching on deciduous trees (such as a maple, which has branches that grow directly across from one another, and oak, which has branches that alternate).
- Compare human tracks to animal tracks.
- Compare compound leaves (which consist of multiple leaflets attached to a common vein on a stem) and simple leaves (which are single leaves attached to a stem).
- Compare and contrast the various things that you experience outside, such as colors, sizes, shapes, textures, and temperatures. For example, is it cooler under the tree than it is in the sun? Is your shadow longer at 2 p.m. than it was at 10 a.m.? Does the soil by the water feel the same as the soil in the grass? Does it smell different outside after it rains? Remember to use a range of senses.

WAYS TO EXPLORE THE DIFFERENT SEASONS

In Wisconsin, we experience the four seasons of fall, winter, spring, and summer. We understand that there are programs in places that rarely—or never—experience snow. In those areas, children might experience a wet season and a dry season (which is, unfortunately, often synonymous with fire season). Preschool teachers are very creative, and we feel confident that you can easily adapt our ideas to the seasons and climates in your locale.

FALL

- Drop leaves off bridges. Do they fall quickly? Do they waft back up on air currents? Count how long it takes each leaf to reach the ground, or just enjoy watching as they make their descent.
- Collect fresh leaves for leaf-printing projects.
- Carve, paint, wash, and repaint pumpkins; roast pumpkin seeds; pound golf tees into pumpkins; roast small pie pumpkins to use in baking projects.
- Make masking-tape bracelets, and use them to collect seeds.
- Take weekly color walks, observing and documenting the changes.
- Follow a compass south as you discuss migration.

- Look for signs of animals eating, gathering, and storing food, such as chewed pine cones and seed caches.
- Stomp, crunch, rake, jump, and play!

WINTER

- Look for animal tracks in the snow.
- Collect snowflakes on sheets of black felt, and study them with magnifying lenses. (Tip: Place the felt in the freezer beforehand.)
- Break up partially frozen ice with sticks.
- Slide down hills, with or without sleds.
- Boot-skate on frozen ponds. (Test the ice first! Ice should be at least 4 inches thick.)
- Take a winter color hike.
- Collect snow, predict how much water it will produce, and bring it indoors to melt.
- Look for winter nests and dens.
- Explore ice formations.
- Make ice sculptures by placing water in Bundt pans. Add birdseed, oranges, and berries, and hang the sculptures from the trees for the animals.
- Gather around a campfire.
- Drink warm-up beverages outside.
- Climb, slide, sculpt, touch, taste, and play!

CHAPTER FOUR: PUTTING INTENTION INTO PRACTICE

SPRING

- Listen to songbirds, raindrops, wind, and so on, and take instruments outside to make music.
- Stomp in post-rain puddles.
- Follow flowing water downhill and see where it leads.
- Identify spring wildflowers.
- Visit ponds to search for tadpole eggs and other aquatic life. Return them to the pond!
- Make your own nests from mud and dried grasses.
- Look for tiny red and brown buds in nature.
- Make your own outdoor mud kitchen. Add dishes, sticks, rocks, and more.
- Sing, dance, jump, spin, and play!

SUMMER

- Catch and release frogs, crayfish, or other local fauna, being certain to do so responsibly.
- Dip nets into ponds, creeks, or tidal pools.
- Take watercolor paints outside.
- Listen to stories under the trees.
- Pound flower petals onto fabric.
- Build fairy houses and gnome homes.
- Search for rocks and fossils.
- Study maps, and make your own!
- Climb trees.
- Watch clouds.
- Explore the woods, prairies, forests, beaches, and more.
- Smell the soil, be still, be loud, be joyful, and play.

A YEAR AT SCHLITZ AUDUBON NATURE PRESCHOOL: A SAMPLE OUTLINE

MONTH	ACTIVITIES
September	• Getting to know each other, our classroom, and our outdoor spaces • All about me: Who am I? What are my interests? • Celebrating our similarities and differences • Getting to know the trails, woods, prairies, ponds, and lake • What is a habitat? • Exploring trail maps • Exploring the micro community beneath a single rock or log • Looking for insects, worms, pill bugs, and slugs • Monarch butterfly migration • Celebrating late-summer wildflowers
October	• Developing strong hiking skills and positive trail etiquette • Introducing our classroom codes and agreements • Identifying deciduous trees • Celebrating the changing colors in nature • Exploring our community: Who lives here? • Autumn leaves and chlorophyll • Animal camouflage • Apples and pumpkins • Seeds and seed dispersal • Weighing, measuring, and counting • Nature journals • Music in nature
November	• Celebrating families, including languages, cultures, and food traditions • Bird migration (geese, ducks, and so on) • Celebrating the harvest (making soup, picking herbs, and cooking bread over a fire) • Nature's kitchen (mud pies, homemade forest recipes, and mud-kitchen cooking) • Chipmunks, turkeys, and squirrels • Exploring the senses • Looking for alphabet shapes in nature • Drawing and writing with feathers, sticks, stones, and more • Understanding place: learning about the many human groups who lived here before us

CHAPTER FOUR: PUTTING INTENTION INTO PRACTICE

MONTH	ACTIVITIES
December	- Weather and light - Winter shadows - Nocturnal animals - The winter solstice - Making gifts for others - Twilight lantern walks - Campfire circles - Crepuscular animals (deer, rabbits, and so on) - Evergreen trees - Animals preparing for winter - Sharing cultural celebrations of winter and the winter solstice
January	- Making friends with winter (how to dress for the elements) - Sledding, boot-skating, and so on - Hibernation - Animal dens - Animal tracks - Active animals - Winter poems - Making snowmelt predictions - Studying snowflake shapes - Studying crystalline structures - Animal coloration in winter - Building snow forts - Winter scavenger hunts
February	- Groundhog Day - Ice formations - Friendship - Letter writing - Finding the color red in nature (dogwoods, berries, birds) - Student photography - Outdoor ice art - Shapes in nature (hearts, stars) - Winter birds and owls
March	- Maple-tree tapping - Sweet maple tea around the campfire - Tree structure: sapwood, heartwood, branching systems, and so on - Animals waking up - Maple sugaring: sap collection, sap tasting, sap boiling, and syrup - Mud play - Photo exhibits - Ash tree art - Celebrating winter and spring (looking for skunk cabbage, winter aconite, and so on) - Pi Day (circles, simple math in nature, mud pies, homemade pie, and so on) - The vernal equinox

PARTNERING WITH *Nature* IN EARLY CHILDHOOD EDUCATION

MONTH	ACTIVITIES
April	• Vernal ponds • Ephemeral flowers • Learning about the wet glacial prairie • Birds, eggs, feathers, and nests • Rocks and fossils • Salamanders • Raptors • Buds, roots, and leaves • Returning songbirds • Early spring aquatic life • Welcome letters to animals • Spring poems • Rain and puddles • Earth Day • Growing beans • Spring bulbs
May–August	• Pond life • Garden • Water play • Reptiles and amphibians • Fairy houses and gnome homes • Beach treasures • Music • Pulling garlic mustard (and other invasive plants) • *En plein air* painting • Giving back to the Earth • Celebration of learning

Ongoing Topics	• Where we are on a map/orienteering
	• Exploring place: Who was here before us? How did they use the land?
	• Exploring the senses
	• Lake Michigan through the seasons
	• Weather
	• Birds
	• Trees and plants
	• Writing and letter recognition
	• Math
	
	   » Counting and numbers
	   » Measuring and weighing
	   » Shapes in nature
	
	• Artistic expression
	• Music and movement
	• Nature stewardship
	• Phenology (exploring the cyclical, seasonal relationships among plants, animals, temperature, and climate)

CHAPTER FOUR: PUTTING INTENTION INTO PRACTICE

A SAMPLE SCHEDULE FOR AN OUTDOOR CLASSROOM

In this section, we describe our daily schedule at Schlitz Audubon. Keep in mind that ours is a half-day program that runs for 2.75 hours in the mornings and again in the afternoons. Classes at our school meet two, three, or four times per week. Programs that run for full days, or five days a week, will of course need to allow time for additional activities, such as snacks, lunch, and naps. There is plenty of room within this sample schedule to add additional activities, including a quiet period of rest and stillness; teacher-led activities, such as reading and singing; and time to return to projects that were perhaps started in the morning or even earlier in the week, to build and expand on them. Note: This schedule assumes a typical morning in which the weather is mild and class is held outdoors.

ARRIVAL (8:45 A.M.–9:15 A.M.)

During the peak of COVID-19, we did not want all of our preschool families arriving at school en masse, and so we established a 30-minute arrival window. Parents appreciated this flexible approach to the start of the school day. Even after some of our pandemic policies relaxed, we opted to keep the flexible start time in place. A more lenient arrival window assured parents that we would consider no one late nor depart on a hike until after the extended arrival window had closed.

Ideally, parents and caregivers use the time just before class begins to take children to the bathroom. We try to instill this habit in our families early on, so that once the children are with us, they can play with their peers outdoors without needing a sudden bathroom break. This also helps reduce the number of "didn't quite make it in time" potty accidents that sometimes occur when the bathroom visit is skipped.

Next, the children "gear up" into their outdoor layers (see pages 98–100 for more information about outdoor gear) and are escorted to their outdoor classroom by their parents or caregivers. Once the children arrive at their outdoor space, they are greeted and signed in by their teachers. Children wash their hands with soap and water at one of our outdoor sinks and place their gear bags at the gathering circle. The parent or caregiver then departs, and the child is free to play and explore.

FREE PLAY (9:00 A.M.–9:55 A.M.)

Each of our outdoor classrooms contains a shed or bin containing seasonal tools and other materials intended to enhance free play. These include watering cans, rakes, shovels, brooms, wheelbarrows, trucks, paintbrushes, and buckets, along with items the teachers may set up in advance, such as bubble wands, scoops, and strainers for outdoor water play. Teachers may also bring out blankets, books, field guides, bug boxes, journals, and construction and art supplies. Free play is such a fundamental part of each child's learning experience that it may easily continue past 10:00 a.m. and may even replace the hike, depending on the day.

CLEANUP (9:55 A.M.–10:00 A.M.)

Each child is expected to participate in cleanup to the best of their ability. During the warmer months, cleanup includes a few large rubber tubs full of water and biodegradable soap. Children dunk their shovels, scoops, buckets, and other items into the water before putting them away. This helps remove excess sand and mud and is a fun way to cool down. As with our outdoor sinks and other forms of water play, this practice is put on hold when outdoor temperatures get colder.

GROUP TIME AT THE GATHERING CIRCLE (10:00 A.M.–10:25 A.M.)

Our gathering circles consist of logs and stumps arranged in a rough approximation of a circle. During the initial days of COVID-19, a few groups rearranged their gathering spots into half circles, as it was unclear whether sitting in an enclosed ring was a health risk. They changed the name of their group time to "rainbow time" to reflect the shape of their circle.

Group time/rainbow time is when the entire class unites as a whole. Classes sing their greeting songs, teachers help guide conversations, and plans for the rest of the day are discussed. At our school, this is also the time when we read stories and pass around our talking sticks. (A talking stick can be any object, in this case a cherished and decorated stick, that is passed around the circle from person to person. Whoever is the keeper of the stick is welcome to speak, while everyone around them listens.)

During circle time, we reveal the day's special helpers and send loving thoughts to anyone who is missing that day. We may also use this time for daily self-care, which includes yoga, tai chi, meditation, and tapping. *Tapping* refers to the therapeutic tapping of different parts of the body to stimulate energy. For young children, we generally use this as a way to direct the desire to touch, squeeze, and release energy through physical movement back onto oneself rather than onto the person sitting next to us. This may mean gently tapping one's own hands, knees, arms, or legs for several seconds or a minute. For some children, these actions can also calm anxiety.

The length of our gathering time may vary. Our youngest students may be able to sit and focus for only about 10 minutes at the start of the year. Our older classes may have gathering times that run well over half an hour.

HIKE PREPARATION (10:25 A.M.–10:30 A.M.)

During this short period, children get what they need from their gear bags to prepare for their hike. We have added this to our daily schedule because we feel our transitions from one activity to

another are just as important as the activities recorded on the lesson plans (and often more so). The "in-between time," which includes washing hands on arrival, putting on gear before a hike, replacing wet mittens, and so on, is when the activities for daily living are best practiced. Organizing one's own belongings and learning to predict and prepare for an upcoming experience are essential life skills, and we do our best not to rush through the process.

HIKE (10:30 A.M.–11:25 A.M.)

Our favorite hikes are often to places where we can relax and play, such as the shoreline of Lake Michigan or to an open space on the edge of the woods filled with logs and stumps that invite climbing and jumping. Hikes may include far-off destinations that lead into the "beyond," such as the forest, prairie, ponds, or other wild habitats, or they may be short, simple jaunts around the nature-center building. Teachers may include teaching tools—nets, field guides, collecting bags, art materials—or the hikes may be unstructured, with each group hiking as far as they want with no preset agenda.

When we head out on the trails, we are expanding our classroom to include new and ever-changing spaces, diverse habitats, and impromptu teachable moments. Not every hike will include an encounter with wildlife or offer up a spectacular rainbow. However, every hike offers opportunities for learning.

We outline a few practical suggestions for leading a successful hike with young children on pages 102–104.

SNACK TIME

If we are offering snacks outside, we often try to do so while hiking, as a few crackers or some string cheese can be a wonderful motivator for getting back up a 100-foot hill. Snacks at our school are usually very simple, and, when possible, we try to ensure they work with our seasonal curriculum. During the colder months, snacks may be eaten around an outdoor fire circle, with hot apple cider to keep us warm. Memorable snacks include homemade soup, fresh fry bread, and hot cocoa cooked over a portable eco-stove, along with maple tea made from maple sap that we collect, filter, and cook ourselves. Because such snacks are preplanned, we can incorporate them into outdoor free play or include them on our hikes so they feel supportive of our overall program.

If we are inside (as we often were before COVID-19), then snack time happens after we come in from our outdoor hike. Children take off their outdoor gear, wash their hands, and sit down at our tables. Snack time provides opportunities for children to socialize and talk about their outdoor adventures. After snack, there is time for free play in the classroom.

CLOSING CIRCLE AND GOODBYE SONG (11:25 A.M.–11:30 A.M.)

Each class ends with a goodbye song. Some classes like to include gratitude at the end of the day or take a few moments to go around the circle and reflect on a highlight or a hope or a thought from each child. Other classes like to document their day with a written chronicle that includes the children's voices and can later be shared with the children's parents. There are also a few classes that end with a story, deep breaths, or yoga. Endings are a thoughtful and calming part of each day. We ask the adults picking up to wait outside the door or beyond the gate until we are ready to dismiss their child.

DEPARTURE (11:30 A.M.–11:45 A.M.)

We try to keep the departure time simple while taking the time to properly dismiss and sign out each child. (This is an important safety and security measure, particularly in an outdoor classroom.) If possible, we also like to take a few moments to connect with each adult. This may mean providing a short verbal summary of the day's activities or simply bidding each adult-child pair farewell with a smile. We try to avoid serious discussions or private conferences at departure time, unless a situation arises during class time that needs to be communicated to the child's parent or caregiver at once.

As is hopefully apparent in this schedule, there are very few forced or abrupt transitions in the school day. This is especially the case when we remain outside the whole time. The children experience long, uninterrupted blocks of play, which allow for them to experience conflict, work through it, and emerge on the other side a little bit wiser and more empathetic. These extended periods also allow for greater exploration of nature. We have plenty of time to study the branching structure of sugar maple trees and to identify fossils on the beach. We can follow rabbit tracks in the snow or listen to the mating trill of spring toads without worrying about racing back to the classroom for the next prescheduled activity.

CHAPTER FOUR: PUTTING INTENTION INTO PRACTICE

HIKING WITH CHILDREN

Hiking with children is a key part—and one of the most enjoyable aspects—of our program. Children should not hear the word *hike* and feel worried about what lies ahead. Hiking is joyful! At the same time, hiking needs to be safe. Children cannot run off and hide, venture down steep cliffs and ravines, or head unsupervised toward open water. Hiking also requires a certain degree of etiquette, as children need to learn to be considerate of other hikers and to be mindful of animal homes and habitats.

PREPARING THE BACKPACKS

Before teachers and children prepare to spend an extended amount of time outside, they should consider what's in their backpacks.

THE ESSENTIALS FOR A TEACHER BACKPACK

- Communication device (walkie-talkie or cell phone): Make sure this has been charged and is in working order. We sometimes wrap our walkie-talkies in plastic baggies on rainy days because they are less effective when waterlogged. We have also found that cell phones and radios struggle after long periods outside in single-digit temperatures or excessive heat. On cold days, we warm them up in our coats. On hot days, it is usually enough to bring them indoors between morning and afternoon programs to cool down.

- The class attendance sheet
- Emergency contact forms for each child
- A first-aid kit containing materials appropriate for your region: This may include bandages, rubber gloves, eye wash, dressing pads, roll gauze, first-aid tape, scissors, safety pins, cold packs, a tick removal kit, and so on. In the warm months, we carry sting-relief wipes, which help with stinging nettle burns and bee stings.
- Hand sanitizer
- Clean tissues and dirty-tissue bags
- Epinephrine injector, such as an EpiPen, and other medications for individual children as required. (These items should be sealed in a bag or container with the child's name, along with the accompanying paperwork, including signed authorization forms and instructions to administer as needed.)
- Camera for documenting experiences

THE EXTRAS (OR NICE-TO-HAVES) FOR A TEACHER BACKPACK

- Paper, crayons, colored pencils, or other art supplies
- Journaling supplies
- Field guides
- Small hoops (such as embroidery hoops) for up-close micro-investigations
- Magnifying boxes and lenses
- An IdentiFlyer for identifying birdcalls (or you may opt for bird and nature apps on your phone)
- Stuffed animals and puppets
- Clippers for collecting natural materials and clearing branches at eye level
- Children's books
- Empty containers, such as clean, empty parmesan-cheese containers, for catching frogs

THE CHILD'S BACKPACK

When our school moved to an all-outdoor model during the pandemic, many families replaced their child's traditional school backpack with a waterproof canoe bag, which allowed their child's gear bag to remain outdoors in all kinds of weather. We so admired these bags that we ended up purchasing them for our staff. In a pinch, a jumbo-sized plastic bag that can fit over the child's backpack also works.

CHAPTER FOUR: PUTTING INTENTION INTO PRACTICE

Either way, the outdoor backpack or gear bag should contain whatever items a child may need for the day. Contents will change based on the weather and location, but generally include:

- Extra socks

- A spare pair of mittens and hand and foot warmers (weather dependent)

- A full water bottle

- Waterproof pants and jackets (if not already being worn, and dependent on your climate)

- Additional clothing (this is important, should a change of clothes or added layer be needed)

BEFORE THE HIKE

Once the teachers and children have the proper equipment, teachers still need to do a little prep work before they embark on their hike. They should familiarize themselves with trails in advance, which means not only mastering their wayfinding skills but also scouting known trails to ascertain their condition. Has a tree fallen across the path? Is a wooden bridge coated in morning ice? How high is the water? How deep is the mud? We may discover that, almost overnight, stinging nettle has grown up all along the edge of a trail. That doesn't mean we won't use the trail, but we do so with knowledge of what to expect and can thus be prepared when we hike it with children.

The children also should know our rules and expectations before the hike and during it. We take time to explain that one adult will be in front, another in back. Children should remain between. We call this a Hiking Sandwich. (The teachers are the slices of bread and the children are the fillings in between.) Depending on the class, this hiking structure can relax over time, but we like to start with stricter guidelines and loosen them as the year progresses rather than allowing too much freedom to race ahead of adults at the start. Of course, children should also be granted some freedom to explore while out on a hike. If possible, do not insist that the children walk in a single-file line (unless the trail is very narrow). If you have to walk single file, make it fun! We say, "Get in a deer family line."

We sometimes use simple stick-figure drawings to introduce what safe hiking looks like. We can pull these out as we hike, especially if we are in need of reminders. Pulling out a sketchbook and creating a quick drawing of the group engaged in safe hiking is a fun activity, and children love it when you can add specific details, such as a baseball hat or pair of braids, to the stick figures.

Consider attaching a sock worm (a sock stuffed with cotton that has googly eyes attached) or perhaps a bright plush bird or puppet to the lead teacher's backpack, so that children can focus on staying "behind the backpack" or, if it's easier, "behind the worm." A sock worm can also be removed and used to help a child who may be reluctant to stay with the group. The child can hold one end of the sock worm, and the teacher can hold the other.

Before you head out, make sure every child has used the bathroom and is dressed appropriately for the weather.

DURING THE HIKE

Stay on the trails unless you have permission to go off or can do so without causing harm. Off-trail experiences are valuable, but so is the conservation of wild spaces. Be mindful that tramping over the soil with our feet each day makes it almost impossible for new plants to grow. We have accepted that some spaces, especially those designated for child play, will never look as pristine as other isolated spots in the woods. It is important to us that the children have spaces where they can roam and run and play and touch. But we also keep other spots as untouched and tranquil as possible.

Give children turns at the front of the hiking group as well as opportunities to decide which way the group should hike. This makes them feel more invested in the experience. We often allow our special helpers to take the lead with the teacher so that every child gets a turn as the leader.

Our school is in a nature preserve, so we may see, touch, and smell most plants but should never pick them. However, there are exceptions. We allow children to pick dandelions, dame's rocket, garlic mustard, buttercups, and other nonnative plants that grow in abundance.

We also do not taste plants. We discourage tasting wild plants with young children, even when we know a plant is safe to eat. Many species of plants look alike, and some of these are toxic. Yet we do allow exceptions. We taste maple sap from the trees, and we also have teaching gardens. The children love picking chives in the spring, and we sample mint and basil. We can do this in a controlled way because our gardens are contained within fenced outdoor classrooms and do not grow wild in the woods.

CHAPTER FOUR: PUTTING INTENTION INTO PRACTICE

Most trees can handle being climbed. But we should also teach children not to break branches, harm nests, or peel bark from living trees.

Finally, be flexible. It is important that teachers be willing to change course. Do not become so invested in what you had planned that children who are struggling feel miserable. Be mindful of what they need rather than what you had planned and end an activity if it isn't working. On the other hand, if something is working, do not call an abrupt end simply to meet an arbitrary timetable. Rather than cutting short a watercolor activity at the pond, in which the children are engaged and focused, to move on to the next preplanned activity, remember that the lesson plan is there to support your intentions. It should not dictate the day. In general, hikes should be less focused on the end goal and instead be open to what you find on the way. A hike that never arrives at its destination is not a failure. The purpose of the hike is the journey.

Here are some tips to help ensure a successful hike:

- Encourage children to use their senses to explore.

- Practice respect for nature, and make this an ongoing part of your daily experiences.

- Encourage children to notice the changes that have happened in nature compared to earlier hikes in the same landscape. You can even bring out photos from different seasons for comparison.

- Take a color hike, matching pieces of colored paper or paint samples to the colors outside.

- Look for examples of camouflage.

- Use "deer ears," "fox ears," or "coyote ears" by cupping your hands behind your ears and listening to nature.

- Discuss and practice trail etiquette, which includes sharing the trail with others coming from the opposite direction. We often use the phrase "tight to the right" to remind our young children not to stand in the center of the path when others are hiking toward us.

- Encourage children to make predictions and then follow up with observations. How high will the waves on the lake be today? Will there be ice on the pond? Will there still be leaves on the oak tree?

- Look for signs of animals, and make guesses about who was there before you.

- Sing as you hike, interspersing this with listening to bird and wind songs.

- Talk about the surrounding habitat. Notice when you go from one habitat to another. What are the differences? Is the light different? What about the temperature? Did the plants change? Is the ground the same? Will there be different animals?

- Actively wonder with the children. "I wonder what happened here." "I wonder whose track that is." "I wonder what created this ravine." "I wonder why the tree died." You don't need to provide an answer to every question. The simple phrase "I wonder" is meant to spark curiosity.

- Find a spot to sit quietly. Listen, observe, rest.

- Take art supplies outside, and draw what you see or simply draw.

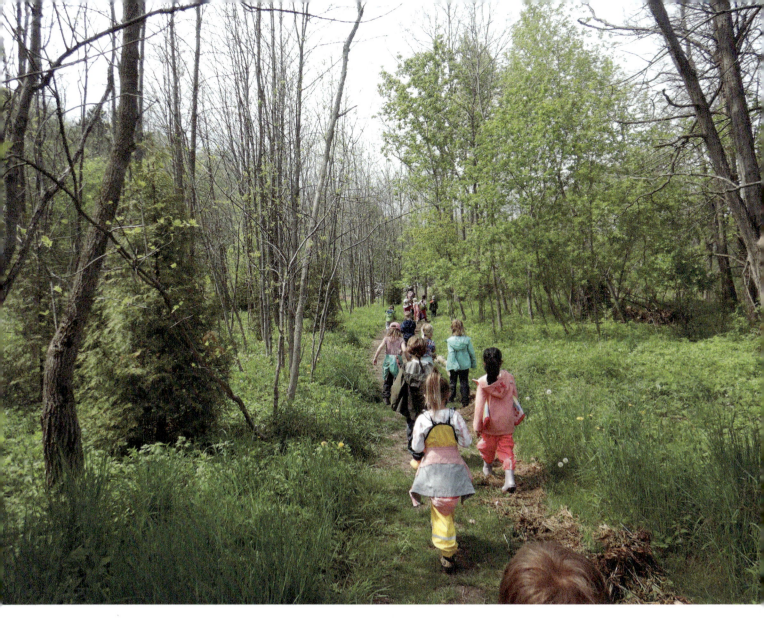

- Find a spot to share a story or book.
- Bring a map of your environment, and look for or add your own landmarks.
- Take along magnifying glasses, bug boxes, or nets to help explore nature.
- Count the things you see along the hike. Talk about quantities. Are there more yellow flowers or more purple flowers?
- Measure things—height, width, and depth—as you hike. You can use sticks with notches as measuring tools or take along measuring tape. Puddles are always fun to measure, especially over a couple of days. (This can lead to good discussions about evaporation.)
- Don't be afraid to talk about scat (animal poop). Children are fascinated. Help the children identify the animal that left it and what it probably ate!

CHAPTER FOUR: PUTTING INTENTION INTO PRACTICE

A SPECIAL NOTE ABOUT SOME OF THE TEACHING MATERIALS

Because we are a part of a nature center, we have access to a number of taxidermy mounts and animal pelts that are a part of our center's educational collections. Not everyone has access to these materials. Others may feel that using real animal pelts or stuffed mounts for teaching is inconsistent with their values. There are companies, such as Kind Fur, that create replicas of animal fur that can be used in teaching. These replicas have the feel of animal skins and furs without using real animals. They are available through a variety of educational-supply catalogs. It is also often possible to borrow or rent trunks, kits, field guides, and other materials from your state's department of natural resources, local environmental education and conservation agencies, and nature centers and natural history museums.

- You may come upon an animal that has died. Use this opportunity to talk about the cycle of life and our personal feelings when we encounter death on the trails.
- Place several embroidery hoops on the forest floor. Have groups of children examine everything within that small, enclosed space. Encourage them to get right down on the ground to look carefully. Depending on the age of the class, they can then document what they see or draw pictures, or you can just let the children observe and then relocate the hoops.
- Provide lots of natural loose parts, such as pebbles, shells, sticks, seeds, or human-made items such as buttons and biodegradable ribbons. See what the children do with them.
- Use natural materials to make outdoor art. A tree cookie, a tray, or a piece of cardboard can provide a backdrop for their creations. Take a picture to record their artwork, then return the natural materials back to the environment.
- Have a picnic hike. This can be as simple as packing a snack and eating it outside, or it could involve a campfire, homemade stick bread (bread dough wound around a stick and cooked over a fire), and soup.
- Share your own awe and your feelings about the things you see.

So far, we have taken a glimpse at some of the infrastructure and logistics involved in taking children outside. Next, we take a closer look at the curriculum. In the following chapters, we introduce a range of topics categorized by seasons. Each topic includes basic environmental concepts, ideas for group activities, art and science activities, and suggestions for sensory bins and indoor/outdoor discovery tables. We preface each section with a brief description of how exploration of these topics might look "in the field" with children.

We provide enough information to get you started, without being overwhelming. We want to emphasize that the topics we selected do not equal the sum total of what we teach. Certain activities, particularly those that relate to Lake Michigan, are so place-specific that we felt obliged to remove them. It is also important to acknowledge that our curriculum is never fixed. Children bring their own interests to school, and the teachers listen, watch, and build on each new provocation. Teachers likewise carry their own energy and ideas into our program. One teacher may have a passion for rocks and fossils; another may be a gifted storyteller. Another may want to explore our connection to place and to the people who lived here before us. Part of the joy in teaching in a nature-based classroom is that we are not locked into a specific and predetermined curriculum. The time we spend on each topic is not dictated by an outside agency. We take our cues from the children and from the natural world around us.

CHAPTER FOUR: PUTTING INTENTION INTO PRACTICE

- CHAPTER FIVE -

The Nature-Based Curriculum in Autumn

It's the first day of autumn! A time of hot chocolatey mornings and toasty marshmallow evening and, best of all, leaping into leaves!

—*Winnie the Pooh* | ***POOH'S GRAND ADVENTURE: THE SEARCH FOR CHRISTOPHER ROBIN***

Our school year traditionally begins a few days after September 1, which is the first day of meteorological fall. For us, this means fresh breezes and cooling air, gardens full of ripe vegetables, and monarch butterflies preparing to migrate. The days are generally mild, allowing plenty of opportunities for *en plein air* painting, outdoor yoga, and music under the basswood trees. We bring out sidewalk chalk, bubbles, weaving looms, water tables, baskets full of books, blankets for sitting, and tables for art and construction projects, and we encourage children to look under logs to see what lives in the dark, damp soil.

We also spend time helping each child adjust to preschool. Fall is an important time to introduce our intentions of kindness and community. Learning to adjust to a new routine, separating from parents, and developing relationships with new teachers and classmates are all a part of this process. Fall is a season of change but also a season of beauty and active preparation as animals prepare for the coming winter. Children are busy too, learning new skills and developing their initial independence away from home.

Topics for fall include (but are by no means limited to) insects, spiders and webs, worms and slugs, monarch butterflies, nature's palette, autumn leaves, seeds, bird migration, squirrels and chipmunks, and harvest time.

CHAPTER FIVE: THE NATURE-BASED CURRICULUM IN AUTUMN

INSECTS

At Schlitz Audubon Nature Preschool, the outdoor classrooms are full of portable stumps, which we use as seating areas. Because the stumps are not rooted to the ground, they can be rolled aside. In our outdoor classrooms, children often look for insects under these movable stumps and exclaim at every discovery of a stink beetle, millipede, earthworm, or slug. Of those four creatures, only one is an insect, but the children don't necessarily know this—not yet. For now, their play is one of discovery and wonder. A rotting oak tree, now on its side and crawling with carpenter ants, might be nicknamed the "Ant Hotel." An old garden bed might become a "hospital" where earthworms and arthropods (invertebrate creatures that include insects and spiders) might safely be transported. We may see clusters of bright red ladybugs emerging in clusters from beneath shaggy tree bark or mud dauber wasps gathering around puddles on the ground in search of mud to secure their homes.

For the first few weeks of school, we often do little more than let the children investigate. We do not necessarily name every insect outright. These initial days are spent noticing, thinking, asking questions, and developing interest and comfort. Eventually, however, we do take the time to introduce insects, along with other arthropods, to our classes.

We may introduce insects to the children with a book. Depending on what has captured the interest of the class, it could be a book about butterflies or one that focuses on insect body parts and biology. The book might raise an ethical dilemma, such as the one proposed in Hannah and Phillip Hoose's *Hey, Little Ant*, which asks children to consider the ant's point of view but leaves the choice about whether or not to step on the ant up to the individual reader.

We may ask the children to name as many insects as they can while we record their answers on a large sheet of paper. We may create a Wonder Circle with a circle of felt on which we place a range of objects related to insects, such as an old paper wasp's nest, mounted butterflies, or plastic insect models. Perhaps we will use an interactive felt board to discuss the many small creatures that live together in the soil, under rocks, under logs, or down in the grass or the prairie plants. There are many ways to begin.

We do not recommend having children handle insects without first demonstrating how to do so gently and carefully. In a temperate forest such as ours, the teacher is always the first to turn over a log or rock as the children gather around to watch. We then observe together. Adults remind the children that we are essentially lifting the roof off someone's house, and we want to do as little damage as possible. Together, we notice how many different creatures we can find. If the habitat is thriving, we might see earthworms, pill bugs, ants, slugs, centipedes, snails, and more, all living together. Although these are not all insects, we celebrate each tiny creature and are careful not to harm them.

Next, our teachers model the best way to pick up, hold, and safely observe each organism. Reusable plastic spoons are ideal tools for carefully lifting and transporting. Old plastic yogurt tubs with a little dirt and leaves make good temporary observation containers. Finally, we show the children how to return each organism to its natural home and replace the "roof of their house" without crushing them.

Of course, not all insects live under logs. In a prairie or field, we may first observe with our ears, stopping to listen as the prairie sings to us. We may decide to lie down in the grass and try to see the world, the ground, and each blade of grass from the perspective of a grasshopper. In a pond, we find insect larvae. Depending on your location, you may find tobacco hornworms, banana slugs, or palo

CHAPTER FIVE: THE NATURE-BASED CURRICULUM IN AUTUMN

verde beetles. You may also find tarantulas and scorpions in certain landscapes, and so lying down on the ground is not necessarily the best idea! Yet the same principles apply. We observe, inquire, and investigate. We celebrate each discovery.

No matter what approach we choose, however, we always have two consistent goals. The first is to give the children plenty of time and space to explore insects safely and respectfully in their natural habitat. The second is to encourage the child's curiosity and comfort.

A FEW KEY CONCEPTS ABOUT INSECTS

- There are more insects on Earth—perhaps as many as 10 million—than any other kind of animal.

- Insects have three body parts: the thorax, abdomen, and head. They have six legs (specifically, three pairs of legs) and two antennae, and they sometimes have wings.

- Most insects hatch out of eggs. Their typical stages of development are egg, larva, pupa, and adult. This process is known as *complete metamorphosis*. In complete metamorphosis, the larva is very active and tends to be ravenously hungry, while the pupa is largely inactive. Caterpillars are a perfect example of larvae.

- *Incomplete metamorphosis* is when an insect has three stages of development: egg, nymph, and adult. With incomplete metamorphosis, the nymph may resemble a miniature adult. One example is a praying mantis.

- Some insects lay eggs on plants; the plant then produces a chemical reaction, forming a protective structure around the eggs called a *gall*. We often find galls on prairie plants or on leaves of deciduous trees. We sometimes find galls on branches, buds, roots, and even fruits and flowers. A "bug" is a type of insect. True bugs—for example, aphids, box elder bugs, stink bugs, cicadas, and leafhoppers—have a straw-like mouth called a *stylet* that allows them to suck the juice from a plant (as opposed to chewing).

- Many animals are insectivores: they depend on insects for food. This is why insects are an essential part of the food web.

- Insects are cold blooded. We do not see them in the coldest months. To survive the freeze, they have adapted to overwinter in different ways and in different stages of development.

- Bees, ants, and termites live in organized groups called *colonies*, where each member has a specific role or job.

- Spiders, pill bugs, worms, and centipedes are not insects but may often live side by side with some of them under rocks and logs.

OUTDOOR EXPLORATION

Make a list of insects you and the children find while exploring outdoors. (You can expand on this by making predictions about what insects you think you'll encounter and later comparing what children expected to see with what they did see.) Go on an insect scavenger hunt and cross off what you find.

On your hike, take tools such as bug boxes and magnifying glasses so children can observe the insects up close. Be sure to look in leaf litter for hidden insects. When the children find an insect, ask what they notice about it and wonder aloud. If they have questions, write them down if you can. You may have to find out the answers together later in a field guide or through an app. Always return the insects to their natural habitat when done.

Take soft butterfly nets to a field, garden, grassy area, or prairie. Teachers can hide laminated butterflies among the plants for the children to find and "catch" with their nets, or you can try to catch real butterflies, as long as you have the appropriate nets to do so (many insect sweep nets are too heavy for butterflies and could damage their wings). You can also use insect nets to sweep high grasses for insects and gently shake what you catch in the nets onto white sheets or pillowcases. Use field guides and/or insect identification sheets to help identify what you find. Observe. Watch ants in an anthill, watch a toad or frog eat an insect, and listen to and count how often a cricket chirps in one minute. Fun fact: At the Schlitz Audubon Nature Center, we have found that the higher the temperature outside, the greater the frequency of a cricket's chirps, at least within a range of 55 degrees Fahrenheit to 100 degrees Fahrenheit. Look for the homes and habitats of different insects, and encourage the children to compare. Hide small plastic insects outside, and let the children try to find them.

IDEAS FOR GROUP-TIME OPPORTUNITIES

- Sing "Head, Thorax, Abdomen" to the tune of "Head, Shoulders, Knees, and Toes."

    Head, thorax, abdomen, abdomen (Touch head, chest, and tummy)

    Head, thorax, abdomen, abdomen (Touch head, chest, and tummy)

    Six legs, two antennae, and usually some wings (Touch legs, hold up two fingers at top of head, and flap arms)

    Head, thorax, abdomen, abdomen (Touch head, chest, and tummy)

- Show children pictures of insects and other arthropods, and discuss how they are alike and different.

- Ask the children to compare photographs of metamorphosis.

- Do a honeybee dance to act out a bee's form of communication. Dance like little bees pretending to pollinate flowers. (Play "Flight of the Bumblebee" by Nikolai Rimsky-Korsakov.)

- Have the children act out the metamorphosis of caterpillar to butterfly using special butterfly props, such as a shiny, soft green fabric similar in appearance to a monarch chrysalis to drape over

CHAPTER FIVE: THE NATURE-BASED CURRICULUM IN AUTUMN

the children as they curl up on the ground. Then give them orange and black ribbons to represent wings when it's time for the new butterfly to *eclose* (emerge as an adult).

- Invite a beekeeper to visit the class and ask them to explain what they do. Or borrow beekeeping equipment to demonstrate for the children. See, touch, and taste a honeycomb.
- Put an insect in a bug box with a magnified top. Pass the bug box around, and have the children observe. Record their comments.
- An insect's outer "shell" is called an *exoskeleton*. To grow, the insect needs to break out of the exoskeleton, a process called *molting*. Wrap paper around a child volunteer and have them try to molt by breaking the paper.

IDEAS FOR SENSORY AND DISCOVERY TABLES

- Fill the sensory table with soil, leaves, sand, or pine needles, and hide plastic insects inside.
- Make a forest floor by creating a table display of bark, tree cookies, green and brown felt, fake trees, and other props. Scatter plastic insects, hiding some and keeping others visible.
- Create a live-insect display in a terrarium filled with materials specific to that insect's natural habitat. Avoid adding predators. Mist with water. Release the insects back outside after a few days.

IDEAS FOR ART AND SCIENCE ACTIVITIES

- Encourage children to draw, paint, and write (with the help of an adult as needed) about the actual insects that they observe.
- Offer children playdough, chenille stems, beads, and other objects for making insect models.
- Hide plastic insects in playdough and ask children to find them.

HOW TO MAKE A SIMPLE TERRARIUM

We prefer to take soil, sticks, moss, rocks, and bark from the same spot where the insects live, essentially bringing the entire habitat indoors for a few days. We may add a single lettuce leaf or other plant material to ensure the insects have a food source. Layer all of this inside a medium-sized glass tank with a mesh lid. Keep a spray bottle nearby, so that the contents remain moist but not saturated. In general, we keep a homemade terrarium active in our classroom for about one week. We might place the terrarium on our discovery table, make use of it during art activities, or surround it with hand lenses to encourage deeper observation.

- Make a table-sized anthill by painting ant tunnels on large white paper. Read about ant "cities" with the children, and have them add ants, eggs, food, and so on while working together cooperatively, as ants do.
- After finding dragonflies and looking at their wings, let children color dragonfly wing shapes with sparkly paint and add a craft stick for the body.
- As a class, create a large papier-mâché insect by using recycled containers as a base and decorating with paint and chenille stems.
- Provide children with tweezers, and dissect an old paper-wasp nest. Make sure there are no wasps left inside first.
- Place cards with pictures of different kinds of insects on a table. Have children sort little plastic insects into categories—ants, beetles, butterflies, grasshoppers, and so on. Ask children to line up different kinds of insects in patterns, such as ant, butterfly, beetle, ant, butterfly, beetle.
- Encourage children to use rubber stamps with images of bugs and stamp pads or to use paint to create a variety of nature scenes to which they can add insect stamps, stickers, or drawings of insects.

SPIDERS AND WEBS

At the Schlitz Audubon Nature Center, we teach the children that spiders exist on almost every continent (except Antarctica) and that there are up to one million spiders on every acre of land. It can be assumed, therefore, that you have spiders where you teach!

Some children are afraid of spiders, but unless you live in an area where spiders are large or venomous, we have found that children's curiosity often outweighs their fear. We often introduce spiders with puppets to demonstrate body parts and behaviors. Some of our teachers are especially gifted at giving our spider puppets a voice, which can make spiders far less alarming for children. Honest, thoughtful, and sympathetic conversations about spiders can go a long way in mitigating concern.

One of our favorite activities following a brief rain (besides jumping in puddles) is to head out in search of shimmering spiderwebs. The droplets catch on the webs, shining in the sunlight. We may have passed that spot earlier in the day and never noticed the web due to the absence of water, but here it is now—a little hidden gem.

We can also do this when the weather is dry by making our own mist with a spray bottle. A fine mist of water will catch on the web, highlighting each strand without damaging the web. We give the children a chance to spray water as well, letting them experience the almost magical reveal of a previously invisible web. Alternatively, we can place dark cloth or cardboard behind the web to make it visible.

Exploring spiderwebs is perhaps the best way to introduce spiders to a class without a living spider or puppet. We simply look for their webs in the corners of fences and in the building, above doorways, and on our hikes. We may then use large spools of yarn to recreate giant webs in our outdoor classrooms. The goal, in this case, is to not only identify and celebrate the artistry of each web but also to develop an appreciation for the spider that created it.

OUTDOOR EXPLORATION

Take tools on your hike, such as bug boxes, magnifying glasses, and water spray bottles. Observe any spiders you may find, returning them to their habitat after a few minutes. Use the water spray bottle to gently mist and highlight any webs you find. (Never spray so hard that you damage the web.) Help children roll over logs to see if they can find spiders, spider eggs, and webs, being careful not to disturb them.

A FEW KEY CONCEPTS ABOUT SPIDERS AND WEBS

- Spiders are not insects. They are *arachnids* (so are scorpions and ticks). An arachnid has two body segments (cephalothorax and abdomen) rather than three.

- Spiders have short hairs on their eight legs and feet that make it possible for them to walk upside down.

- Spiders come in an array of vivid hues, including red, pink, orange, yellow, blue, and green. Many, but not all, spiders make webs, which they rebuild every day. The web is used to catch and contain insects for food. It usually takes a spider one hour to weave a web.

- Spiderweb silk begins as a liquid inside the spider's abdomen. Once the spider releases it, it becomes solid, emerging as a thread. Spiderweb silk is five times stronger than a piece of steel of the same size.

- Spiders eat insects, such as mosquitos, that bother humans and spread disease.

- Spiders have small mouths, so they do not chew their food. They inject a digestive enzyme into their food that makes it liquefy (like a milkshake!) so they can drink it.

PARTNERING WITH *Nature* IN EARLY CHILDHOOD EDUCATION

HOW TO MAKE A SIMPLE WEAVING LOOM

You can purchase loom kits, but these are often more sophisticated than what we need. A far simpler and less expensive approach is to use tree cookies—we prefer a section approximately 8 inches across—which we then drill using a very fine bit. We drill approximately eight to ten holes around the outer edges of the tree cookie and then hammer in nails. We attach a long piece of colored thread to one nail, or perhaps multiple pieces in many colors, which the children can wrap across and around the nails however they choose.

Take a spider puppet on a hike, and have the children try to find an ideal place to spin its web. You can follow up on this by using yarn to weave one or more webs between trees with the children. Then have the spider puppet express its delight. You can also make a child-sized spider web using rope and challenge the children to crawl through it without touching the sticky sides.

IDEAS FOR GROUP-TIME OPPORTUNITIES

- Read books about spiders, and have the children share their feelings about spiders.
- Sing "The Itsy Bitsy Spider." Don't forget to do the movements as well.
- Give children a mix of plastic insects and spiders, then ask them to sort the two groups.
- Talk about ways that spiders benefit us, including eating insect pests such as mosquitoes. Spiders also teach us more about engineering and weaving as we study their web designs. Spider venom is even used in some medicines.
- Sit outside with weaving looms and try to make your own spiderwebs.

IDEAS FOR SENSORY AND DISCOVERY TABLES

- Fill a sensory table with silky ribbons, yarn, tape, and colorful plastic spiders.
- Build a web between two branches in the discovery table, and secure a plastic spider on the web.
- Add children's books about spiders, spider puppets, and models to the discovery table to help take away some of the fear children may have about spiders.

IDEAS FOR ART AND SCIENCE ACTIVITIES

- Encourage children to illustrate, write (with adult assistance as needed), and dictate about the spiders they find outside.
- Bring in a live spider in a terrarium (a lot of nature centers have tarantulas) for the children to observe and draw.
- Have children make imprints of plastic spiders in playdough or plaster and count the legs.
- Cut out spider shapes, and encourage the children to paint them using bright colors.
- Provide children with playdough, beads, and chenille stems to make spider models.
- Give children oil pastels to draw brightly colored webs on dark paper.
- Ask children to create webs on paper using lines of glue and then sprinkling the glue with biodegradable glitter.

WORMS AND SLUGS

One of the basic truths we know at our nature preschool is that worms and slugs will waylay the best of plans. There isn't much that can compete with the slippery feel of an earthworm or a sticky slug in the hands of a child.

Children are often simultaneously delighted and repulsed by worms and slugs. Many of our preschoolers struggle with two conflicting emotions the first time they encounter a big, wiggly worm: a deep,

primal fear of touching it and an equally deep desire to know just what it feels like. We can sometimes measure a child's growing comfort with nature and growing confidence at preschool by their willingness to hold a worm. This is exciting to behold, but we have also learned over the years that we may need to check a child's pockets for worms!

Worms provide a wonderful starting place for encouraging kindness and empathy. We do our best to make sure that worms are handled safely, and we talk to the children about how to keep worms from drying out and safe from harsh sunlight and to never, ever cut them into pieces! We sometimes turn our flowerbeds into "worm resorts" and encourage the children to carry worms to where the soil is nice and fluffy, should they find one washed up on the sidewalk or struggling in the sandbox.

Slugs generally come in second to worms at our school, but that can change when teachers teach children how to hum to a slug. They will gather the children around while holding a slug in the palm of their hand and hum gently. We also do this with snails. Slugs and snails will frequently respond, raising their eyestalks as a sign of alertness. We often find children clustered together in tiny groups, humming to the slugs. The practice of humming to slugs and snails dates back many generations. In coastal areas of New England, the common periwinkle snail is beloved by children, who are taught to hold it carefully in their palms while humming to coax it out of its shell; local lore suggests that humming or singing helps snails to relax. Scientists debate this, suggesting it may simply be the act of being held that causes snails and slugs to raise their heads. What is less debatable is that children take great delight in humming to snails and slugs.

A terrarium is one of the best ways to introduce children to worms and slugs, because it allows you to look through the glass and watch as they tunnel through soil and leave slime trails on bark without doing long-term damage to either animal. If you do something like this, know the difference between invasive slugs and native slugs. Here in Wisconsin, the leopard slug is invasive and feeds on

A FEW KEY CONCEPTS ABOUT WORMS AND SLUGS

- Slugs and worms play an important role in nature by eating decomposing vegetation. Some slugs help break down wood and other natural materials. Worms are beneficial for gardens due to their ability to improve the quality of the soil. Earthworms, which have segmented bodies that enable them to tunnel through the ground, can loosen up compacted soil and improve drainage. Composting worms, which have smooth bodies, help break down organic matter at the top of the soil, adding the nutrients back into the ground in the form of castings.

- Worms have no eyes and can dry out if left in the sun. They prefer the damp, dark soil.

- Worms have both male and female reproductive organs. Worm eggs are carried in an organ that looks like a collar around the worm's body; baby worms emerge from this collar fully formed.

- Worms have five hearts, although some scientists prefer to call them "pseudohearts" as they are more like chambers than organs.

- Worms do not have lungs. They breathe through their skin.

- Contrary to common belief, cutting a worm in half does not create two worms. It usually results in the worm's death.

- A slug will leave a trail of slime as it travels. When the slime trail dries, it leaves a silvery track, which the slug can use to find its way home. A slug's slime enables it to glide without difficulty over sharp objects.

- Slugs can raise and contract the eyestalks on their heads, enabling the slug to have a better field of view.

- Slugs use their sense of smell to navigate.

native slugs. We do not want to mix them in a common container. If you bring a homemade terrarium indoors, be sure to check and double-check the lid. We came into school one memorable Monday morning to find the lid to our terrarium had been left ajar all weekend. There were slime trails from our classroom slugs across the carpet, across every classroom potted plant, and even up the walls and ceiling!

A fun way to introduce worms to your class is to make a worm composting bin, which will allow you to compost food scraps in your classroom. The worms consume the food scraps and then excrete *vermicast* (essentially manure), which serves as a nutrient-rich, soil-enhancing fertilizer. Over several weeks or even months, you can add bits of vegetable and fruit matter to your bin, checking daily to make sure the organic matter is breaking down and that the soil is neither too dry nor too moist. You can then use paper plates or newspapers to scoop out the worms, observe them up close, discuss their body parts and movements, and gain a deeper understanding of how they benefit the earth. The preferred worm for composting is the red wiggler due to its practice of remaining at the top of the soil, where it will consume organic waste. Earthworms function better outdoors, where their segmented bodies and practice of burrowing deep into the ground allow them to aerate the soil.

Although you do not need a commercially made worm bin, there are several available for less than twenty dollars. There are also several different guides to worm composting online. We are partial to the book *Worms Eat My Garbage: How to Set Up and Maintain a Worm Composting System* by Mary Appelhof and Joanne Olszewski, which we consider the definitive guide to *vermicomposting* (using worms to convert organic waste into fertilizer).

OUTDOOR EXPLORATION

Go on a slug hunt or worm search by turning over logs in different wooded areas. Get down low to find hidden slugs and worms in the dirt. Be sure to teach children how to protect and to hold slugs and worms safely and carefully: we do not put them in our mouths or pockets, nor do we harm them by squashing them with rocks.

Allow children who are nervous around slugs and worms to look, then touch, then hold them only when and if they feel comfortable doing so. Use magnifying glasses to look at silvery slug trails or to see worm body parts up close. Talk about the texture and feel of a slug or worm (compare and contrast).

IDEAS FOR GROUP-TIME OPPORTUNITIES

- Read a book about slugs and worms, such as *Under One Rock: Slugs, Bugs, and Other Ughs* by Anthony Fredericks.
- Make up a funny slug or wiggly worm song.
- Teach the children the sign for *slug* in American Sign Language: raise your pointer finger and pinky, fold the thumb over your middle two fingers, then move your arm forward to imitate a slug crawling.
- Chart the different sized slugs and worms you find outside with the children. Record where you found the most slugs and worms and whether you found more slugs and worms on dry days or wet ones.
- Have everyone try to move like a worm! Get on your belly and try to go forward.

IDEAS FOR SENSORY AND DISCOVERY TABLES

- Fill a sensory table with soil, leaves, sand, or pine needles, and hide rubber worms inside. (Bait shops often sell rubber worms.)
- Line a table or sensory bin with plastic wrap, then cover the wrap with a little baby oil. This mimics the slimy feel of a slug and is a fun sensory experience.
- Make a forest floor in your discovery table by creating a table display of bark, tree cookies, green and brown felt, fake trees, and so on. Scatter plastic insects, worms, and slugs around, hiding some and keeping others visible.
- Create a live slug or worm display with a terrarium. Note: Make sure the lid is secure! Release the slugs and worms back outside within a week or two.

IDEAS FOR ART AND SCIENCE ACTIVITIES

- Encourage children to draw, paint, and write (or dictate) about slugs and worms.
- Provide children with silver paint to make "slug trails" on black paper. They can also use fingerpaint on slippery paper to make slug trails.
- Encourage children to make worms from playdough.

CHAPTER FIVE: THE NATURE-BASED CURRICULUM IN AUTUMN

MONARCH BUTTERFLIES

We are fortunate that, at our nature preschool, the beginning of the school year overlaps with monarch migration. Our prairies often serve as waystations for monarchs migrating to Mexico, so every few years we are gifted with the sight of hundreds of orange and black butterflies arriving in droves to rest up and eat before heading over Lake Michigan. Fun fact: A group of butterflies is called a *kaleidoscope*.

On a typical late summer day, we spot monarchs passing through our play spaces, flying above us on the trails, or alighting on New England asters and sunflowers. We always take time to stop, watch, and enjoy them. The teachers bring books to our circle times that tell the story of monarch life cycles and their annual migration. We also share maps, design art projects, sing songs, and physically act out their life cycles.

In addition, the teachers prepare for the first weeks of school by scouring for milkweed leaves and bringing the leaves that hold monarch eggs into the classroom. We prepare multiple butterfly houses, doing our best to have only one egg (and eventually one caterpillar) per house. These are placed throughout the classrooms, and the children are invited to watch the process of each instar over several weeks. (Each interval between a caterpillar molt is called an *instar*. In all, a monarch caterpillar will go through five instars before it reaches the chrysalis stage. We recommend visiting the websites Monarch Joint Venture (https://monarchjointventure.org/) and Monarch Watch (https://monarchwatch.org/) for more information.)

When at last the day comes that a butterfly house has a monarch flying inside of it, we carry the house outside to the gardens and release the butterfly as a class.

A FEW KEY CONCEPTS ABOUT MONARCH BUTTERFLIES

- Monarch butterflies can be identified by their bright orange wings with black and white markings. Male monarchs have two visible black spots on their wings (these are their sex glands); the females are missing these spots. Females generally have thicker wing veins and are often slightly darker in color

- Monarchs range from South America through Central America and up through North America as far as southern Canada. Monarchs also live in in Hawaii, Australia, and the Pacific Islands.

- Monarchs feed on the nectar from milkweed plants, which grow in fields, marshes, and along roadsides. Before the milkweed blooms in summer, monarchs will visit other flowers, including lilac, clover, and thistles. In the fall, they visit goldenrod, blazing stars, and sunflowers.

- Monarch caterpillars eat milkweed exclusively. By feeding on milkweed, which contains a substance poisonous to birds and other predators, monarchs become toxic. Birds see their warning colors and leave them alone.

- Monarchs east of the Rocky Mountains adapt to changing weather by migrating from Canada to Michoacán, Mexico, in the fall. There they roost in mountain foothills by the millions. Descendants of these butterflies will begin the journey back north in the spring. A smaller migration takes place on the western side of the United States, when monarchs overwinter along the west coast from California to British Columbia.

- Monarch caterpillars hatch out of eggs, which are laid on the underside of milkweed leaves. The caterpillar goes through five growth stages called *instars*, shedding and molting its skin between each stage. After the fifth instar, the caterpillar makes a chrysalis.

- A chrysalis differs from a cocoon. A cocoon is woven around the body; the chrysalis is a part of the body itself. The chrysalis begins when the caterpillar attaches its back end to a support such as a plant, table, or container lid, and its body hangs in the shape of a *J*. The inside of the caterpillar's body then changes as it splits its skin to form a chrysalis. The chrysalis is green with gold markings. Inside the chrysalis, the body continues to change. After about two weeks or longer, the adult butterfly emerges (scientists use the term *eclosion* for the emerging process).

asters, paid for with a joint grant from the U.S. Department of Agriculture and the nonprofit group Monarch Watch. Obviously, a native pollinator garden will vary depending on location and climate, but a butterfly way station is a wonderful addition to any program, as it can serve as a laboratory, a classroom, a place to play, and even an artistic landscape for many years to come.

Even without a pollinator garden, if you have access to milkweed, you can explore monarchs. Each year, our teachers collect monarch eggs from the common milkweed plants that grow along our trails, bringing them into our classrooms. Each egg is placed in its own container, and by the time the school year begins, we have multiple containers in each room with caterpillars in various stages. A large part of the first month of school includes the study of monarch butterflies, which includes their life cycles and migration patterns. By late September, each class has released at least one, if not many, monarch butterflies into the prairies. If you do not have monarchs where you live, most of these activities can easily translate to other butterflies.

OUTDOOR EXPLORATION

Look for monarch butterflies on your hike. Ask the children where they find them and what flowers they prefer. Many monarchs will cluster around the bright purple and yellow prairie flowers just before migration. In the egg-laying season, they look for milkweed plants.

Depending on the season, the children may find the eggs of monarch butterflies on the underside of milkweed leaves. Give children butterfly nets to sweep through fields and try to catch butterflies. Heavier nets will damage the butterflies' wings, so be sure to use soft, light nets designed for butterflies.

If you raise or catch a monarch, consider tagging it and tracking its flight with the children (see https://monarchwatch.org/ for details). Even if you do not tag a monarch, releasing one can be a moving and exciting experience for children. Release it on a warm day, as monarchs struggle to fly in temperatures below 55 degrees Fahrenheit. Before releasing your monarch, try to survey the scene to ensure that there are no predatory birds in the immediate area.

Take a monarch puppet on your hike, and have the puppet visit flowers for nectar. You can also put paper butterflies in bushes and grasses and encourage the children to "catch" them in butterfly nets.

Act out the monarch butterfly life cycle by having the children lie down in the prairie. Cover them with shiny green cloths to represent the monarch chrysalis. As they "sleep," place orange and black ribbons by their side. Remove the cloth, have them open their eyes, and then "fly" through the prairie with their brand-new wings.

IDEAS FOR GROUP-TIME OPPORTUNITIES

- Play music and let the children fly around the room. Provide them with black and orange streamers or ribbons to make wings.
- Observe a real caterpillar going through metamorphosis by bringing in an egg on a leaf, placing it in a secure terrarium, and watching the process over several weeks. Release the butterfly into nature.
- Look at a map of North America. Have the children place monarch stickers (these can be purchased, or you could make your own) on the map, following the path of migration to Mexico.

IDEAS FOR SENSORY AND DISCOVERY TABLES

- Fill a sensory table with dried flowers, then hide plastic or paper butterflies inside.
- Place a laminated map of North America on the discovery table. Draw a line from your location to the Central Highlands of Mexico or to the western United States. Place plastic monarch butterflies on the map so the children can move them from place to place.
- Make a prairie scene with goldenrod, sneezeweed, milkweed, and asters on the discovery table; place plastic monarchs among the flowers.

IDEAS FOR ART AND SCIENCE ACTIVITIES

- Paint monarch butterfly shapes with orange paint. You can have children add strips of black paper and puffy white fabric paint to make the details or simply give them free reign with the materials.
- Provide children with monarch butterfly puzzles on a table or carpeted area.
- Make "stained glass" monarchs by making outlines with a thick, black permanent marker. Have children use oil pastels or watercolor paint to fill in white spaces with shades of orange and yellow.
- Use orange, black, white, and yellow paint to cover large sheets of paper, then cut the paper into butterfly shapes.

NATURE'S PALETTE

Exploring nature's palette means spending time observing and celebrating the colors of nature. It is a deceptively simple activity and can be a fun way to learn about colors. For example, you could explore primary colors, pastels, color mixing, or color wheels. You could also introduce children to the far more complex concept of phenology (discussed in more depth in chapter seven).

Conversations about color can also lead to conversations about camouflage, warning coloration, mimicry, and even seasonal coat coloration, which is when certain northern animals, such as weasels, hares, and ptarmigans, turn white in the winter to blend in with the snow.

Phenology is the study of seasonal changes in nature. It involves looking at the same landscape week after week and noticing subtle changes in color as the seasons and temperatures change, certain plants vanish or go dormant, and the days grow shorter or longer.

One of our favorite ways to explore nature's palette is to head outside with paint-sample cards from our local paint shop and ask the children to match their cards with things they find on the trails. It isn't enough to hold a single blue card up to a blue flower and declare it a match. We may have many blue cards in our mix, and we're

A FEW KEY CONCEPTS ABOUT NATURE'S PALETTE

- Certain animals, such as bees and butterflies, are attracted to colors, and they see colors differently than we do.

- Warning coloration usually involves bright colors, particularly yellow, red, and orange. This is often contrasted with black, so the bright colors are even more striking. Venomous and poisonous animals frequently have warning colors so others will leave them alone.

- *Mimicry* is when nonvenomous or nonpoisonous animals adapt color schemes that are similar to more dangerous animals. Predators mistake them for the more dangerous animal and avoid them. This is another form of protection.

- *Camouflage* is when an animal's colors and markings allow it to blend into the surrounding landscape. Some animals have seasonal colors, which means they can change colors when the surrounding landscape changes. Examples include ptarmigans, ermine, and snowshoe hares.

- Autumn leaves show us their true colors when they lose their green chlorophyll. The oranges, reds, and yellows underneath are only revealed when their chlorophyll is gone.

looking for the best match we can find. The blue of the sky is a very different color than the blue of bottle gentian flowers. We look through the cards and discuss shades and hues and note that one shade of blue looks almost purple while another is pale enough to be almost white. We can also take advantage of this slower activity to identify different plants. This may inspire new names for our paint cards: Bottle Gentian Blue, for example, or Prairie Crabapple Red.

We may also introduce nature's palette by heading out on the trails each day in search of a particular color. Red Day might have us searching for red buds, highbush cranberries, crabapples, dogwood branches, rosehips, cardinals, and red-headed woodpeckers. We may create color books with the children, in which we list the items we find on our color walks and have the children paint each page with the corresponding color, which the children mix themselves. Some years, we have taken dozens of photographs during the height of autumn, when the maples, oaks, and other deciduous

CHAPTER FIVE: THE NATURE-BASED CURRICULUM IN AUTUMN

trees are at their most spectacular, and combined these with photographs of the children's boots, mittens, raincoats, and so on. We have then created beautiful color wheels made up of these different photographs.

By taking regular photographs of a particular landscape, the photographs later become a visual record of a specific moment in a specific season. Here in Wisconsin, a grove of paper birch trees will be yellow in autumn, snow-covered in winter, brown in spring, and green in summer. The bark may remain the same throughout, but the surrounding colors change constantly. This is a striking reminder of how transformation in nature can be viewed through something as simple as color.

OUTDOOR EXPLORATION

Encourage children to notice the colors in nature by picking one color to explore each day. By zooming in on purple, for example, you may be surprised by how many different objects in nature feature shades of purple, including leaves, shells, water, storm clouds, flowers, and rocks. Help the children make a list of the things they find, and take pictures. You can do this with all the colors in nature: on a color walk together, take pictures and make a list of the things you find in nature that are specific colors. If you experience distinct seasons, pass out photos from the summer and fall and see how the landscape has changed colors in the winter.

Look at the different colors of the birds. Explore with the children why some are brightly colored and others are duller shades of brown and gray. You can repeat this activity with rocks: look for different colors in rocks, noticing how colors deepen and change when the rocks are wet.

Carry paint sample cards on your hike and encourage the children to match the colors with what they find in nature. You can also bring watercolors or oil pastels and paper outside and ask the children to mix colors on paper while trying to recreate the different colors they see. Together, make a color guidebook that connects colors to specific features in nature. In the winter, give the children spray bottles with colored water to use on snow. You can also make colorful ice cubes in different shapes and sizes and add these to your outdoor play areas.

IDEAS FOR GROUP-TIME OPPORTUNITIES

- Discuss and show examples of warning colors on animals, such as snakes and insects. (We use photographs or models rather than actual venomous animals.) Yellow, orange, or red side by side with black usually means danger. You can also show examples of animals that use color to camouflage.
- Talk about the specific order of colors you find in rainbows.
- Place different colored sheets of paper or cloth on the carpet. Together, you can sort objects by color. For example, place a red plush cardinal on the red paper, a yellow shell on the yellow paper, a purple flower on the purple paper, and so on.
- Read books and sing or listen to songs about colors.

IDEAS FOR SENSORY AND DISCOVERY TABLES

To your sensory table, add items such as:

- purple or orange sand,
- water with food coloring (you can change the color daily),
- scissors and different colored ribbons (we like biodegradable paper ribbon),
- shells and pebbles, and
- flower petals (we often use flower petals swept up from our neighborhood garden center).

IDEAS FOR ART AND SCIENCE ACTIVITIES

- Set up paint-mixing experiments using, for example, blue and yellow, and ask the children to experiment to see what color they get.
- Have the children make dot paintings based on the colors they see outdoors.
- Pass around colored lenses, and encourage the children to look at everything around them through rose, blue, green, or yellow lenses.
- Give children eyedroppers to add small drops of food coloring or paint into water to see how the colors mix.
- Place freshly trimmed white roses (or white carnations or daisies) into clear glasses of water. Ask the children to add different food colorings to the water and then wait for the white flowers to change color.
- Set up a loom in the classroom. Add different colored ribbons each day for children to weave.
- With the children, make paper lanterns by watercoloring sheets of paper and rubbing them with oil. Use darker colors, such as green, purple, and blue, on one sheet of paper and brighter colors, such as orange, red and yellow, on others. When the oil dries, shape the paper into a cone, and secure it with tape or staples. Place a battery-operated candle inside the cone. Some lanterns will have daytime colors and others will have nighttime colors.

AUTUMN LEAVES

At our school, autumn is our showiest season, and we aim to spend as much time as we can enjoying this glorious time of year. We can sit outside with art supplies, musical instruments, and books, and they are generally safe from the elements. Throughout the days and weeks of autumn, we collect leaves and make gorgeous leaf-print shirts and bags using acrylic paints. (Tip: You can refrigerate leaves, preserving their freshness for upcoming art projects.) We drop leaves from bridges and towers, sometimes timing how long it takes leaves to reach the ground and sometimes just watching them dance

CHAPTER FIVE: THE NATURE-BASED CURRICULUM IN AUTUMN

on the currents. We identify lobed leaves (leaves with deeply indented margins) versus toothed leaves (leaves with small, tooth-like edges).

The best way to introduce autumn leaves is to head outside in autumn and look around at the trees. The first step should simply be to notice the colors, the shapes, the sounds, and the smells. Encourage sensory experiences. Collect leaves as you walk. Look for the smallest, the largest, ones that are green, leaves with two colors, leaves shaped like hearts, and so on.

We sometimes cut long strips of paper and fasten them into headbands for the children. As we hike, children collect leaves and we secure them to each headband, creating autumn leaf crowns, using a stapler we have brought with us.

That said, far and away our most popular leaf activity is really the simplest of all: we rake leaves into piles and jump in. We use light, wooden rakes designed for children instead of ones with metal teeth. We tend to need to reorder them every few years. Raking is a wonderfully satisfying activity: it allows children to see immediate results, and it's extremely cooperative. We'll often start with small, individual piles, then work in teams to bring our piles together. We hold off on jumping in the piles until they're really big; letting the anticipation build is part of the fun. The physical movements required in leaf-raking are cross-body, which means children are crossing the midline. This supports brain development. But the main reason we love this activity is because it's just so fun and joyful. It is delightful to run, jump, hide, fall into, and toss bright red, orange, and yellow leaves. We enjoy throwing them in the air together, hearing them crunch underfoot, and letting them catch us before we hit the ground.

In our experience, it isn't necessary to browse Pinterest or other sites looking for autumn crafts. Just head outside to a group of trees after the majority of their leaves are down, and hand each child a comfortable rake. Monitor them just enough to make sure the rakes don't turn into jousting poles (or, if they do, that they're being handled responsibly), and let the children rake and jump over and over for as long as they want. It's simple, easy, and full of joy!

PARTNERING WITH *Nature* IN EARLY CHILDHOOD EDUCATION

128

A FEW KEY CONCEPTS ABOUT AUTUMN LEAVES

- Leaves require sunlight, water, chlorophyll, and carbon dioxide to make food for themselves. Chlorophyll is what makes leaves green and what allows plants to absorb energy from light (*photosynthesis*). When the weather gets colder, leaves produce a coating that blocks their water source. Without water, leaves can no longer make chlorophyll.

- In the fall, plants and trees are preparing for the coming cold. They begin to absorb the nutrients in the leaves. As green chlorophyll is consumed, the leaves reveal their true colors, often shades of orange, yellow, and red. After these true colors appear, the leaves will eventually die. This process helps to ensure that the tree itself survives the winter.

- Leaf imprints from prehistoric times exist in fossil records. (The leaf itself did not turn into a fossil, but the outline and print it left in the mud filled in with minerals and fossilized.)

OUTDOOR EXPLORATION

Look for autumn leaves. Look for leaves that are smooth, shiny, prickly, and have different shapes and colors. Ask the children to select a leaf and describe it using many different words. Chart the different colors they list, or give the children paints and brushes to paint each color they see. Ask the children to try to catch a leaf as it falls.

With the children, lie down under a tree and look up into the branches. Take a deep breath and enjoy! Ask each child to choose one leaf from all the many leaves. Give them time to study the leaf. If you put all the leaves in a big pile, can they find their own leaf again?

Start a class tree journal. Ask the children to choose a tree in the autumn and watch it through all the seasons, perhaps taking photographs or sketching it every three months.

Play the Chlorophyll Game. As children hold colorful leaves, have them hide beneath a green sheet (representing chlorophyll), which can be held aloft by two teachers like a canopy. Recite the words "Chlorophyll, chlorophyll, go away! Autumn colors come out to play!" Then whisk the green sheet away, and let the children run around with their leaves.

IDEAS FOR GROUP-TIME OPPORTUNITIES

- Read a book about autumn leaves. Our favorites include *Fall Is Not Easy* by Marty Kelley, *Leaf Man* by Lois Ehlert, *Goodbye Summer, Hello Autumn* by Kenard Pak, *It's Fall!* by Linda Glaser, and *We're Going on a Leaf Hunt* by Steve Metzger.

- Hand each child a paper leaf, making sure there are two of each kind. Have the children find their match.
- Pretend to dance like falling leaves, adding colorful streamers if you wish.
- Place a variety of leaves onto a large, black felt circle. Have the children help sort them as you compare the shapes and colors of leaves.

IDEAS FOR SENSORY AND DISCOVERY TABLES

- Fill a sensory table with dried leaves or colored sand (yellow, red, or orange) to match the colors outside, and hide small plastic insects.
- Make an autumn leaf display on the discovery table.
- Place a small tree on the table and hang silk leaves from it.
- Place colored sorting baskets on the table so that children can sort leaves based on color and shape.

IDEAS FOR ART AND SCIENCE ACTIVITIES

- Put a sealable plastic bag over a live leaf, and observe later how much water it gives off.
- Have the children make leaf rubbings. (For younger children, put leaves in envelopes so they can more easily do this.) To make leaf prints, ask them to paint the veined side of leaves and press them on paper.
- Ask the children to arrange leaves by size from smallest to largest.
- Provide the children with cookie cutters of different leaves that they can dip into trays of paint and then place on a paper banner.
- Make a matching game with leaves. Use clear plastic tape, lamination, or clear contact paper to adhere different leaves (two of each kind) onto note cards. Ask the children to match the leaves that are the same.
- Let children collect leaves and place them between clear contact paper. Cut into shapes if desired, then hang the leaves in the windows.
- Read *Leaf Man* by Lois Ehlert, then make your own autumn leaf collages by spreading leaves, stems, acorn caps, and other materials on dark paper or sheets.

- Give each child a large leaf shape cut from orange or yellow paper. Set out bowls of dried leaves. Let the children brush glue on their leaf shapes, then crumble the dried leaves and sprinkle them over the glue.
- Cover a table with black felt, and place empty picture frames on it. Have the children arrange autumn leaves, pine cones, acorns, goldenrod, asters, and so on, in the frames. Photograph their fall pictures.

SEEDS

It can feel challenging to introduce a topic like seeds to a group of children, perhaps because, when compared to dinosaurs, seeds are not as exciting. By their very nature, seeds are quiet, small, and seemingly less spectacular than, say, volcanic eruptions. However, when approached with the same energy and fascination one might show for volcanoes, seeds can be truly amazing.

Just imagine the energy and power required for something so tiny to create a living organism as mighty as a cottonwood or a redwood!

You can dissect seedpods from wildflowers with the same fascination and level of scrutiny you might use for digging up ancient fossils. Cutting open a pumpkin or other fruit and seeing what's hidden inside is always delightful. Children who enjoy lift-the-flap books or looking under logs and rocks are sure to find pleasure in splitting open a thick milkweed pod and watching those fluffy white seeds burst out.

Seeds are wonderfully interactive. In the right season, you can blow on some seeds, such as milkweed and dandelion, and send them flying. You can attach burdock seeds to soft fleece vests or stick them onto your socks inadvertently. You can crush dried bergamot seeds to release the oil. Coneflower seeds smell like peppercorns; sneezeweed seeds smell like pineapple.

Too often, children are cautioned not to touch nature. But most seeds invite touch. Walk through the woods on a warm day and pick a fallen pine cone from the ground. Have children remove the outer scales, which protect the hidden seeds within. Do the same activity on a very cold day to compare. Pine cone scales tend to close up tight when the weather is inhospitable to seed growth. Find an oak tree and hunt for fallen acorns. The caps are wonderful for art projects, instruments, fairy houses, or sorting activities. Prying the caps from the acorns is also good for fine motor dexterity. It's fun and satisfying.

Often, our very first step outside at our center includes a walk through the prairie on a golden autumn day. Of course, not every program has a prairie at their doorstep. Luckily, seeds are all around us. Whether your program is urban, suburban, or rural, if you have any trees, shrubs, or even weeds nearby, chances are you have seeds. The goal is to find a spot where you can look, touch, and even sniff different seeds. You may be surprised to find how many seeds have a distinctive smell.

Once we have spent a few days observing, we head out again with the goal of collecting. To protect ourselves from potentially sharp or irritating seeds, we like to don fuzzy mittens. We may even place clean socks on our hands. This has the added advantage of helping us collect seeds that are so small and inconspicuous we might otherwise have missed them. By running your mittened hands across a myriad of plants—asters, burdock, or, depending on your location, maybe rabbit brush, pigweed, or broadleaf dock—you can collect dozens of tiny seeds often nicknamed "hitchhikers." Carefully remove the seeds and spread them out on large sheets of paper. Using magnifying lenses, explore their shapes and textures.

Which ones float on the breeze? Which ones attach best to coyote fur? Use field guides to determine which seeds are the most nutritious for the animals that live in your region. Finally, return the seeds to the earth by blowing, brushing, or scattering them back among the plants, replenishing the prairies for the following spring.

Seeds are small and secretive, which can make them fascinating. Children are often captivated by tiny things. In our experience, they are more mesmerized by a single stone at the beach than they are by the vast stretches of pebbles and sand. Collecting seeds feeds this love of tiny things. Give children time and space to collect tiny basswood seeds or pluck seeds from dried-out sunflower heads, then provide

A FEW KEY CONCEPTS ABOUT SEEDS

- A seed is the part of a plant that can grow into a new plant. Some plants make lots of seeds, some only a few.

- A typical seed includes an embryo, nutrients, and a seed coat. Seeds begin in a dormant stage, which means they are resting inside their seed coat. When the seed is ready to develop, it requires water, air, and warmth. As the seed develops, it will grow into a seedling that requires water, air, space, and sunlight.

- Seeds grow into the same kind of plant from which they came.

- Plants need to disperse their seeds in a new location to make new plants.

- Seeds travel in many ways! Some seeds float on the wind. Some are sticky or have spikes and attach to animals. Some are poppers. Some are eaten by animals and then pooped out in new locations.

- In autumn, many plants stop growing and die. This is when they spread their seeds so new plants can take their place the next spring.

- Most fruits contain seeds. A coconut is technically a seed!

them with tools such as scissors and tweezers so they may dissect a range of flowers and fruits. Seeds are like tiny presents; unwrapped by eager hands, they turn into treasures.

OUTDOOR EXPLORATION

Go on a seed scavenger hunt and see how many different seeds the children can find. You can give children sticky tape (maybe as bracelets) to see how many seeds they can stick on as they hike. Offer them a magnifying glass to look at their seeds, and discuss how they may have been dispersed. Children can also look for signs of animals that use seeds for their food (for example, pine cones that have been chewed). Allow them to take the seeds from dried plants and scatter them about.

Leave seeds for the birds or corn for the deer on the trail or in some special spot. Come back to the same location and see whether it is still there. You can also put out a birdfeeder and fill it with seeds, watching the different birds that visit.

If present in your area, look for milkweed pods, sunflowers, or field corn cobs. Encourage the children to open the milkweed pods and examine the seeds before distributing them into the wind. Have children use their fingers to remove the kernels from field corn cobs or dried sunflowers.

CHAPTER FIVE: THE NATURE-BASED CURRICULUM IN AUTUMN

Ask the children to pretend to be squirrels, and give them paper acorns to hide. Can they find them all later?

Play the game Will It Grow? In this game, some children will be seeds, some will be water, some will be sunshine, and some will be soil. One or two children could also be birds. (You can give them pictures to help them remember their role.) Create three "bases" and then have the children run around for one minute. Then announce that it's time to find a base. Once the children are at a base, have them stand still. Now see if each base has a seed, sunshine, soil, and water. If one of those things is missing, will that seed grow? If there is only one seed and a bird, will that seed grow? What if there are too many seeds and not enough soil and water? Repeat, and compare results.

IDEAS FOR GROUP-TIME OPPORTUNITIES

- Role-play the life of a seed from hiding in the ground to sprouting to putting out leaves to catch the sun. End with them stretching up as tall as they can.

- Make a list of all the different seeds children can name.

- Place different kinds of seeds on a felt circle, including seeds that disperse on the wind, seeds that stick and cling, and seeds that flutter to the ground. Brainstorm with the children how the seeds disperse and why.

IDEAS FOR SENSORY AND DISCOVERY TABLES

- Fill a sensory table with unusual seeds like putka pods from India or dried corn cobs, beans, or dried sunflower heads filled with seeds. Provide scoops, tongs, and tweezers for the children to use.

- Make a seed display in the discovery table. Interesting seeds to include are dried wild indigo, basswood seeds, and different sizes of pine cones.

IDEAS FOR ART AND SCIENCE ACTIVITIES

- Ask the children to estimate the number of seeds in an apple, then count to see how close they are. You can also cut open different kinds of fruit and let the children find and talk about the seeds. Are the seeds tiny or big? Are there many seeds or just one? Record their discoveries.

- Pop popcorn and munch on the exploded seeds (for ages four and up), or toast sunflower seeds or pumpkins seeds for snacks.

- Soak lima beans in water overnight, then provide the children with tweezers to dissect them. They can remove the seed coat, open the two halves of the *cotyledon* (the embryonic leaf) and remove the embryo.

PARTNERING WITH *Nature* IN EARLY CHILDHOOD EDUCATION

- Plant bean seeds in little cups and watch them grow. With the children, measure daily and make a chart to show growth. Alternatively, plant lima beans or sunflower seeds in baggies with a wet paper towel, and hang them in the window to watch the process. You can also grow wheat grass in large, low containers filled with soil. When it grows tall, children can cut it with scissors.

- Ask the children to grind different seeds using a mortar and pestle. How do different seeds smell?
- Help children classify seeds and sort them in ice cube trays.
- Plant the same kind of seeds in several containers. Give one water and another no water. Give one light and another no light. Try sand for one, and compost for another. Ask the children to observe and discuss which grows the best.
- Add large tree seeds, such as locust tree pods, to your art materials.

BIRD MIGRATION

One of the biggest challenges when exploring bird migration is that the birds themselves are so far away. If we see them migrating at all, it's often from a great distance or at a considerable height. A more realistic approach is to notice their presence in the late summer months and to compare this to their absence in late fall. We may spot groups of birds in the sky, or we may simply take a hike one day and find that most of our local birds have gone. The ducks, geese, and blackbirds have all flown away, and the barn swallows have vacated the eves of the building.

Often, during migration season, we hear rather than see the effects of migration. The landscape is suddenly quieter, and often we hear only the chickadees or perhaps a stray cardinal who continue to sing near our spaces. It is interesting to compare the quiet days to the change in light and temperature. Migration is a wonderful opportunity to explore phrenology a little more deeply. What other changes are taking place all around us as autumn slowly gives way to winter?

We may celebrate bird migration by learning to mimic the call of the Canada goose. We teach children how to form a *V* as a class, and we may flap our wings and soar across a grassy field, moving and honking in imitation. It is fun to do this and then look up and see great flocks of geese flying in similar formation. If we are tired from running, this is a good time to lie on our backs and watch the flight overhead.

One of our favorite approaches to introducing bird migration grew from a compass game designed for older children. The purpose of the game was to master the use of a compass and to follow a map across the nature center grounds. For much smaller children, we keep it simpler, but there is still an element of orienteering combined with bird migration.

Borrowing a box full of compasses, we teach the children how to first hold a compass (flat in the palm), and how to put Red in the Shed, meaning line up the appropriate arrows on the compass, which should always point to magnetic north regardless of which way you're walking. We then use the compass, along with our surrounding landmarks, to determine which way is south. We locate a landmark south of where we are standing and walk toward it.

Most years when we do this activity we end up at the grassy pavilion overlooking Lake Michigan. There, one of our volunteers meets us with a feast of water, cookies, and fruit. The purpose, besides providing a snack as a reward for outstanding compass use, is to illustrate the purpose of migration: most animals migrate to find food. The birds are not necessarily flying away because it is too cold; they fly away because their food sources are vanishing. Birds are better equipped to handle cold weather than we may imagine. It is the frozen water

A FEW KEY CONCEPTS ABOUT BIRD MIGRATION

- Some animals need to migrate or move away when their food source is gone.

- Migrating birds include geese and ducks, which often travel in groups, forming large *V* shapes. Geese and ducks do not fly away because they are cold; their feathers keep them warm. They migrate because of their need for open water, grassy fields, and other dependable food sources.

- The smallest migrating bird is a hummingbird. This tiny bird can travel up to six hundred miles each year. Its migration path includes flying across the Gulf of Mexico.

- Some birds will migrate as far as 16,000 miles at speeds of 30 miles per hour. This means they may travel for more than two months, flying eight hours a day to reach their destination!

- Migrating birds need access to fresh food and water.

- Before they migrate, birds prepare for the journey by building up their body fat. We can help them by filling feeders, hanging out suet, and providing plenty of fresh water.

- Some migrating birds fly at night, when it's cooler and there are fewer predators.

- Migrating birds face many dangers, including hawks, owls, dehydration, starvation, storms, man-made structures such as power stations and windmills, and human events such as war and environmental pollution.

- Birds' inner compasses helps them navigate. They use the stars, sun, and the Earth's magnetism to help them find their way.

- Many migrating birds return to the place where they were hatched, which means you may see the same bird in the same place year after year.

- Not all birds migrate! Some of the most common nonmigrating birds in North America include cardinals, chickadees, pileated woodpeckers, common ravens, and blue jays.

and the lack of fruit, insects, larva, and seeds that propels them to migrate. (Depending on the age of your classes, this is also a wonderful opportunity to discuss that many migrating birds can detect the axis of Earth's magnetic fields in their brains, while we depend on a physical compass.)

Schools in other regions may not run this activity in quite the same way. Perhaps the birds in your state don't migrate in autumn. Perhaps there is an influx of songbirds and others arriving at your school from the faraway north. Even in Wisconsin, we see the arrival of certain owls from northern Canada. But regardless of location, you can pull out a compass and mimic the flight paths of birds specific to your region.

OUTDOOR EXPLORATION

Pretend to be geese migrating. If you'd like to differentiate between male and female geese, know that the female makes a "hink" call that is higher pitched and faster than the male's call. The male's call is lower and slower and sounds more like the "honk" we associate with the Canada goose. You can also use a long rope to form a *V* that children can carry as they hike to walk in a *V* formation.

Play the Migrate, Activate, and Hibernate trail game. As the children hike, the leader holds up a picture of an animal. If that animal hibernates, the children all pretend to sleep. If the animal migrates, they pretend like they are birds flying away. If the animal is active all winter, the children jump and leap about.

Take a compass outside and navigate your way south. How do birds and other animals know in which direction to fly? Follow the compass south and have a little treat ready for your class when you reach your destination. You can also divide the class into two groups to take two routes that go south and meet at a prearranged destination. Compare what each group saw along the way.

IDEAS FOR GROUP-TIME OPPORTUNITIES

- Play Who Migrates? Choose local birds and make cards for each, showing what that bird eats. Each child is a bird and draws a card to see what that bird eats: mosquitoes, worms, berries, fish, squirrels, frogs, ants, mice, snakes, insects, caterpillars, and so on. As you hike, each child can determine whether the food their bird eats is still available or whether they need to migrate.

- Look at maps of bird migration routes.

- Listen to a recording of migrating geese.

- Give each child a stuffed animal that lives in your area. Mark three large, plastic hoops or boxes as "Migrate," "Hibernate," or "Active." Let the children decide where their animal belongs.

PARTNERING WITH *Nature* IN EARLY CHILDHOOD EDUCATION

IDEAS FOR SENSORY AND DISCOVERY TABLES

- Fill your sensory table with water, and place plastic ducks and geese in the water. Freeze plants in ice, then add them to the water to see how ducks and geese struggle to find food once it is frozen.
- Use geese silhouettes to make a *V* shape. On your discovery table, place them on top of blue cloth for the sky, and add white fabric for the clouds.

IDEAS FOR ART AND SCIENCE ACTIVITIES

- Make bird feeders for the birds that do not migrate.
- Invite someone who bands birds to visit the class and explain how they do it and why. Make "bands" for the children by covering cut paper-towel tubes with aluminum foil and attaching them to their wrists.
- Ask the children to keep track on a chart of the birds they see outside. Which birds stay in the winter, and which migrate?

- Provide children with pencils or crayons to make still-life drawings of geese or ducks.

SQUIRRELS AND CHIPMUNKS

Our program is based in Wisconsin, which means squirrels and chipmunks are a common sight. We recognize that these native mammals may not be present in other places, but throughout North America, squirrels and chipmunks are widespread. We encourage programs that have their own native mammals to take these ideas and rework them so they more accurately reflect your own local fauna.

Because these mammals are, for us, so common, we typically have daily sightings. Squirrels, in particular, are present even in the winter, and we see evidence of ground squirrels, tree squirrels, and chipmunks almost every day of the year. With the children, we parse out information about these animals a little at a time, pausing each time we see one to learn just a little bit more about their lives and behavior. There are also plenty of days when we do not discuss their natural

history at all. We simply let the children watch, ask questions, or perhaps just play in their spaces and mimic the animals' behavior.

We have found that by having a few special spots on the trails and grounds dedicated to some of the animals we see most frequently, the children form deeper connections to these creatures. At Turtle Pond, we try to spot the turtles. At Raccoon Tree, we wonder about the resident raccoon and what it may be up to. Whenever we stand on Chipmunk Bridge, we take a few minutes to look for the chipmunks and to speculate about why we may or may not see them that day. We talk about their homes, which consist of an underground tunnel system with multiple entrances and exits, carefully concealed among the rocks. We discuss who their neighbors might be. Do they share the ravine with snakes and weasels? Do they have to look out for circling hawks or the owls who may live in the trees? How do they know when it's safe to come out and scamper across the rocks?

Eastern chipmunks hibernate in winter, and as the seasons advance, we may stop to wonder if the chipmunks are safe and sleeping in their underground tunnels. We may wonder whether they've awakened to eat a few nuts or seeds and whether they have enough leaves to keep their snuggeries warm and cozy. We may read several children's books about chipmunks or even sing a lullaby from atop the bridge on a chilly day in November, just in case they're still awake but are settling in for the winter.

In addition to Chipmunk Bridge, we also have the Squirrel Kitchen, which is an area of towering pines where we find hundreds of chewed-up pine cones, along with squirrel *dreys* (nests) high in the trees. The children love climbing the pine trees, which we allow as long as they follow our safety guidelines. They love raking through the many piles of pine-cone scales that lie in heaps on the ground. Teachers may bring out a squirrel puppet and teach the children the song "Grey Squirrel, Grey Squirrel, Shake Your Bushy Tail," which can easily be adapted to "Red Squirrel, Red Squirrel" or "Black Squirrel, Black Squirrel."

OUTDOOR EXPLORATION

When you hike with the children, record how many squirrels and chipmunks they see. Encourage the children to look for chewed pine cones (a red squirrel might be nearby), holes in trees (possible homes for red or flying squirrels), or dreys in the treetops. Encourage the children to make their own

A FEW KEY CONCEPTS ABOUT SQUIRRELS AND CHIPMUNKS

- Squirrels and chipmunks are rodents, just like rats, mice, and beavers! Chipmunks are part of the squirrel family.

- Squirrels and chipmunks are mammals. Mammals have specific characteristics: they are warm blooded, most are born alive, they provide milk for their offspring, and they have hair or fur.

- There are more than two hundred species of squirrels. Squirrels live on every continent except Australia and Antarctica.

- Most, but not all, squirrels climb trees.

- Tree squirrel nests are called *dreys*; they are made of leaves and twigs and are usually built in the forks of trees or in tree cavities. Some incomplete dreys are actually just sleeping platforms, used by a solitary squirrel in hot weather.

- Most tree-dwelling squirrels are solitary, but they will group together for warmth in the winter. Chipmunks also live alone, except when they give birth.

- Early spring is the most challenging season for squirrels and chipmunks due to lack of food.

- Squirrels are mostly herbivores, but they will also eat eggs, caterpillars, and small insects. Their preferred foods are nuts, seeds, fruit, fungi, grains, plants, roots, bulbs, and tree bark. Chipmunks eat seeds, nuts, and fruit and mostly forage on the ground. They can store large amounts of food in special cheek pouches.

- Prairie dogs and ground squirrels are both members of the squirrel family, even though they look and act differently than tree squirrels.

- There are twenty-five species of chipmunks in North America. They live in mountains, forests, plains, and deserts.

- In the fall, chipmunks stockpile food by taking it into underground burrows for the winter. One chipmunk can gather up to one hundred sixty-five acorns in a day. After two days, they usually have enough to last the winter.

- A chipmunk burrow is called a *den* or *snuggery*. They consist of underground tunnels with multiple front and back doors. Chipmunks keep their refuse in different "wings" far from their sleeping quarters.

- Chipmunk babies are called *pups*. They are born in late spring. Mother chipmunks give birth to four or five pups at a time.

- Eastern North American chipmunks hibernate, but western ones do not.

drey using twigs and leaves or collect acorns and put them by a tree that they think a squirrel might frequent.

You can also leave a little field corn out before you take a hike and return to the same spot later and see if it is still there. In the winter, follow squirrel tracks to the base of a tree. Let children hide paper acorns. Come back later and see if they can find them all. Will the ones not found grow into paper oak trees?

IDEAS FOR GROUP-TIME OPPORTUNITIES

- Cut interlocking foam pieces to make a Chipmunk Tunnel. Give each child a piece of the foam and have them assemble the tunnel. Include special areas for sleeping and refuse. Using a chipmunk puppet, have it move and talk its way through the tunnel.

- Place laminated squirrel tracks on the floor and have them lead to an indoor tree or special hiding spot. Or take the laminated tracks outside, and have them lead to a tree with a drey in it.

- List all the mammals children can name. Discuss what makes something a mammal. As an extension to this idea, go on a mammal scavenger hunt outside.

- Distribute stuffed animals among the children and then decide as a group whether the animal is a mammal. You can sort the animals in piles: birds, reptiles, mammals, and so on.

- Give each child a picture of a different animal. Place two large, plastic hoops in the circle with a "yes" sign in one and a "no" sign in the other. Have each child decide if their animal is a mammal (put it in the "yes" hoop) or not a mammal (put it in the "no" hoop).

- Sing the squirrel song.

    Grey squirrel, grey squirrel,
    Swish your bushy tail.
    Grey squirrel, grey squirrel,
    Swish your bushy tail.
    Wrinkle up your little nose,
    Hold an acorn in your toes,
    Grey squirrel, grey squirrel,
    Swish your bushy tail.

- Change to red squirrel and pine cone or chipmunk and skinny tail.

IDEAS FOR SENSORY AND DISCOVERY TABLES

- Place branches, dried leaves, and grass in the sensory table for making squirrel dreys.

- Fill the sensory table with real pine cones, plastic or real acorns, dried grasses, squirrel and chipmunk puppets, and tongs.

- Set up a woodland scene in the discovery table with different plastic mammals.
- Make a mammal-tracks display on the discovery table.
- Set up stuffed-animal chipmunks and squirrels along with trees, burrows, dreys, and rocks on the discovery table so that children can place them in the appropriate habitat.

IDEAS FOR ART AND SCIENCE ACTIVITIES

- Provide children with old nature magazines, scissors, glue, and paper to make a mammal collage.
- Invite children to draw a favorite mammal and tell a story about it.
- Take children outside and ask them to draw the homes of squirrels and chipmunks.
- Mount a mailbox outside and write postcards back and forth with a chipmunk, who can describe how it gets ready for winter! The children can draw pictures that they send to the chipmunk along with dictated letters with the child's own signature.

HARVEST TIME

In almost every climate and in almost every culture, there is a time to plant and a time to harvest. Harvest time can be observed in a myriad of ways with young children, but the most straightforward is to literally head out to the garden to gather fruits and vegetables. Doing this also requires a six-month head start, depending on your growing season.

As mentioned earlier, over the years we have planted tomatoes, potatoes, cucumbers, eggplant, tomatillos, pole beans, and basil in our gardens, with a mixture of success. One of the greatest challenges we face is that, being part of a nature preserve, our gardens attract dozens of wild turkeys, ground squirrels, and rabbits. We can pour endless amounts of time and money into our gardens with little to show for our efforts. We also struggle with our growing season, which begins as our school year is ending and ends with a new group of children the following fall. It is difficult for the children to feel a connection to their harvest when they were not involved in the entire process.

However, it is still possible to make harvest time meaningful, even with an abbreviated season. We keep raised herb beds and give the children ample opportunity to play with, cut, taste, and cook with herbs such as basil, rosemary, mint, chamomile, and thyme. We plant cherry tomatoes late in the season and often begin the school year just as they are ripening.

We also visit farmer's markets, bringing in local vegetables, and we invite children to bring vegetables to school. We devote time in the classroom to cutting our vegetables into bite-size pieces; the children assist with this using safety knives and adult supervision. We then either make the food right away into soup or freeze the vegetables for later. Our goal, ultimately, is to make stone soup, a community soup consisting of many ingredients.

Due to some children's serious food allergies, we are very careful to control the foods that parents may want to bring to school. However, we try to create space in our program for families to share their own cultural traditions. Over the years, we have enjoyed latkes, figs, saffron bread, pumpkin pie, snow crackers, and even dandelion fritters, all in observance of special holidays and festivals. It is one way of honoring every child in our school.

In some programs, observance of any religious or cultural holiday may be strictly forbidden. One of the great advantages of a harvest celebration is that it is possible to remove the human element, if you must, and focus on animals. Harvest time does not apply strictly to people.

Throughout the harvest season, we take walks in the woods in search of animals getting ready for winter. We look for evidence of chewed plants and food caches. We read books and stories about gathering food for the coming cold and may even go out on the trails with handfuls of seed corn, scattering little bits here and there for the wild turkeys, chipmunks, and squirrels. Harvest time is a chance to hang bird feeders, if you have not done so already, or to make your own suet and seed feeders.

A FEW KEY CONCEPTS ABOUT HARVEST TIME

- In Wisconsin, we can pick apples, pumpkins, fall greens, and other goodies from the garden. Look at what's available in your growing season (for example, citrus in the winter in Florida, Arizona, and California) and make that part of your program's harvest-time activities.

- There are different kinds of apples, and they do not all taste the same.

- Apples grow on trees, in orchards. Pumpkins and gourds grow on vines on the ground.

- Gourds can come in many shapes; some are especially funny and lumpy!

- During our Wisconsin harvest time, the animals are also busy gathering food for the winter. Animals need the food that nature provides to fatten up before the cold, whether to provide nourishment for their long migration or to save and store for the upcoming winter.

- In earlier times, many people would prepare food for the winter by smoking, pickling, drying, making jams, and finding other ways to make their fall foods last during the long winter months.

- Because there is a lot of food this time of year, it is a tradition to gather with family and friends to eat. This is a good opportunity to express our thanks.

- Every group that has lived on this land has had to adapt, learning how to manage the seasons, using what nature provides, and teaching the next generation.

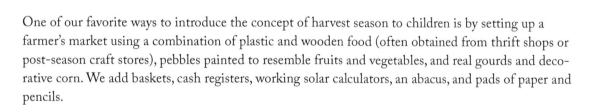

One of our favorite ways to introduce the concept of harvest season to children is by setting up a farmer's market using a combination of plastic and wooden food (often obtained from thrift shops or post-season craft stores), pebbles painted to resemble fruits and vegetables, and real gourds and decorative corn. We add baskets, cash registers, working solar calculators, an abacus, and pads of paper and pencils.

We also may combine our farmer's market with our outdoor mud kitchen, supplementing our "produce" with dried grasses, wood chips, autumn seeds, and more. We might compose nature cookbooks using recipes the children create at the mud kitchen. Children love to celebrate food, even when it's make-believe.

CHAPTER FIVE: THE NATURE-BASED CURRICULUM IN AUTUMN

OUTDOOR EXPLORATION

Encourage the children to look for acorns, hickory nuts, crabapples, berries, chewed pine cones, and so on. Pick any final herbs or vegetables from the gardens, and have an outdoor picnic. If it is too cold, consider transitioning to a campfire, cooking over the fire, and gathering to eat warmer foods and drinks.

IDEAS FOR GROUP-TIME OPPORTUNITIES

- Make a list of the different foods the children find outdoors. Remember, what is edible for animals is inedible to humans.
- Read books about apples and pumpkins (or the fruit or vegetable that is harvested in your area).
- Cut open apples and look for the star.
- Create a list of the children's favorite dishes made from apple, pumpkin, and other local fruits and vegetables.
- Cut vegetables for making harvest soup, and invite families to join you for a Harvest Soup Party.
- Make stick bread, fry bread, warm tea, chai, or hot cocoa over an outdoor fire.
- Invite families to share their own special food traditions, if policies and protocols allow.
- Read books and sing songs in celebration of food and family.
- Make stone soup. If you cannot make the real thing, use a pot and have every child add a play vegetable as you tell the story (or read it aloud from a book).
- Bring pumpkins and gourds into the play areas. Cut some open and scoop out the seeds. Let the children cut some with safety knives. You can also carve a pumpkin together; lay down plenty of newspaper first.
- Leave some gourds scattered around for the animals. Check them each day for evidence of animals eating.
- Bury a small pumpkin or gourd in the garden; label it. Return in the spring to see if it has decomposed.

IDEAS FOR SENSORY AND DISCOVERY TABLES

- Fill the sensory table with dried corn, pine cones, or putka pods, and add scoops, measuring cups, and food scales.
- Provide water and soap at the sensory table for washing pumpkins and gourds.
- Make a farmer's market on the discovery table using dried corn, gourds, baskets, and so on.
- Hang plastic apples from a small tree on the discovery table. Use this as a calendar, adding a new apple every day.

PARTNERING WITH *Nature* IN EARLY CHILDHOOD EDUCATION

- Place pumpkins and gourds on the discovery table along with scales.
- Make an autumn color sorting discovery table that includes apples, gourds, and pumpkins.

IDEAS FOR ART AND SCIENCE ACTIVITIES

- Do a taste test with different kinds of apples, and graph which ones the children like best.
- Cut one apple lengthwise and another crosswise. Ask the children to describe how they look different.
- Play the sink and float game in your sensory table using gourds, pumpkins, crabapples, autumn leaves, acorns, acorn caps, pine cones, and other seasonal materials.
- Make red or orange playdough, and provide children with apple and pumpkin cookie cutters.
- Prepare for your class's harvest soup party. Have the children decorate invitations; create centerpieces using wreaths, dried flowers, and turkey feathers; and make tablecloths using large sheets of paper that they have painted with rollers and leaf rubbings.

- Make seasonal treats such as beet brownies, pumpkin cake, zucchini bread, and applesauce.
- Have the children measure and weigh your garden produce.
- Provide pumpkins and gourds to paint; set up a washing area to rinse them, then let the children repaint them if they wish.
- Create classroom cookbooks featuring family recipes, mud-kitchen recipes, or both!

- CHAPTER SIX -

The Nature-Based Curriculum in Winter

Winter is not a season, it's a celebration.

— *Anmika Mishra* | **AUTHOR AND TRAVEL BLOGGER**

Teaching outdoors during winter in Wisconsin can be challenging. Even the most winter-hardy teacher may need to take a deep breath and brace herself against the elements when heading out on a cold, icy day with a group of tiny three-year-olds. It's hard to see and harder to hear with all the layers around one's face and ears. There are days when you can hardly tell one child from another, they're so bundled up against the cold.

On the other hand, winter can be magical. The entire season feels like a pause: the air becomes still and silent, and the morning after a nighttime snow is about as peaceful and calm as one will ever experience with a group of lively preschoolers.

Winter can feel like a secret, a chance to be awake and present during a season of rest. It offers moments of exquisite beauty. Often, when we look back on our school year and reflect on some of the most profound moments, we discover that they happened in winter. So often, winter is the season when we truly begin to feel like a community, gathered together around a blazing fire, drinking warm teas, and huddling just a little bit closer in our circles. Winter is when we witness the spectacular ice formations on Lake Michigan, showing us the kind of fleeting beauty that exists in no other season. Winter is also when we learn about owls and other nocturnal animals, appreciate the beauty of evergreen trees, explore cold-weather adaptations, experiment with snow and ice, and celebrate the solstice, the myth of the groundhog, and, most of all, our friendships.

Topics for winter include (but are by no means limited to) evergreen trees, nocturnal and crepuscular animals, the winter solstice, winter adaptations, snow and ice, hibernation and animal dens, animal tracks in snow, friendship (Valentine's Day), winter birds, and owls.

EVERGREEN TREES

Evergreen trees, as the name implies, are trees that retain their green foliage year-round. (There are also evergreen plants.) Evergreens are often overlooked in autumn, when their showier cousins, the deciduous trees, are at their most glorious. We tend to take the quiet green pines and spruces for granted in our rush to collect those brilliant orange and red maple leaves before winter covers them with snow. But come the winter, we are grateful for the tall, stately evergreens, with their sticky sap, protective boughs, and wonderfully collectible cones.

Pine trees are a common type of evergreen that feature wonderful branches for climbing. Children can climb their ladder-like boughs and hang from sweeping branches. The children in our program will spend hours climbing pine trees throughout the winter months. Apart from the many physical benefits that children gain from this, there is a connection taking place between the child and the tree that is wonderful to see. Far from feeling that they've "conquered" the tree, most children seem to understand that it is an honor and privilege to climb it. They embrace the feeling that, just like a squirrel or a bird, they have a second, wild home among the branches of the evergreens. Keep in mind, however, that

in many cases, these lower branches are dead or dying, which means it is very important to test the strength of the branches and to teach children to climb closer in, toward the trunk of the tree where the wood is strongest.

One of the best ways to introduce children to evergreen trees is to simply walk among them. Look down on the ground and collect their many cones, sit beneath them as you read books, and gather around them on snowy days to see how the large green boughs capture the snow and act as a shelter for those who stand beneath them. Shake the branches, and you can create a small snowstorm. Gather fallen branches from the ground, and turn these into paintbrushes. Inhale the scent of pine pitch, or carefully collect some and use it to light a wintertime campfire. Adopt a special evergreen tree, and visit it often. Decorate it for the solstice and again for

A FEW KEY CONCEPTS ABOUT EVERGREENS

- *Evergreen* is a common term to describe trees and plants that retain their green foliage throughout multiple growing seasons. There are many types. Examples include cedars, pines, cypress, spruce, redwood, hemlock, and yew.

- Evergreen trees keep their leaves in winter; deciduous trees lose theirs.

- Evergreen trees provide a warm place for animals to shelter in the winter.

- Evergreen trees come in all shapes and sizes; some have needles (spruce trees, scotch pines) while others have scales (cedar trees).

- Some evergreen trees produce cones of differing shapes and sizes; these are called *conifers*.

- Confusingly, certain types of cedar trees, such as junipers, produce berries. However, these are not true berries but rather a type of cone with a fleshy, berry-like exterior. These serve as a useful food source for birds, squirrels, and so forth. (Juniper berries can also be dried and used as a flavoring in cooking and distillation.)

- Pine trees grow mostly in the Northern Hemisphere. They prefer temperate and subtropical climates. Although they do not require much water to thrive, they do require full sun. Most pines can live at least 100 years, if not much, much longer.

- Pine needles are photosynthetic, which is why they remain green year-round. They are bundled into clusters called *fascicles*. The number of needles per cluster can be anywhere from one to seven, depending on the species, but in most temperate zones, two and five clusters (on red and white pines, respectively) are the most common.

Valentine's Day. Celebrate the evergreen tree as you would a maple or an oak. It can be a source of joy, of shelter, of adventure, and of peace. Give it the reverence and love that it deserves.

OUTDOOR EXPLORATION

Look for signs of animals near evergreen trees. Encourage the children to find pine cones and see if squirrels have been snacking on the seeds. The children can also decorate evergreen trees with food for animals (birdseed, popcorn garlands, dried fruits). Bring along a magnifying glass, paper, and crayons so the children can study tree bark, make bark rubbings, and compare prickly and tickly needles.

CHAPTER SIX: THE NATURE-BASED CURRICULUM IN WINTER

Snuggle under a conifer tree to keep warm. Compare this to the area underneath a deciduous tree on a cold, winter day. Which kind of tree offers greater protection from the elements?

Look for signs of animal activity around an evergreen tree in winter.

On hikes, look for triangle shapes. Encourage children to turn into a conifer tree or a deciduous tree by saying "conifer tree" and putting their hands over their heads or "deciduous tree" and spreading fingers apart up in the air.

IDEAS FOR GROUP-TIME OPPORTUNITIES

- Create a Wonder Circle by placing a circle of black felt in the middle of the group. Add to it some of the identifying features of different evergreens: cones of varying sizes, needles, and bark. Next, add contrasting nature items, such as palm fronds, oak leaves, and tree fruit. Invite the children to wonder aloud. The purpose of the Wonder Circle is to invite observation and discussion. It is a time for wondering, not direct instruction. The great thing about a Wonder Circle is that you can easily adjust the items you showcase. This same activity could be done using only pine cones from different parts of the country, for example, and comparing shapes and sizes.

- If you have access to a small, artificial pine tree (commonly sold at Christmastime), you can create your own woodland scenes. Give children plush animals and ask them who might call an evergreen tree home. Do birds nest in its branches? (Great horned owls are partial to conifers.) Do mammals seek shelter under its boughs? What about insects, such as ladybugs, overwintering under the bark? Invite the children to place their plush animals in and around the tree. You can also do this with plastic animals or even paper cutouts.

- Create a sensory bottle filled with fresh evergreen branches. Pass it around (children can close their eyes) and ask the children to describe the scent.

- There are many wonderful books about evergreens. Two beautiful children's books are *The Snow Tree* by Caroline Repchuk and *Night Tree* by Eve Bunting.

- Another wonderful book that is not about evergreens specifically but invites children to form beautiful, personal connections to trees is Toni Yuly's *Some Questions about Trees*.

IDEAS FOR SENSORY AND DISCOVERY TABLES

- To your sensory table, add evergreen needles, pine cones, bark, and branches, or add fake evergreen trees and snow, along with plastic animals that are active in winter.

- Fill the sensory table with evergreen-scented water; dye it green for added fun!

- Add fake evergreen trees and animal pelts to your discovery table. Animal pelts can be ordered from various nature-based classroom catalogs but can also often be borrowed from local nature centers and department of natural resources teacher kits. Before bringing real animal pelts into your classroom, it is a good idea to share with the children and their families how these wild animals died and the educational benefits of touching and examining their furs. Some teachers prefer not to work with taxidermy or animal pelts at all. Kind Fur is a company that creates fur replicas using synthetic materials.

IDEAS FOR ART AND SCIENCE ACTIVITIES

- Encourage children to paint with evergreen branches. They can also roll pine cones in paint and then roll them on paper. (We often use white or silver paint on black paper, which looks very dramatic when painted with evergreen branches and cones.)
- Make evergreen-scented paint or playdough that the children can use to make evergreen sculptures.
- Add pine cones and pine-needle clusters to the playdough area to make imprints.
- Cut triangle shapes to make templates. Invite the children to trace, cut, and then glue the triangles into pine-tree shapes on paper.
- Have the children sort prickly and tickly needles into baskets.
- Cover a table with black cloth, and place empty picture frames on it. Invite children to create nature pictures by filling the frames with different styles of pine boughs, branches, cones, cedar leaves, and juniper berries.

- Give children plain white paper and black ballpoint pens. Invite them to make still-life observational drawings of different evergreen branches. They can then add a light wash of watercolor to make these unique illustrations jump off the page.

NOCTURNAL AND CREPUSCULAR ANIMALS

Exploring nocturnal and crepuscular animals can be challenging at nature preschool because we are usually away when night falls. In addition, hiking in the pitch black with very young children is not ideal, which means we need to take a different approach when it comes to exploring nocturnal animals. We like to begin simply. As the days get shorter and the light grows dimmer, we often keep the lights off indoors, turning instead to candles. (Depending on your policies, these may need to be electric candles, but they are still effective.)

Outdoors, we may seek the darkest spots we can find—inside our homemade wigwam, for instance, or in the shadows of the Secret Forest outdoor classroom. We talk about the animals that come out at

night and think about the special adaptations they need. We may bring out books about nocturnal animals and play recordings of their calls. Perhaps we'll even go for twilight hikes, bringing adult family members along, seeing how the trails we know so well in the daylight look and feel different when the sun is setting.

If a twilight hike isn't possible, we instead look for the signs the animals leave behind: coyote tracks and scat, owl pellets, raccoon prints by the pond, and so on. These are all reminders that when we are tucked in our beds, other creatures are just getting up. It's an invitation to wonder what they do when we're not there and to try to imagine the nighttime sights and sounds of the land we know so well during the day.

OUTDOOR EXPLORATION

- Look for places where nocturnal animals could sleep hidden from view during the day. For example, look for mouse homes in the prairie, owl nests and cavities in the woods, or outdoor bat boxes.
- Encourage the children to keep their eyes open for raccoon, deer, coyote, and other tracks.
- Compare bright areas to dark ones: Is there a change in temperature? Can you see as far?
- Play the camouflage game (similar to Hide and Seek). Is it easier to hide in the dark or in brightness?

IDEAS FOR GROUP-TIME OPPORTUNITIES

- Place a felt sun (daytime) on the carpet and a dark felt circle or square (nighttime) next to it. Give every child a stuffed animal (including plenty of nocturnal animals and a few crepuscular ones) and encourage them to sort the animals onto the appropriate fabric. For the crepuscular animals, you can either create an additional swath of fabric (perhaps using sunrise and sunset colors) or simply place the animals between the day and night panels, representing the time in between.

A FEW KEY CONCEPTS ABOUT NOCTURNAL AND CREPUSCULAR ANIMALS

- *Nocturnal* animals are active at night. Some examples of nocturnal animals include bats, salamanders, raccoons, flying squirrels, catfish, opossum, and mice. Nocturnal animals in other parts of the world include leopards, black rhinos, Tasmanian devils, hedgehogs, hyenas, and honey badgers.

- Many nocturnal animals live in the desert. Being nocturnal allows them to avoid the intense heat of the desert sun. Well-known desert-dwelling nocturnal animals include kangaroo rats, coyotes, scorpions, peccaries, bobcats, and owls.

- Nocturnal animals often have special eyes that help them see better in darkness.

- Nocturnal animals may have colors designed to help them camouflage during the day.

- *Crepuscular* animals are those that prefer twilight. These animals include rabbits, deer, foxes, skunks, rattlesnakes, hummingbirds, moths, and trout.

- Many felines, including lions and jaguars, are nocturnal yet border on crepuscular.

- We are more likely to see crepuscular animals because, as humans, we are generally more active during sunrise and sunset, and because these animals are often more active throughout the day when it is overcast.

- *Matinal* animals are crepuscular animals that are only active at dawn; *vespertine* animals are only active at dusk. *Diurnal* refers to animals that are active during the day.

- Turn out the lights and give the children flashlights with red plastic over the protective lens. Encourage them to look around the room using their flashlights. You can also hide nocturnal stuffed animals around the room that children can try to find.

- Read children's books about nocturnal animals and crepuscular animals, such as *Daylight Starlight Wildlife* by Wendall Minor, *When It Is Night, When It Is Day* by Jenny Tyers, and *The Sunset Switch* by Kathleen Kudlinksi.

- Play recordings of nocturnal animals. There are plenty of websites that will allow you to do this, or you can use the wonderful book *Night Sounds* by Frank Gallo. This book allows you or a child to press a button corresponding to each nocturnal animal in the book, which will then play a recording of its call.

CHAPTER SIX: THE NATURE-BASED CURRICULUM IN WINTER

IDEA FOR THE DISCOVERY TABLE

Create a display of nocturnal and crepuscular animals, using either plastic or stuffed animals; include a few pelts, either real or synthetic. Arrange the display into day/night and sunrise/sunset zones so the children can sort the animals.

IDEAS FOR ART AND SCIENCE ACTIVITIES

- Provide the children with dark paper and oil pastels. Encourage them to make a nighttime scene.
- Purchase a bat box that the children can paint, then let them help find a place to put it up.
- Help the children cut out suns and moons that they then paint. Turn these into mobiles.
- Have children trace, cut, and paint simple paper shapes of nocturnal animals native to different regions and habitats. These could be used to create a bulletin-board display.
- Give the children watercolor paints to paint the sunrise and sunset.
- Ask the children to collage glass jars with tissue paper. Use dark colors in shades of blue and purple to create nighttime lanterns and bright colors in shades of yellow and orange to create daytime lanterns. (Baby food jars can be repurposed for this project.)
- If possible, set up an overnight video camera outside your school to observe nocturnal wildlife. If this isn't possible, there are similar types of footage available on the internet showing nighttime animals across different regions.

THE WINTER SOLSTICE

Although we shy away from celebrating most major holidays, we embrace the winter solstice. We see the solstice as a time to embrace the coldest days of the year and to find solace in quiet and stillness.

We use the solstice as an opportunity to talk about darkness and light, to highlight crepuscular animals, and to discuss the Earth's relationship with the sun. We take comfort in slowing down. We do not dive deep into the solstice's pagan origins or discuss connections with other religious traditions, but we may note that ancient archeological ruins show evidence of people marking the solstice on stone calendars, which can make us feel more connected to human cultures across time.

In the classroom, we turn off our overhead fluorescent lights and turn on battery candles or flashlights in the far corners of the room. We may track on a chart the daily times for sunrise and sunset, particularly in the weeks leading up to the solstice.

A FEW KEY CONCEPTS ABOUT WINTER SOLSTICE

- The word *solstice* comes from the Latin words *sol*, meaning "sun," and *stit*, meaning "stand" (Merriam-Webster, 2022). The word *solstice* means, broadly, "the sun stands still." This is because the sun is so low in the sky it appears to rise and set in the same spot for several days surrounding the solstice.

- As the Earth travels around the sun, it tilts closer to the sun for half of the year and away from the sun for the other half of the year. When our part of the Earth is tilted away from the sun, our area becomes colder and darker.

- Because less sunlight reaches our part of the Earth at that time, the days become shorter, with the solstice marking the shortest day and longest night of the year.

- Every day after the winter solstice sees the return of a little more light (until the summer solstice).

- The date of the winter solstice varies from year to year, falling from December 20 to December 23 in the Northern Hemisphere. However, it generally falls around December 21.

- For those who live in the Southern Hemisphere, December 21 marks the first day of summer, and June 21 marks the first day of winter.

- On the winter solstice, if you stand outside at noon and look at your shadow, it will be the longest shadow you cast all year (Encyclopedia Britannica, 2020).

We may read books about the shortest days and longest nights of the year and ask the children to consider how the changing light makes them feel.

We often make solstice-themed gifts for our families. Over the years these gifts have included painted or collaged glass lanterns; dried oranges strung with cinnamon sticks; pine cones dipped in silver paint; solstice poems; and homemade frames decorated with berries, pine trees, and acorn caps featuring photographs of the children in the class. We also invite families to join us for stories and songs in honor of the solstice, embracing the season by creating an atmosphere that is cozy and inviting.

By far our favorite way of introducing the winter solstice is by taking a hike on the actual solstice, departing at dusk and returning in darkness. This generally means heading out with the children and their families at 4:15 in the afternoon. Before we depart, we give each child (including siblings, cousins, and any other nonenrolled children) a paper lantern. Each lantern is attached to a lantern wand,

CHAPTER SIX: THE NATURE-BASED CURRICULUM IN WINTER

which runs on batteries. The wand acts as a holder and a light, providing a soft glow in the darkening twilight. The lanterns come in all shapes, colors, and sizes, and when we head out on the trails in groups, it is a lovely sight to see the mix of lanterns bobbing along the paths.

Note: This activity could also be structured to include time before the solstice during which every child makes their own lantern. Lanterns can be made from repurposed glass jars or, if glass jars are a safety concern, from plain white paper lanterns that can be purchased in bulk and painted with soft watercolors.

It is still light when we depart, although the sun is very low in the sky. We generally head down to Lake Michigan in groups, each led by a teacher. Once on the beach, the teacher may read a story about the solstice or briefly describe what the solstice is, and then the children are invited to sing a special solstice song (using an approximation of the tune for "Twinkle, Twinkle, Little Star"), which we learn at school:

> *We are all a part of nature*
> *Every season 'round the sun.*
> *Winter, spring, summer, autumn*
> *Happy solstice everyone.*
> *We are all a part of nature*
> *Every season 'round the sun.*

After the hike, families return their lanterns, gather around an outdoor fire, and are treated to a few warming cups of hot apple cider before heading home. It is a beautiful, peaceful activity that feeds the spirit. After the first year we tried it, we knew it would become an annual tradition for years to come.

OUTDOOR EXPLORATION

Take a color hike and compare the colors of December with photographs taken of the same areas from earlier in the year, such as some taken in September and October. While hiking, you can also talk about nocturnal animals and animals getting ready for winter. Make a solstice sculpture using natural materials, such as driftwood and rocks, to mark this as a special day. Celebrate the solstice by inviting the children to play a range of musical instruments (shakers, tambourines, drums, bells, and so on) outdoors.

IDEAS FOR GROUP-TIME OPPORTUNITIES

- Cut out a yellow felt sun and lay it on the ground. Next, use a small globe to show how the Earth travels around the sun. Demonstrate how it tilts away from the sun in winter, making our part of the Earth colder and darker. (Explain how across the globe, some countries are experiencing summer while we experience winter.) Encourage the children to ask questions or add their own thoughts.

- Read *The Shortest Day* by Susan Cooper, *The Longest Night* by Marion Dane Bauer, *The Return of the Light: Twelve Tales from Around the World for the Winter Solstice* by Carolyn McVickar Edwards, or another winter solstice book.

- Listen to the song "Light is Returning" by Charlie Murphy and Jami Sieber. (This is a gospel-style song that references the winter solstice. There are many versions on the internet.)

- Read *The Snow Tree* by Caroline Repchuk, and decorate a tree, either in the classroom or outside, with the ornaments from the story, including icicles, berries, pine cones, amethyst, and a gold star.

- Sit in front of a fire and read a story, sing, or play music. Talk about what makes us feel warm, both physically and emotionally.

- Invite families to come in at the end of class time and light candles together.

IDEAS FOR SENSORY AND DISCOVERY TABLES

- Add different kinds of rocks and gemstones to the sensory table.

- Fill the sensory table with snow, and provide the children with spray bottles of diluted food coloring.

- Fill the sensory table with black sand. Add scoops and funnels.

- Create a discovery-table display featuring different illustrated children's books about the winter solstice.

- Cover the discovery table with sheets of black paper, taped in place, and add a small basket of white oil pastels, which children can use to add illustrations of moons, stars, or anything else.

IDEAS FOR ART AND SCIENCE ACTIVITIES

- Paint heavy watercolor paper with watercolors. Once dry, paint a thick coat of vegetable oil over the paper until it becomes translucent. Cut or tear the paper into strips. Wrap strips of the paper around a mason jar and place a battery-operated candle inside.

- Use a food dehydrator or oven to dry orange slices. Invite the children to string a dried orange slice with gold and silver beads and add a fragrant cinnamon stick.

- Paint pine cones with gold or silver paint, and dip the edges with glue and biodegradable glitter. (Tip: Do this outside!)

- Help the children compose solstice poems on heavy paper and then wash the paper lightly with paint.

CHAPTER SIX: THE NATURE-BASED CURRICULUM IN WINTER

WINTER ADAPTATIONS

We begin the discussion of animal adaptations in mid-to-late autumn, as the days get colder. We start with one simple question: What do animals do to get ready for winter? If no one is sure, then we turn the question inward: How do we get ready for winter? We may wear warmer coats and add hats and mittens to our daily routine. We may sleep with extra blankets. Buildings switch from fans and air conditioners to heaters. We may want to eat warmer foods. (This generally leads to conversations about our favorite hot foods.)

For animals, getting ready for winter is much the same, except that they can't turn a switch and change the heat controls. They don't wear clothes, so they depend on their bodies to adapt and change. Those who can grow thicker fur do so. Those who don't have fur or other ways of keeping warm in the cold will find different ways to survive. This might involve traveling to where it is warmer, sleeping through the long winter months, or eating as much food as possible during the harvest season to live through the scarcity of winter.

For us, winter adaptation is an ongoing topic. We do not head outdoors with the intention of discussing it for a day or a week, with the goal of then moving on to the next winter subject. We touch on it whenever it is relevant. If we spot the entrance to an underground den, it's an opportunity to talk about who might live there and why that would make a good home in winter. We talk about who hunts in winter and who is asleep and therefore needs to stay safe. When we find tracks, we remind the children that there are many animals active in winter. What foods do they eat? How do they stay warm?

One particularly fun activity is to divide our stuffed-animal collection into categories. We may start with three sheets of paper labeled "Migrate," "Hibernate," and "Activate." We then hand every child a stuffed animal, and together we sort out which animal belongs in which pile. Because not all songbirds migrate, we can then mentally note which birds we may still see in winter: Chickadees? Yes. Cardinals? Yes. Red-winged blackbirds? No. The study of winter adaptations is also a wonderful time to explore vocabulary. So many science words are associated with this theme. *Hibernation, migration, hibernaculum,* and *snuggery* are just a few of our favorites.

A FEW KEY CONCEPTS ABOUT WINTER ADAPTATIONS

- All living things adjust for cold weather, but they do it in different ways. Animals may migrate, hibernate, stay active, or become dormant to survive winter.

- Snowflakes are six-sided ice crystals that vary in form, size, and structure.

- Winter is an excellent time to find animal tracks in the snow.

- Water changes to ice when it is cold enough.

- Plants and trees also adapt to winter by going *dormant*, which means they slow or stop growing, cease making food for their leaves, and store less water in their roots.

OUTDOOR EXPLORATION

Go on a winter hike, and look and listen for animals that stay active in the winter, such as squirrels, deer, and winter birds. Ask the children to try to find the animals' homes and food they would eat. Encourage them to follow the tracks of active animals in the snow. If you have birdfeeders near your school, have the children help the birds by making sure the feeders are always full.

Ask children to look for evidence of animals that are dormant in the winter, such as skunks, chipmunks, and raccoons (for example, look for holes in the ground). They may see these animals during mild spells of weather. Children can also look for evidence of insects in the winter. They may find cocoons or galls, insects hiding under logs, or anthills covered in snow.

Visit a place where animals may be hibernating. Snakes, groundhogs, turtles, and frogs can hibernate. You may not see them or even see evidence of them, but the children could sing a lullaby to them while they sleep.

If your program setting experiences snow and ice, have the children search for icicles. Where do they form? Watch as water drips down and freezes. What happens when you bring an icicle inside? Encourage children to catch snowflakes on black felt to enjoy their beauty and compare the differences in the flakes.

If possible, go boot-skating! Our program used to exchange letters with a nature preschool in Austin, Texas. After we shared pictures of our children boot-skating on the frozen ponds, the teachers in Texas creatively froze large trays full of water to make ice. They then put the ice sheets together to create a small, temporary ice rink for their students. They sent back pictures of their own Texas-style outdoor ice rink. We were thrilled to see our pen pals boot-skating in shorts and T-shirts on a mild winter day in Austin.

CHAPTER SIX: THE NATURE-BASED CURRICULUM IN WINTER

IDEAS FOR SENSORY AND DISCOVERY TABLES

- Fill a sensory table with ice, snow, and water; add plastic animals or scoops and shovels, mittens, spray bottles with water, eye droppers, and so on.
- Freeze water in differently shaped containers, and put the ice in the sensory table. Add food coloring if desired.
- Freeze blocks of ice, then place them on trays or in the sensory table. Let children pour warm, colored water on the ice and see what happens. What happens if you use salt water?
- Make winter scenes in your discovery table using a mirror for ice; fake snow, such as Buffalo Snow; plastic evergreen trees; and plastic winter animals.

IDEAS FOR ART AND SCIENCE ACTIVITIES

- Make boot rubbings from winter boots. Depending on your location, these may be hiking boots or rain boots.
- Cut two large mitten shapes out of construction paper. Punch holes around the edges, and invite the children to lace the sides together with string or yarn. (This is an excellent fine motor activity that mimics sewing.) Use Jan Brett's website (https://www.janbrett.com/) to print out pictures of all the animals in her book *The Mitten*, then use a paper mitten to have the children help to tell the story again.
- Ask the children to help you graph temperatures in different places and on different days.
- Make a winter camouflage scene by placing illustrations of ermine, arctic fox, snowshoe hares, snowy owls, and ptarmigan—animals that turn white when it snows—against white paper. You can replace the paper with other colors to show how the surrounding landscape will either help the animals blend in or stand out.

SNOW AND ICE

Snow is one of the greatest gifts for any nature preschool teacher, assuming you live in a cold-weather state. Those few winters in our program when we did not get real snow were difficult indeed, accustomed as we are to at least six weeks of a snow-based curriculum. (Sledding in mud is just not the same.) This section may not be relevant for those programs in warmer climates, so we invite you pick and choose which activities are most appropriate to the cold-weather signs in your area.

Ice is a part of our program as well. We may experience ice as early as October, when the first frost arrives. Our boardwalks ice over in the early morning, and the wood chips in our outdoor classes freeze into a hard, almost uniform surface. This is usually the first warning we get that winter is coming. It's time to install our patio heaters outside, disconnect our outdoor hoses and sinks, and trade our rubber rain boots for insulated boots and thick wool socks.

Our philosophy with snow and ice is similar to our feelings on rain and mud: as long as we are dressed for it, the possibilities for play and discovery are almost boundless. We take walking sticks on our hikes to crack the thin sheets of ice forming across partially frozen puddles. We fill containers—Bundt pans, molds, ice-cube trays—with colored water, flower petals, and pine cones and take them outdoors to freeze. The resulting ice sculptures make wonderful loose parts and colorful decorations in our outdoor spaces.

There is no need to introduce snow to children. We simply go outside and experience it. When we get enough snow to cover the dried plants on our nearby hill, we head outside with sleds. The children could happily spend their entire class time sledding, climbing snow hills, rolling, and otherwise playing in snow. There may be no need to hike, given the amount of movement that can happen in a single spot following a snowy day.

Snow also invites investigation. We catch snowflakes on frozen felt and peer at the flakes with magnifying lenses. We learn that snowflakes are formed on a piece of dust and make predictions about how much water will remain when a snowflake melts. We follow tracks across the prairie, look for signs of vole tunnels, and talk about camouflage in winter.

CHAPTER SIX: THE NATURE-BASED CURRICULUM IN WINTER

We also differentiate between the different kinds of snow. Why, in some cases, does snow stick and allow us to form snowballs; whereas, on other days, snow is powder light and will not stick no matter how much we try? We may even learn some of the different types of snow, including wet snow, dry snow, sugar snow, and different kinds of snow events, such as a flurry, snowstorm, or blizzard.

OUTDOOR EXPLORATION

Children can do so many things in the snow. They can look for animal tracks and mouse holes or tunnels in the snow. They can shovel snow, roll balls of snow to make them bigger and bigger, make boot prints, dig under the snow and see what the plants underneath look like, make snow angels, and create designs in the snow with squirt bottles filled with colored water. They can also just stop and listen to the quiet of the snow.

There are also math and science activities that make use of snow. Ask the children to measure the depth of the snow with notched sticks. Where is the snow the highest? Where is it the lowest? Why are there height differences? Have children catch snowflakes on black felt and look at the shapes with a magnifying glass.

Fill small canisters with snow, and ask the children to observe what happens when you put them in a pocket, in your hand inside a mitten, in a backpack, in a snow pile, or back in the classroom. How long does it take for the snow to melt? On a snowy day, put containers in different spots outside. Let the children decide where to place them. Check them later and compare the amounts of snow.

Children enjoy making an igloo or snow wall with snow bricks. Pack snow into loaf pans to make bricks. After the bricks are released, spray them with water when it is freezing outside to make the bricks stronger.

A FEW KEY CONCEPTS ABOUT SNOW AND ICE

- Water can take different forms, including snow and ice.

- Snow is formed from water vapor, just like rain. For snow to form, the surrounding atmosphere must be cold enough that the water vapor freezes into tiny ice crystals. These crystals stick to particles of dust, forming individual snowflakes.

- Snowstorms are the result of dry, cold air mixing with wet, warm air. The moisture gets so cold that it forms snowflakes. The snowflakes are too heavy to remain in the sky, and so they fall.

- Snowflakes have six sides, but each can look very different.

- Snow provides a blanket of warmth for many plants and animals by adding a layer of insulation over the ground.

- Snow waters the ground in winter, just as rain does in other seasons.

- Some animals have adapted to live most or all of their lives in snow.

- Ice melts and changes shape due to heat, salt, and wind.

Play Fox and Geese in fresh snow. First, make a big circle track in the snow. Then make more tracks that cut the circle into quarters. One person is the fox, and the rest are the geese. The fox chases the geese and tries to tag them (to make them foxes), but everyone needs to stay on the tracks in the snow.

Many outdoor activities can also be done with ice. Give children magnifying glasses to find bubbles or other objects stuck in ice. Pour water colored with food coloring into different containers and take them outside to freeze. See what the children create. You can also freeze colored water in balloons to create cylinders and spheres. Cut off the balloon wrappings, and roll the frozen cylinders and spheres up and down hills or along flat, frozen surfaces.

Take pie plates filled with water outside. Ask children to add natural objects such as sticks, leaves, and berries to the water, then add a circle of string sticking out of the water for a hanger. Leave these outside to freeze, and then hang the children's creations outside.

CHAPTER SIX: THE NATURE-BASED CURRICULUM IN WINTER

IDEAS FOR GROUP-TIME OPPORTUNITIES

- Have children pass a snowball to their friends without dropping it.

- Put on music and ask the children to dance like snowflakes.

- Play the Snowflake Matching Game. Create two sets of snowflake cards. Give one card to each child and have them find their matching snowflake.

- Read books on winter, snow, and ice, such as *The Snowy Day* by Ezra Jack Keats.

IDEAS FOR SENSORY AND DISCOVERY TABLES

- Fill a sensory table with snow and mittens. Add ice-cream scoops and squeezable bottles full of colored water, and encourage the children to explore.

- Fill a sensory table with colored ice in different shapes. Add eyedroppers and bowls of salty water.

- Make a snow and ice scene in the discovery table using a mirror; fake snow, such as Buffalo Snow; miniature pine trees; and plastic winter animals.

IDEAS FOR ART AND SCIENCE ACTIVITIES

- Bring snow into the classroom, and weigh or measure it. Ask the children to predict how much water there will be when it melts. (Bonus: Is the water clean or dirty? Why?)

- Make "snow" by putting a bar of unwrapped Ivory soap in a microwave (other types of soap will not work). Be sure to place it in a microwave-safe container. Microwave it for 1–2 minutes on high. The soap will splinter apart and turn fluffy. Cool the resulting "snow," mix it with finger-paint, and let children create snow scenes on a table. Alternatively, use an unscented shaving cream, and let children spread it across a smooth surface with bare hands.

- Offer children "snow dough," biodegradable silver glitter added to white playdough. Provide snowflake cookie cutters, rolling pins, and other tools.

- Invite the children to fold a white paper circle in half, then in thirds, and then in half again. Snip little pieces out of the edges, and then unfold to find a beautiful snowflake. (Younger children may need help with this, but five-year-olds and older can generally manage once they see a demonstration.)

- Have the children make a snowman shape from paper, and add natural objects to decorate it and turn into the snowman of their own design.

- Cut pictures of snowflakes in half. Have the children match the sides to put the snowflakes back together again.

- Give children construction paper and an ice cube. Sprinkle a little powdered tempera paint on each child's paper. Encourage the children to rub their ice cubes over the powder. As the ice melts, it will turn the powder into liquid paint.

- Place an ice cube in a glass of cold water. Ask the children how they could lift the cube out of the water without touching it. (The trick is to soak a piece of thread in cold water. Lay the thread on top of the ice cube, then sprinkle the ice cube and the thread with salt.) Then ask the children to help you count to ten. Carefully lift up the string; the ice cube will be attached!
- Fill paper cups partway with water and freeze. Give each child a cup, and have them put their cups in different spots in the classroom or outside. Check on the cups every 5–10 minutes. Which one melts the fastest? Which is the last to melt?
- Weigh ice, snow, and water in containers that are the same. Have the children compare weights.
- Set out a bowl of ice cubes and a variety of insulation materials, such as tissue paper, aluminum foil, newspaper, plastic wrap, and fabric. Wrap an ice cube in each material and set it in a bowl. Check in one hour, and discuss with the children which ice cube has melted the most and why.

HIBERNATION AND ANIMAL DENS

Because we go out on the same trails all year long, children develop an excellent understanding of the animals and plants that live in the various habitats at the nature center. As the weather gets colder, children notice which animals are no longer around. We explore the woods and look for dens where familiar animals might be hibernating. Not all hibernators are deep sleepers. Even though chipmunks hibernate, they can be seen scampering about when the sun streams down on a warmer winter day.

Noting how often we see some animals in the winter helps children to think more deeply about the lives of animals and the mechanisms at work to keep them alive. On a very cold winter day, if we can find holes in the ground with crystals of ice around the edges, we can imagine which animal might be hibernating in the den beneath. Their warm breath melts the snow around the edges of the hole and then it freezes into crystals.

As the snow piles up at the edges of the parking lots (from being cleared and pushed into a giant pile), we start to create our own dens. One year we dug out a cave with the help of several adults, which we then used for several weeks. The children found the cave very warm, as it offered magnificent protection from the howling winter winds. What better way to reinforce how animals survive in winter than experiencing it firsthand!

One of our most elaborate and memorable activities was created for us by one of our elementary educators, Moya. It became known as the Jello-Baby Game. This activity generally takes place once a year, always on a very cold day. To begin the activity, the teacher places children in groups of two or

A FEW KEY CONCEPTS ABOUT HIBERNATION AND ANIMAL DENS

- Hibernation is a way some animals survive the winter cold.

- During hibernation, animals go into what looks like a deep sleep. But it isn't a true sleep, the way people sleep.

- During hibernation, an animal's heart rate and breathing slow. Its body becomes inactive to conserve energy.

- Hibernators get ready for the winter by eating a lot. They need the added fat to help survive the weeks and months when they do not eat.

- Some hibernators also collect food to store with them as they sleep. Some, like chipmunks, will stir, wake up, eat, and then return to their hibernating state.

- Hibernating animals prefer dark, secure, and quiet dens. They may move underground, find a cave, or dig down into the mud at the bottom of a pond.

- Many hibernators will add fur, grasses, feathers, and other soft materials to make their winter dens extra warm and cozy.

- Hibernating animals respond to the outside weather. When the weather warms up, that tells an animal it is time to come out of hibernation. A few warm days in winter followed by another wave of cold can be dangerous to animals if they come out of hibernation too early. On the other hand, if there is a polar vortex or another deep freeze, some animals must wake up and move their bodies to avoid freezing to death. Luckily, animals that hibernate have adapted to a range of weather and temperature inconsistencies.

- Bears, ground squirrels, frogs, turtles, chipmunks, and many insects hibernate during the winter. (Remember that *hibernation* is an overall term that looks different depending on the species.)

three and gives each group an empty plastic honey-bear container filled with gelatin powder mixed with hot water. (Moya called it their "Jello Baby.")

Next, the teacher sets out baskets full of animal pelts (you can also use fabric scraps), downy feathers, cotton fluff, and other natural materials and states the purpose of the game: Each group must find a place outside where their Jello Baby can keep warm and safe. Children need to find or build some kind

CHAPTER SIX: THE NATURE-BASED CURRICULUM IN WINTER

of shelter using loose branches, stumps, bushes, logs, and so on. They need to consider whether their shelter is protected from the wind and rain. They can also use the materials in the basket to supplement their shelter, adding additional protection. The teacher gives the groups about thirty minutes to complete their task. Once their Jello Babies are in their spots, the whole group heads out for a hike.

After about forty minutes or so, they return and retrieve their Jello Babies. Those that had been tucked away in protected shelters and wrapped in fur, cotton, or down are still warm and in their liquid state. Any Jello Baby left out in the cold, however, has solidified, turning to jiggly gelatin. (Moya always made a point of placing her own Jello Baby in the cold to illustrate the outcome.) The teacher then asks the children to discuss what happened.

While this particular activity is not something we do with our youngest groups, those who are five years old find it not only engaging but also memorable. They talk about it for weeks afterward, especially as the winter weather grows harsh and the outdoor temperatures plummet. They understand what the animals are up against and feel more invested in their survival. The children who complete this game are often quicker to find evidence of dens and burrows. They follow tracks to see where they lead. They express an interest in adding food to the feeders. A few will make even deeper connections, such as understanding that this is why baby birds are seldom born in the winter, or this is why mammals grow thicker coats, or this is why some animals hibernate.

OUTDOOR EXPLORATION

When you go outdoors, encourage the children to listen for animals. Where do they think they are? Look for places outside where animals might build dens, burrows, or nests. What makes a good place to hibernate? Are there nuts and berries nearby? If it is sunny, take a shadow hike. Encourage the children to pretend they are a groundhog just waking up from hibernation (do this on or close to February 2). If there is a pond or creek nearby, sing lullabies to the frogs and turtles sleeping at the bottom of the pond or creek.

Play a hibernation trail game. As you hike, call out, "Freeze. It's winter!" The children stop and listen. If you name an animal that hibernates, children pretend to sleep. If you name an animal that stays active during the winter, the children continue to hike. You can also hide a plush bear, chipmunk, turtle, or something similar in the woods and give clues to find it. Once the children have found it, have the group decide on a good hibernating place outside.

IDEAS FOR GROUP-TIME OPPORTUNITIES

- Have a hibernation party when children can wear their pajamas to school. Turn an area of the classroom into a cozy place to hibernate.
- Ask the children to sort stuffed animals into active and hibernating (or active, hibernating, and migrating) groups.

- Turn out the lights, provide blankets, and let children act out hibernation, finding cozy spots underneath tables and in corners.

- Ask the children to pretend to be any hibernating animal. When you play music, they can dance about. When the music stops, the children find a place to hibernate.

- Read a book about hibernation, such as *Bear Snores On* by Karma Wilson, *Time to Sleep* by Denise Fleming, *Over and Under* by Kate Messner, or *Under in the Mud* by Laureanna Raymond-Duvernell.

IDEAS FOR SENSORY AND DISCOVERY TABLES

- Fill the sensory table with soil or pine needles; add rocks, bark, and tree cookies of different sizes. Add plastic animals such as bears, skunks, turtles, snakes, and so on. Let the children build caves and dens for the animals.

- Put water and plastic fish in the sensory table, and let the children try to catch the fish with "bear paws." (We use paw-shaped salad tongs.)

- Create a winter scene with snow, trees, caves, dens, and water on a discovery table. Add active animals and hibernating animals. Divide the table into active and hibernating areas, then let the children sort the animals.

IDEAS FOR ART AND SCIENCE ACTIVITIES

- Obtain a very large cardboard box, such as a refrigerator box, and turn it into a bear den for the children to enjoy.

- Help the children make bear caves out of paper bags. Cover the top of the bag with cotton balls for snow, and add construction paper stones or branches. Place plush or plastic bears inside the dens.

- Provide children with kinetic sand or playdough for making make dens, caves, nests, and so on for plastic animals.

- Place a box turned into a cave on a table, and fill it with animals that sleep all winter.

- On top of a dark blanket on a table, place sleeping stuffed animals, then cover them with another piece of dark fabric and with white snow. Ask the children to find the sleeping animals.

- Go on an indoor bear hunt: tape images of a bear's paw prints to the floor, leading to a cozy spot where a plush bear is asleep inside a den (or box). Ideally, place the den in another part of the building so that children must follow the tracks for several minutes. Note: This activity can easily be adapted to represent other hibernating animals. You could even do this activity more than once, using different animals, so that the children have to guess what the hibernating animal might be based on its track prints or other clues that you add along the way.

ANIMAL TRACKS

Although our daily hikes provide opportunities for children to find animal tracks in all seasons and conditions, such as in wet sand and spring mud, the best time to find tracks is after fresh snow has fallen. Animal tracks are particularly intriguing because the animals themselves are often hard to find. The tracks they leave behind are clues to a mystery that is begging to be solved. The shapes, sizes, patterns, and locations begin to tell a story as children identify and interpret what they see. To help children with their interpretations, we use the three *P*'s of tracking: print, pattern, and placement.

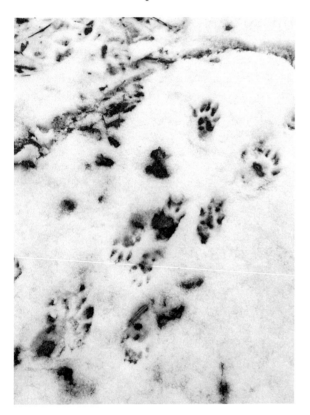

Print refers to the individual track's size and details. We might compare a wolf print to that of a domestic dog, noting the similarities in shape and significant difference in size. We might look at a bear's and a mouse's footprints. We might count the number of toes that a squirrel has compared to those of a deer. We might look at the visible claws on a dog's footprint compared to a cat's, where the claws are retracted and therefore not visible when the cat leaves tracks.

Pattern refers to how an animal moves, such as walking, bounding, or waddling. The space between the footprints denotes how fast the animal is moving. (Closer together denotes a slower pace, while farther apart is faster.) Some animals, such as a fox or a cat, walk in a straight line with one foot in front of the other. Animals that bound or hop leave unique track patterns in which the hind feet are in front. A squirrel's front feet will land next to each other, but a rabbit's are spaced asymmetrically. Bears, skunks, and raccoons are waddlers, meaning that they move one whole side of their body simultaneously, resulting in tracks that show a front and hind foot close to each other and the same pattern (on the opposite side) for each step. We can try to mimic some of these movements by using a large sheet of white paper on which we draw these different track patterns. The children can then be the animals and walk, hop, waddle, or bound across the paper.

Placement refers to where the tracks are found, such as by a pond, in the woods, or on a prairie. The more the children spend time in different habitats, the more they will use the clues to figure out the identity of the animals that made the tracks they find. A bounding track that ends at a tree is most likely a squirrel, not a rabbit, because rabbits do not live in trees.

A FEW KEY CONCEPTS ABOUT ANIMAL TRACKS

- Animals leave tracks that we can find and interpret.

- Size, shape, and even number of toes differ greatly between animals. Learning these differences will enable us to "read" their tracks more easily.

- Bird tracks are usually forked or arrow shaped, and mammal tracks will resemble paws, usually with four or five toes.

- Walkers include deer, foxes, and coyotes. Their front and back legs and feet are the same size and length, and they make a consistent pattern. Most walkers will step their back feet into the same tracks left by their front feet.

- Deer walk in a "deer family line" for a variety of reasons, one of which is for easier footing along undefined trails. (In other words, only the deer at the front has to break the snow.) All the rest walk in the footsteps of those in front of them. This conserves energy.

- We can often tell a dog track from a coyote track by looking at the patterns: dogs are more likely to play and run in circles, enjoying the snow. Wild canines need to conserve energy for hunting, and so their tracks are usually straightforward.

- Waddlers are rounder, shorter animals, such as porcupines, skunks, beavers, and bears, who shift from side to side as they walk. Their front and back feet are different shapes and sizes.

- Bounders move by placing their front paws down first and swinging their larger back paws around to land in front. This allows them to move quickly. Their track marks are unique in that they will show their back feet in front of their front feet.

- Some bounders, such as squirrels, land with their feet side by side. Rabbits, however, land with their feet slightly askew. This is one of the easiest ways to tell rabbit tracks from squirrels once the snow melts a little. The other way is to follow the tracks. Squirrel tracks will lead to a tree; rabbit tracks will lead to a burrow.

There are several children's books that we use to help the children decipher the clues left by animals. Some of our favorites are *Whose Tracks Are These?* by Jim Nail and the Who's Been Here? series by Lindsay Barret George.

Searching for animal tracks in the snow, mud, or sand is one of the most exciting, nature-based activities we know of that teaches children to truly read and understand the land.

CHAPTER SIX: THE NATURE-BASED CURRICULUM IN WINTER

OUTDOOR EXPLORATION

When hiking with the children outdoors, look for tracks and search for animal shelters or dens to see if there is animal activity. If you find tracks, ask the children to try to identify them. Drawing a circle around a track or placing an embroidery hoop around it may help young children focus on the track. If possible, use plaster of Paris to preserve the tracks. Encourage the children to look for other signs animals might have left behind, such as scat, pieces of food, antler rubbings, and so on.

Play a tracking game. One team hides, leaving sticks or footprints pointing the direction that they went. The second team tries to find the first group by following the clues.

On a snowy day, encourage the children to move like different animals, running, hopping, and walking. Then they can see what the tracks they made look like.

IDEAS FOR GROUP-TIME OPPORTUNITIES

- As a class, examine and discuss a poster showing different animal tracks.
- On a large roll of paper, draw tracks showing the different patterns made by animals hopping, bounding, or walking. Have children try to duplicate this way of moving.

IDEAS FOR SENSORY AND DISCOVERY TABLES

- Place snow or damp sand in the sensory table; add plastic animals or rubber tracks.
- Make an animal-track display, matching pictures of tracks with stuffed animals.

IDEAS FOR ART AND SCIENCE ACTIVITIES

- Paint children's bare feet, and have them walk along a long sheet of butcher paper.
- Ask the children to help you make a track-identification book using track stamps and ink pads. Write the name of the animal and add a picture to each track.
- Make handprints in salt dough.
- Use track stamps to make animal tracks on a large piece of paper. Encourage the children to create a "story" using just the tracks. For example, how could the tracks show one animal escaping from another, or one going to a tree and one going to a pond? Invite the children to narrate their track stories.
- Provide children with paint and rubber models of animal tracks to press on a piece of paper or on a T-shirt.
- Use rubber track casts to create plaster of Paris molds of different animal tracks. (Many animal tracking supplies, including rubber casts and molds, are readily available through natural science supply companies.)

PARTNERING WITH *Nature* IN EARLY CHILDHOOD EDUCATION

FRIENDSHIP (OR VALENTINE'S DAY)

When we started the nature preschool in 2003, there was a tall, dead tree that stood just outside the front play area. It was a remnant of what once was the king of our trees. It still had some branches that towered overhead and a large enough circumference that it took a circle of children to reach all the way around it. We named it Grandpa Tree. As the children were learning about trees, they would give them special designations. There were *baby trees* (with a small enough circumference that a hand fits around it) and *sister and brother trees* (of a size that children's arms could reach all the way around and hug the tree). There were *mom and dad trees* (so large that it took at least two children to encircle the tree). But the most impressive of all were the *grandma and grandpa trees* (really large, so a circle of children were needed to reach all the way around the trunk).

Grandpa Tree was beloved by all the children and families at nature preschool. As classes began their daily hikes, they would stop to hug Grandpa Tree. Grandpa Tree became the focus of many activities, but the most celebrated one occurred on Valentine's Day, when the children created hearts and strung them up around the tree. This was an opportunity to develop an attachment to a special tree and experience caring feelings for something other than oneself. (Inevitably, all dead trees break down, and

Grandpa Tree was no exception. The tree slowly decomposed, providing yet another learning experience for the children.)

Friendship is an important concept that we focus on throughout the year, but it takes center stage in February. Ironically, for us February is often the coldest, greyest month of the year. The excitement of the winter holidays is long over, and spring still feels like a long way off. Friendships are tested in February. We often have to take a few steps back, rediscovering what it means to be a kind and caring community. Thankfully, the work we put in at this time of year will yield its own rewards later. By learning how to work through conflict, by discussing different points of view, and by communicating our own needs while learning to listen to those of others, the children begin to develop a deeper, longer-lasting understanding of what it means to be friendly and what it means to be friends.

What is the difference between being friendly and being a friend? Nature preschool provides numerous opportunities for children to demonstrate acts of affection, from stringing hearts on a tree to being kind to plants and animals. But we are hoping to instill a deeper understanding of compassion that is often less demonstrative. The simple acts of making sure no one is left behind when we hike, that someone helps another to their feet after they stumble and fall, and that one child initiates play with another are all core goals of our program. We do not require everyone to be friends. That is not realistic. But we do want to create a space in which everyone feels safe and valued and where beautiful friendships can grow. We also want children to understand that they can have more than one friend, and that friendship itself is not a limited resource. It is possible, and quite wonderful, to make friends with nature.

OUTDOOR EXPLORATION

Invite the children to create valentines for nature and then visit a favorite tree or plant to hang them on. You can also write friendly letters from the animals to the children and hide them along a trail.

Create a communal art project to which everyone can add a piece. This could be a giant collage on paper, or each child could make an ornament to hang on a tree. If it is cold enough, create an outdoor ice mosaic using colored pieces of ice.

To celebrate Valentine's Day, take a red hike: Look for buds, berries, red osier dogwoods, cardinals, woodpeckers, and more. Look for heart shapes in nature. You can find this shape in the fallen leaves of certain deciduous trees, succulents, cacti, and palms, as well as in tree bark, moss, snow mounds, mud, ice, and clouds.

IDEAS FOR GROUP-TIME OPPORTUNITIES

- Read books about friendship. We absolutely adore the Elephant and Piggie books by Mo Willems. No matter which book in the series we read, the friendship between the two protagonists is at the heart of every story

A FEW KEY CONCEPTS ABOUT FRIENDSHIPS

- There is a difference between being a friend and being friendly. While a *friend* may be a particular person with whom you feel safe and share interests, being *friendly* implies a welcoming and inclusive mindset and treating others with consideration, which is possible even if two people do not connect to each other as friends.

- Being friendly allows us to form a more peaceful and cohesive preschool community as we recognize that not everyone is automatically friends.

- Friends need not be alike or even agree all the time.

- Disagreements can be resolved; friendships do not necessarily have to end because of them. Sometimes, a friendship can be even stronger after a disagreement because there is a deeper understanding of differing points of view.

- A person can have more than one friend at a time.

- Some people may want a friend but do not know how to make friends with others. This could be because they are still learning, do not yet have the words to express what they mean, or are shy. They may need others to invite them into play and friendship.

- Friendships can take place in families, in school, and between humans and animals.

- One special thing we can do during winter is take time to show our love for nature.

- Create music. Hand out a range of simple instruments, and give each child a chance to play a solo. Then mix all the instruments together.
- Have every child think of something they love (in nature or otherwise) and write it on a paper heart. Help as needed.

IDEAS FOR SENSORY AND DISCOVERY TABLES

- Add red or purple sand, along with buckets and plastic or wooden hearts, to the sensory table.
- Fill the sensory table with water dyed red or purple.
- Make a display on your discovery table featuring red nature items.
- Set up a special mailbox in your discovery center with a new letter from an animal to the class each day.

CHAPTER SIX: THE NATURE-BASED CURRICULUM IN WINTER

IDEAS FOR ART AND SCIENCE ACTIVITIES

- Provide children with paper and scissors, then show them how to cut simple heart shapes.
- Ask the children to make and deliver valentine cards to the entire class.
- Have the children write or dictate letters home, then visit a post office or mailbox to mail them, if possible.
- If the children keep journals, ask them to write or draw about something they love in nature or about a special person they love.

WINTER BIRDS

Children have already learned that birds who are unable to find food in the winter need to migrate or change their diet to survive. Setting up a bird feeding area is especially helpful because birds typically have difficulty finding food in the winter.

Watching the feeders can quickly become a daily ritual. Blue jays and cardinals, downy woodpeckers, and tufted titmice provide a diversity of activities that allow children to denote differences among bird shapes, bills, colors, and crowns. Feeding winter birds can be a highlight of the winter season.

Birds can be difficult to see as they flit among the trees during warmer seasons, but in the winter, the leafless branches give way to allow more sightings. Colorful feathers contrast with winter white and gray, standing out against the snow. Bird feeders placed in strategic areas outside the classroom windows provide a viewing area that is accessible for children. Setting up a bird-watching area next to a window focuses children's attention. We include pictures of the birds we typically see, as well as baskets of binoculars and bird field guides, on our side of the windowpane.

OUTDOOR EXPLORATION

Visit your bird feeders and ask the children what birds they see. Bring a bird identification guide to help. When going outside, encourage the children to look for places that birds may be nesting, such as shrubs, trees, and holes in trees. Try to observe birds from different locations and elevations. Offer the children binoculars to observe birds up close. Ask the children to compare the different kinds of birds seen in various habitats, such as lakes, prairie, ponds, and forests. Go on a listening hike. Listen for bird calls and use a bird song IdentiFlyer to learn their songs.

A FEW KEY CONCEPTS ABOUT WINTER BIRDS

- Some birds stay where they are for the winter, while others migrate. We recommend reaching out to your state department of natural resources, as well as to any statewide or local environmental groups or nature centers, for details about which birds in your area migrate and which remain in place throughout the winter.

- Examples of winter birds in the Upper Midwest and New England include the black-capped chickadee, northern cardinal, downy woodpecker, hairy woodpecker, goldfinch, dark-eyed junco, blue jay, white-breasted nuthatch, crow, mourning dove, purple finch, house finch, great horned owl, screech owl, barred owl, snowy owl, red-tailed hawk, and bald eagle.

- Birds that overwinter in cold places have special adaptations. An *adaptation* is any trait or behavior that provides an advantage when it comes to survival.

- Many birds consume more calories in cold weather and remain less active so as not to waste energy.

- Some birds will store any surplus of food in special caches, which they can eat later when food supplies are low.

- Many birds have an elevated body temperature, which allows them to survive very cold air. Some also have blood flowing down to their claws, which means their unfeathered feet can remain warm in cold weather.

- Most birds will fluff out their feathers to trap more air, which is then heated by their bodies. This provides added warmth.

- Some bird species will cluster together in tree cavities and under evergreen boughs, which gives them protection and additional heat during the cold winter nights.

- For more on how birds survive the winter, we recommend the book *Birds in Winter: Surviving the Most Challenging Season* by Roger F. Pasquier.

IDEAS FOR GROUP-TIME OPPORTUNITIES

- Discuss the birds seen outside, then make a list with photographs or pictures.
- Read and listen to *Bird Calls* by Frank Gallo.
- Ask a naturalist to bring a live bird to the class, or if this is not possible, try to arrange a virtual visit with a bird through a local nature center, zoo, or wildlife center.

CHAPTER SIX: THE NATURE-BASED CURRICULUM IN WINTER

IDEAS FOR SENSORY AND DISCOVERY TABLES

- Provide feathers; nesting materials, such as sticks, grass, and so on; and toy birds in the sensory table.
- To your discovery table, add small baskets, toy birds, feathers, and small logs with holes for birds to nest in.

IDEAS FOR ART AND SCIENCE ACTIVITIES

- Paint with feathers.
- Create feather prints on T-shirts, bags, or other fabric items. Do this by carefully pressing sturdy feathers into paint and then carefully onto fabric. (We purchased ours at a craft store, as this requires very strong feathers.) Cover with paper, press down, and remove.
- Set up a feeder watch near a window in the classroom. Create a bird list (with pictures). Ask the children to put a check mark on the list when they see a corresponding bird at the feeder.
- Make winter bird feeders using pine cones. Peanut butter is often the preferred base. Spread it over the pine cone and then roll the pine cone in birdseed. Because ours is a nut-free school, we prefer to use vegetable shortening. Other nut-butter alternatives include lard, suet, or solidified coconut oil. You can also use sesame butter, although you will again need to be mindful of allergies. Not all commercial birdseeds are nut-free, so do read the labels. You may wish to secure some kind of stick to the pine cone so that small birds have a perch on which to stand. Hang these bird feeders from tree branches with twine.

OWLS

At Schlitz Audubon, there is a raptor center on the nature center property. At least once a year, each class gets a behind-the-scenes tour of the raptor building. The building is home to owls, eagles, a vulture, and various other birds that have been injured and, for various reasons, can no longer live in the wild. The tour includes areas that are not open to the public. Many, many parents sign up to help with the class on these days, as they have never seen these areas before. Our raptor educators travel the state, presenting programs at schools and events across Wisconsin. Even before COVID-19, they offered live virtual programs nationwide.

Although it is a wonderful resource, it is not necessary to have access to a raptor center to learn about raptors. As mentioned earlier, over the years, a very outgoing eastern screech owl has regularly paid us a visit in one of our outdoor classrooms. We sometimes see Cooper's hawks at our feeders. On very special occasions, we may even spot a bald eagle soaring high overhead. There are often hawks sitting on lampposts overlooking the highways. There are owls in the cemeteries throughout many major cities. Raptors, including owls, are often all around us. They are just very good at staying hidden.

It is far more likely that we will find the signs and evidence they leave behind than it is that we will see the birds themselves. One of the things we are hoping to encourage in the children is an increase in observation skills. Searching for the signs left behind by a camouflaged owl can be both a treat and a challenge that helps to hone those skills.

Owls do not digest fur and bones of the animals that they eat. Instead, they swallow the prey whole and regurgitate the fur and bones in a small mass called an *owl pellet*. We sometimes find pellets on the ground, usually beneath very tall conifers. We do dissect owl pellets with the children; however, we leave the ones we find outside on the ground. Instead, we order specific teaching pellets through scientific catalogs. (We do this because the commercial pellets have been sanitized for the classroom.)

By dissecting the owl pellets, children can discover what the owl last ate before it ejected the pellet. Using tweezers and toothpicks, the children take the owl pellet apart (great fine motor practice) and pull out the tiny bones inside. We sometimes use an electronic microscope to look more closely at the bones. Helped by field guides and identification charts, the children figure out what animal the bones came from. There might be more than one animal's bones in the pellet. This is also a great introduction to the food chain.

OUTDOOR EXPLORATION

When outdoors, encourage the children to look in tall trees where owls could make strong nests. Play a camouflage game while hiking, in which the teacher is an owl looking for hidden mice to eat (these are the children walking behind her). When she turns around, the mice freeze so the owl doesn't see them.

If possible, visit a wooded area at night, as this is a place where owls often hunt. Teach children and their families different owl calls or bring recordings of calls. Call the smallest owls (such as the screech owl) first, because if they hear the call of a great horned owl, the smaller ones won't answer (a larger owl might eat a smaller one). Visit an open area and have the children fly and soar silently. Then have them lie down and pretend to sleep when the morning comes.

A FEW KEY CONCEPTS ABOUT OWLS

- Most owls are solitary and nocturnal. But some, such as the snowy owl, live in areas where the sun doesn't set during certain months of the year. Hence, snowy owls are not nocturnal.

- Owls are birds of prey; they hunt for their food and prefer to eat small mammals, insects, fish, and birds.

- Owls specialize in silent flight. They have serrated wings that help them fly without noise.

- Owls have large eyes to help them see in the dark.

- Owls have strong beaks and powerful talons.

- Owls are excellent at hiding because their feathers camouflage them extremely well.

- Owls regurgitate pellets, made up of undigested matter. Contrary to popular belief, owl pellets are *not* owl poop.

IDEAS FOR GROUP-TIME OPPORTUNITIES

- Bring in owl parts (wing, talon, pellets, and so on) and talk about their special adaptations. A lot of nature centers and natural history museums have these types of materials available to loan to teachers. Companies such as Acorn Naturalists often sell replicas of owl skulls and other raptor skeletons.

- If possible, contact your local nature center and ask them to bring in a live owl or arrange a virtual program.

- Read some nonfiction owl books such as *All About Owls* by Jim Arnosky and *White Owl, Barn Owl* by Nicola Davies.

- Read fictional children's books about owls such as *Owl Babies* by Martin Waddell and *Owl Moon* by Jane Yolen.

- Turn out the lights and listen to different owl sounds while resting.

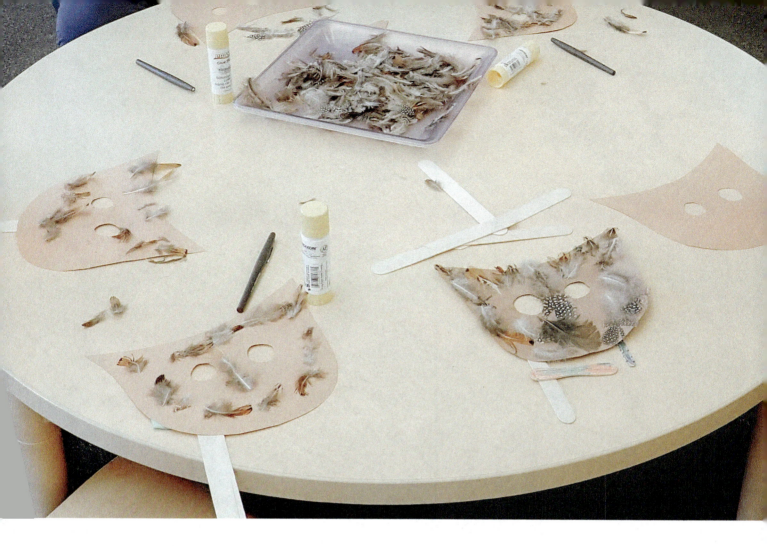

IDEA FOR A DISCOVERY TABLE

Make a natural history display using owl pellets, owl puppets, and other owl parts either purchased or borrowed from environmental organizations.

IDEAS FOR ART AND SCIENCE ACTIVITIES

- Cut out owl shapes from paper, and give each child an owl to decorate with feathers.
- Provide the children with tweezers and toothpicks to dissect owl pellets. (Sterilized owl pellets are easily available through biological science catalogs.)
- Create owl masks using printable templates. There are many offered at no charge on the internet.
- Create pine-cone owls by adding googly eyes and tiny paper beaks made from paper to medium-sized pine cones. The pine cone has an uneven surface, so use a hot glue gun (adults only). Add a feather tuft on top to turn the pine cone into a great horned owl, or fill in the gaps with fake snow, such as Buffalo Snow, turning it into a snowy owl.

CHAPTER SIX: THE NATURE-BASED CURRICULUM IN WINTER

- CHAPTER SEVEN -

The Nature-Based Curriculum in Spring

Spring's greatest joy beyond a doubt is when it brings the children out.

— Edgar Guest | POET

In our part of the world, spring has two distinct halves. The second half is warm and sunny, typically marked by green leaves and flowering trees, busy songbirds, and brilliant blue skies. The first half is a time of bare branches; cool, grey skies; and a mostly muddy landscape. At our school, the first half of spring is also known as *mud season*.

Mud season is sometimes called the "fifth season" in places such as New England and the Upper Midwest. It coincides with the rapid melting of winter snow and arrival of spring rains. It can be a very bleak time of year. The lack of color, the dark nights, and the ongoing mist can be depressing for some. For others, mud season is almost spiritual. It is the season when nature is shifting from one stage to another, and we can witness its transformation in detail. We may be the very first to spot the tips of skunk cabbage rising out of the bogs or to witness ephemeral flowers poking their heads through the snow. It can often feel like a pause, a quiet moment in between the more distinctive and showy times of year. Certain activities, such as maple sugaring, can only be experienced in this season.

As much as we have learned not to rush through the transitions in our school days, we have learned to appreciate the cool, damp spring. As eager as we may be for warm days and sunshine, this is a special and unique time of year. Topics in this season include maple sugaring; signs of new life and growth; ponds; spring ephemerals, birds, eggs, feathers, and nests; rocks and fossils; gardening; Earth Day; and phenology.

CHAPTER SEVEN: THE NATURE-BASED CURRICULUM IN SPRING

THE GIFT OF TREES (MAPLE SUGARING)

Trees give us so much. In places such as Washington, DC, and Philadelphia, people come out in droves to celebrate the cherry blossoms. In New Mexico and Arizona, generations of families come together to harvest piñon nuts. Apple picking is a tradition across much of North America. Oak trees, often associated with longevity, are used as memorials in honor of a loved one after death.

In this section, we are going to focus on maple trees, specifically on the early spring practice of maple sugaring. Although we recognize that maple sugaring is not an option for everyone, we have opted to include it in this book for the simple reason that sugar maples are widespread across eastern Canada, New England, the American Midwest, Mid-Atlantic, and as far south and west as Tennessee and Missouri. If sugar maples do not grow in your area, we urge you to study the cultural history of a tree or plant that does grow in your region. Saguaro cacti, pawpaw trees, palms, redwoods, and more each come with their own unique stories and *ethnobotanical* histories (related to the plant lore of Indigenous cultures) that are worthy of exploration.

Our deeper intentions within the maple-sugaring program include developing wonder and understanding about the transitional time between winter and spring; nurturing connections to trees as living, generous, much-needed organisms; and learning about Indigenous traditions that continue in the present time. We also celebrate the sense of accomplishment that comes from producing a product from nature without destroying the source of the raw materials. All of these intentions can be transferred to other trees as well.

Maple sugaring originated with the Native Americans in the northern regions of the continent. It is not known exactly when or who first started the practice of cooking maple sap into syrup; it was likely done among a range of groups. The Iroquois, or *Haudenosaunee*, are often credited with the original practice, likely due to the maple-sugaring legend of Chief Woksis. He was said to have stuck his axe into a maple tree overnight, inadvertently letting loose a flood of maple sap. However the practice actually began, there is certainly no question that maple sugaring was a prominent part of the early spring harvest for several centuries among groups such as the Ojibwe, Mohawk, Oneida, Onodaga, Cayuga, and Seneca peoples, and it remains a part of contemporary Native American culture in many parts of the United States and Canada today.

In our preschool, maple-sugaring season comes just in time to sweeten our spirits. It arrives at a time when winter has lost its luster amid a sea of mud and slush, when cabin fever is epidemic and spring is still only a dream. The very nature of maple sugaring invites the concrete, sensory, exploratory learning style inherent in every young child.

All trees make sap. To describe the process of photosynthesis (very briefly)—during the growing season, sunlight, water, carbon dioxide, and minerals in the soil combine with chlorophyll to produce sap. Sap is the sugar water that is the lifeblood of trees. Some tree sap is made into latex or rosin; sap from maple trees is made into syrup due to its high sugar content. Sap rises and falls in response to the temperature. In fall, shorter, cooler days signal to trees that it is time to prepare for winter's rest. Sap glucose converts to starch and is stored all around the dormant tree, especially in the roots. In late winter, in response to longer, warmer days followed by cold nights, the dormant sap "wakes up" and moves through the *cambium* (inner bark) to prepare for the new growing season. This is when the sap flows.

We begin the maple-sugaring season with a focus on trees. This may begin months in advance, as we get to know the trees in our area and understand what they need to live. We often draw comparisons between the trees and our own bodies. We breathe out carbon dioxide, which the trees take in. They then give off oxygen for us to breathe. We might stand near a tree and imagine our feet are roots that go deep into the ground. We might make our bodies like tree trunks, standing straight and tall. We look at the bark of a tree and compare it to our skin. Does our skin heal when we get a cut? Can we find evidence of bark having healed from a wound? Our arms become branches, and our fingers become leaves. We act out a year in the life of a deciduous tree through all the seasons, dropping leaves in the fall, sleeping in the winter, and popping out new leaves in the spring.

Changes in snow consistency, temperature, and animal behavior provide clues that let us know it is maple-sugar time. Two examples of animal behavior that children can observe are grey squirrels gathering hardened sap from broken branches or woodpeckers hunting for bark insects in late winter.

Sugar snow, which is late winter granular snow that has been frozen and thawed repeatedly due to the warmer days and colder nights, is another clue. Such clues help children observe the often-incremental details that denote the transition from winter to spring.

The period in which to collect sap and produce maple syrup is rather limited, usually a four- to six-week window. At the end of maple-sugaring season, we always gather around the trees and thank them for their gifts. We then remove the spiles, sometimes hanging messages of love from the branches with a promise to care for the trees in return for all they have given us.

CHAPTER SEVEN: THE NATURE-BASED CURRICULUM IN SPRING

A FEW KEY CONCEPTS ABOUT MAPLE SUGARING

- Sap is a liquid inside a tree that contains sugar.

- Maple trees have a higher percentage of sugar in their sap than other trees. This is why we tap maple trees rather than oaks. However, maples are not the only trees that can be tapped. Birch sap, for example, can also cooked into syrup. Different tree syrups will have different flavors.

- Maple syrup is made by heating sap until most of the water in the sap has evaporated and a large concentration of sugar remains.

- Maple sugaring season is temporary. As winter ends and temperatures get above freezing, the sap begins to move up the tree. This is also when the sugar content is especially high. We can tap the trees during a short window of time, but once the temperatures are consistently warm, the tree will need all its sap to survive and grow new leaves.

- Not all maple trees can be tapped. It is generally illegal to tap a city tree. Additionally, many city trees take in salt and pollutants through their roots.

- Maple trees should be, minimally, ten inches wide in diameter to be tapped.

- It is possible to over-tap a tree. When considering where to place a spile, a good rule of thumb is four-and-a-half feet above the ground. However, if there are unhealed holes at this height from previous years, it is better to begin a pattern of tapping six inches up and over, to give the tree adequate time to heal from each hole.

- Maple sap should be heated to 219 degrees Fahrenheit to become syrup.

- Another delicious treat, which does not require a thermometer, is to cook maple sap into maple tea. This is simply sap boiled until it turns amber in color and tastes strongly of maple sugar. It is still very much a liquid at this stage and is best enjoyed warm in a mug.

OUTDOOR EXPLORATION

Hug trees on your hike and measure their circumference. Look for sumac branches and birch trees. Native Americans used hollowed sumac branches to make spiles and birch-bark buckets to collect sap. Listen to the trees with a stethoscope. When the sap is flowing and the conditions are right, the children may actually hear the sap flowing inside the tree.

Tap a maple tree by drilling a hole into the sapwood layer and hammering a spile into the tree. If the sap is flowing, the children can taste the sap directly from the tree. (There are lots of books explaining the details of this process.) Hang a sap bag or bucket from your spile to collect the sap. Before your hike, predict how much sap you think will be in your sap container. When does the sap seem to flow the fastest? Make a chart that includes the daily temperatures.

Once you have collected several buckets of sap, invite the children to help you cook it down over a campfire. You can pour the sap into a cast-iron pot and enjoy s'mores or maple tea as you watch the sap boil. Take note of the steam rising from the pot: this is the water in the sap evaporating away. The process of making syrup is essentially one of subtraction. Through this process, you can also share Native American stories and legends about maple-sugaring season around the campfire.

IDEAS FOR GROUP-TIME OPPORTUNITIES

- Maple trees are not the only trees that give gifts. Read books and brainstorm with the children about other trees that give gifts. You can bring in persimmons, oranges, plums, cinnamon sticks, figs, coconuts, and other foods that come from trees, always being mindful of allergies.
- Have children act out the sap flowing from the roots to the tips of the branches.
- Fill a mystery box with things associated with maple sugaring, such as spiles, maple leaves, stethoscopes, twigs with opposite branching, maple-syrup jugs, hand drills, and so on. (Or use items related to trees in your area.) Place the items on a black piece of felt, and let the children figure out what they have in common.
- Show pictures of the steps involved in making maple syrup, and ask the children to put them in the correct order. (You could easily do this sequencing activity with other trees as well. For example, use images of the steps in making apple cider or olive oil.)

- Play the What's Missing? game with objects having to do with maple sugaring. Place items on a table and let the children see the objects. Cover the objects with a cloth, remove one while the children aren't looking, and see if they can remember which item is missing once the cloth is removed.

- Read books about maple sugaring such as *At Grandpa's Sugar Bush* by Margaret Carney, *Sugar Snow* by Laura Ingalls Wilder, *Ininatig's Gift of Sugar: Traditional Native Sugarmaking* by Laura Waterman Wittstock, and *Sap to Syrup* by Inez Snyder. For books that talk about the gifts of trees in general, consider *A Tree Is Nice* by Janice Udry, *Be a Tree* by Maria Gianferrari, and *Thank You, Tree* by Fiona Lee. We also enjoy *Mama Panya's Pancakes: A Village Tale from Kenya* by Mary and Rich Chamberlin, which is related to maple season peripherally.

IDEAS FOR SENSORY AND DISCOVERY TABLES

- To the sensory table, add maple (or lemon, orange, or apple) scent to water, along with scoops, strainers, empty maple-syrup bottles, funnels, and syrup ladles.
- Create a maple-sugaring display on the discovery table with all the tools needed to make maple syrup: cooking area, ladle, felt bag, bottles, strainers, spiles, blue bags. Alternatively, make a display related to a tree in your area, such as citrus, coconut palm, olive, cherry, avocado, apple, or peach.

IDEAS FOR ART AND SCIENCE ACTIVITIES

- Encourage the children to look at the inside of a tree by examining a tree cookie. They can use a magnifying glass to see the small holes where the sap flows and count the rings to see how old the tree was. Painting the tree cookie with water will temporarily accentuate its rings.
- Have the children put white flowers or celery into colored water and observe what happens.
- Do a taste test comparing real maple syrup and store-bought maple-flavored syrup. Make a graph depicting the children's preferences.
- Ask the children to dip apples, pretzels, and even pickles into maple syrup. Which do the children like the best? Graph the results.
- Make pancakes with the children, and enjoy them with some real maple syrup.
- Make a maple-sugar camp in the dramatic play area with a camping tent, a tree trunk, and a bucket hung from a spile. Add a camp stove, camp chairs, and a pretend fire ring.

"WAKING UP": SIGNS OF NEW LIFE AND GROWTH

In Wisconsin, spring often requires a few false starts before it really gets going. It is, therefore, common to see winter aconite, skunk cabbage, wild leek, or trillium coated in heavy, wet snowflakes.

Part of the fun for us is treating spring like a quest: we are searching for any sign of this elusive season that we can find. Every day is another chance for us to assume the role of stealthy nature detectives spotting evidence of trees and animals waking up.

We may find a place in the woods not too far from the trail where we brush aside the leaf litter and look for tiny green shoots. (Once spotted, we gently cover them back up so they are protected from the cold.) We may visit our

A FEW KEY CONCEPTS ABOUT SIGNS OF NEW LIFE AND GROWTH

- The first day of spring is called the *vernal* or spring equinox. It marks the day in which the amount of sunlight and darkness is equal. The spring equinox typically occurs on March 20 or 21.

- The first day of spring in the Northern Hemisphere is the first day of fall in the Southern Hemisphere.

- Spring has long been a symbol of rebirth. There are festivals and holidays throughout the world to mark the arrival of spring. In China, the coming of spring coincides with celebrations for the Chinese New Year. In Japan, the cherry blossoms opening in March or April signal the start of spring. The Persian new-year celebration, Nowruz, occurs on the first day of spring.

- As the days get warmer, hibernating animals start to wake up, and migrating animals return from the south.

- Spring is often a rainy season. The rain, combined with increased warmth and sunlight, can catapult new growth, helping seeds to sprout.

- Flowers literally grow faster in the spring. There is also evidence that children also grow faster in the spring (Dalskov et al., 2016).

- Many mammals and birds have their offspring during this season, when food sources are more abundant and the temperatures are milder.

- Bears generally give birth in winter but do not emerge from their dens until spring.

- Snakes and other reptiles emerge from brumation in the spring. (*Brumation* is similar to hibernation but refers specifically to cold-blooded animals.) Their emergence is based on the temperature of the air.

low rock walls and learn the wonderful word *hibernaculum*, which is any place a creature may overwinter but which we use most often to describe winter snake dens.

There is no need to introduce the topic of looking for signs of new life and growth, as simply going outdoors daily will expose young children to everything spring has to offer. They can experience for themselves the warming air, the shift in light, and everything else that accompanies the gradual change in season.

One of our favorite spring activities is to head out to the ponds as the ice is thinning. We bring long poking sticks and allow the children to break the ice. They love the dramatic and satisfying crack—the noise it makes and the beauty of the fragments. They also understand more fully the properties of water. Out of consideration for the animals that live in the pond, we do not toss our sticks in the water, nor do we step foot on the fragile ice ourselves.

We continue our visits throughout the spring. Eventually we can see new life in the water: painted turtles climbing onto logs, ducks and geese returning and making nests, and tadpoles hatching by the thousands.

Perhaps one of the most satisfying things for teachers is to see the new growth in our students. They have certainly grown in the most literal sense possible: many no longer fit into their rain pants and boots from the fall. But they have also developed into stronger hikers, grown closer as a class, shown their resilience through snowstorms and rain, and developed a much deeper connection to nature and an understanding of environmental concepts.

So much of what we do in the spring is the direct and logical extension of what happened in fall and winter. We see the pond ice melting, see new life waking up, and understand that from eggs will come tadpoles and then frogs. Likewise, we see children who know the trails backward and forward, children who have worked through social conflicts, mastered their gear, and grown in their own confidence. Spring in Wisconsin is a time of metamorphosis: from ice and cold comes mud and slush, and from that comes brilliant color and life. While not a perfect metaphor, in many ways, the season's changes mirror our own experience as teachers watching the children grow and blossom in small, seemingly magical ways, every single day.

OUTDOOR EXPLORATION

Ask the children to focus on one particular thing each time you go on a hike. For example, take a listening hike, and ask the children what new sounds they hear. Take a smell hike, and learn what new smells they discover. Go on a green hike, and look under the brown leaves for little signs of green and tiny tree seedlings; take a red hike, and look for new red buds on branches, along with red-headed woodpeckers, cardinals, and red-winged blackbirds. Remind children to be gentle to fragile new plant growth and mindful that animals are making new homes. As a class, create a Signs of Spring list and go on a scavenger hunt, checking off the items the children find. If possible, visit a pond, lake, or creek, and look for signs of new life.

Take musical instruments on a hike. Play music to welcome back the spring. Go on a hike during and after a rain. Encourage the children to try to catch a raindrop on their tongues. Look for mushrooms after a rain. Look for animal tracks in the mud. Ask the children to measure the depth of rain puddles. And of course, everyone must splash in a puddle!

IDEAS FOR GROUP-TIME OPPORTUNITIES

- Introduce the children to a rain stick to simulate the sound of rain.
- Invite the children to rub, tap, and clap their hands to simulate a rainstorm.
- As a class, make a list of all the changes spring will bring, and discuss or journal about the ways spring makes us feel.
- Encourage the children to make up a dance or a song to celebrate spring.
- Read books about spring, such as *Bear Wants More* by Karma Wilson, *The Dandelion Seed* by Joseph Anthony, *Ruby's Birds* by Mya Thompson, *Who Likes Rain?* by Wong Herbert Lee, *A New Beginning* by Wendy Pfeffer, and *City Green* by Dyanne Disalvo-Ryan.
- Record sounds such as birds singing, rain falling, children playing, and thunder booming. Let the children listen and describe what they hear.
- Use plastic models to demonstrate animal life cycles. There are some wonderful life-cycle kits available through educational catalogs that feature the stages of development of frogs, butterflies, chickens, grasshoppers, ladybugs, and snails, among others. Most kits are child friendly and encourage sequencing and fine motor skills.

IDEAS FOR SENSORY AND DISCOVERY TABLES

- Place silk flowers, vases, and green floral foam in the sensory table.
- Add feathers in the sensory table.
- On the discovery table, make a spring display featuring live flowers and models of robins and red-winged blackbirds. Alternatively, create a display with colored birds' eggs and different kinds of nests.
- Put recordings of spring sounds, such a toad trills, spring peepers, and chickadees, on the discovery table.

IDEAS FOR ART AND SCIENCE ACTIVITIES

- Paint children's hands with brown paint so they can make muddy handprints on construction paper. They can also paint with actual mud (use sticks to create frames around their mud paintings).
- Bring tree buds inside and put them in water. Ask the children to notice the changes that take place daily and watch

the buds open. Provide the children with tweezers so they can dissect the tight buds to find the little leaves inside.

- Invite the children to paint a still life of branches with buds in a vase or a bouquet of flowers.
- Ask the children to color and cut out a chipmunk and glue it onto a craft stick. Give them a paper-towel roll "tunnel" so they can pretend they are chipmunks waking up from hibernating and popping out of their tunnels.
- Help the children dye eggs to look like wild birds' eggs: use plant dyes and oil to get a realistic effect.
- Set up a counting and sorting game using construction-paper nests and painted cardboard eggs.
- Help the children collect water from rain puddles in different tubes. Label the tubes, and observe the contents with magnifying lenses.
- Have the children make a rain picture by putting powdered paint on construction paper and taking it outside during a gentle rain. Let the rain paint the picture, then bring it inside to dry.

EARTH DAY

There is a popular expression that says "Every day is Earth Day." This saying is particularly apt in a nature-based classroom. Earth Day falls on April 22, eight months into our school year. If we waited until April to address environmental issues in our classroom, we would be doing a poor job. By the time April rolls around, the children already know that we need to reduce our collective footprint. They understand that we don't pollute our water systems or throw trash on the ground. They know that we compost our snack scraps and recycle and reuse what we can. They realize that we all have an active role to play in protecting and conserving nature.

For us, Earth Day is also a local event. It was created in Wisconsin by Senator Gaylord Johnson and was first observed in 1970. Part of the original vision was to galvanize the energy of the nation's youth, although this quickly expanded to include religious groups, community groups, and all citizens. In 1990, Earth Day became a global event, and it is now recognized as one of the largest secular celebrations in the world. It would be a missed opportunity if our school did nothing to celebrate or observe this occasion!

We honor Earth Day by combining self-expressive and creative experiences with practical service projects spread out over the course of the week. We don't want to focus

A FEW KEY CONCEPTS ABOUT EARTH DAY

- We need to care for our Earth.
- The Earth's resources are finite.
- Everything in nature is interconnected.
- We can work together to sustain the environment by reducing, reusing, and recycling.
- We can host clothing and toy swaps rather than constantly buying things new.
- Being mindful of resources, reducing water use, picking up trash, and so on doesn't have to feel like a burden. It can actually make us feel happier to take care of our environment.

too much on the gloom-and-doom message that the Earth is being damaged by an overabundance of pollution and trash or suggest this is a problem that falls on preschoolers to fix. We want to focus on what is beautiful and wonderful about the planet. We also want children to take pride in leaving a patch of land better than when they found it and to feel satisfaction and empowerment with small acts of kindness.

We may read books that celebrate the Earth; apply swirls of green, white, and blue paint on paper Earth shapes; and dictate messages that express our own thoughts and feelings about nature. We may also hike down to the lakefront with mechanical grabbers and a trash bag, picking up trash washed ashore on the waves or blown down by the wind. We may spend an hour pulling out invasive garlic mustard and hiking it over to the organic dump or visit the compost bin to see where the remains of our snacks, weeds, branch clippings, and coffee grounds end up. Most important, we ask the children how they would like to observe Earth Day. Should there be a special food treat? Should we do something we love and enjoy, or should we try something we've never done before?

Over the years, we have created unusual, experimental snacks for Earth Day, including edible "Earth balls" made with sunflower butter, jam, and cookie crumbs. We have created mixed-media art exhibits featuring photographs, paintings, and sculptures built from recycled and salvaged materials from our classroom. We have invited families to join us while we read books and, better yet, have shared our own class musings about the message of Earth Day. There is a tendency for Earth Day to become somewhat preachy, so we try to infuse it with a feeling of fun, energy, and experimentation. We don't want it to be an adult-driven event, with each activity focused on recycling or cleaning up other people's messes. Earth Day is about giving back. We want the ideas and the actions to come from the hearts of the children.

OUTDOOR EXPLORATION

Encourage the children to examine a decaying tree to feel how the hard wood is being recycled into new dirt. Ask the children to look for animals that are helping to recycle the tree.

Set up a compost bin and visit it often. Talk with the children about decomposers, such as bacteria, fungi, pill bugs, earthworms, and snails, as well as scavengers, such as turkey vultures. Bury different types of materials in the fall—some paper, an apple peel, a foam cup, and a candy wrapper. Mark the spot, uncover it on April 22 (if the ground isn't frozen), and see how each thing has changed. Use photographs to record the differences and to share the results with others. Ask the children to dig for worms in the garden, then talk about the role worms play in creating healthy soil. (Be sure to return them after a few minutes.)

IDEAS FOR GROUP-TIME OPPORTUNITIES

- Ask the children to problem solve about ways we can help reduce waste, and document their ideas.
- Make a big Earth using recycled paper. Have the children paint it, and then ask them what they love about the Earth. Write their responses on paper hearts, and secure each one to the Earth. Display this for families to see.
- Read books that celebrate the Earth, such as *The Earth and I* by Frank Asch, *Listen, Listen* by Phillis Gershator, *My Friend Earth* by Patricia MacLachlan, and *We Are Water Protectors* by Carole Lindstrom.
- Write your own class book. Use recycled or homemade paper for the pages, then add photographs of the children engaged in Earth Day projects. Invite parents to join you on an Earth Day hike, and share your class book!

IDEAS FOR SENSORY AND DISCOVERY TABLES

- Fill the sensory table with shredded paper (save scraps from the recycling bin) and add water; you can premix it in a blender to create slurry. Add scoops and funnels to complete the experience.
- Make an Earth Day display out of recycled objects on your discovery table. This could be a mishmash of tiny boxes, used wrapping paper, or paper-towel tubes. Allow children plenty of time to play and sort these materials. Another option is to save worn-out toys, such as puzzles that are missing pieces, incomplete life-cycle kits, and so on, and create a fun and interactive exhibit of battered but beloved objects.

IDEAS FOR ART AND SCIENCE ACTIVITIES

- Using leftover art supplies, create individual and group collages.
- Have the children make Earth bracelets with blue beads for water, green beads for plants, and white beads for clouds and ice. You can also use blue, white, and green polymer clay to mix your own mini Earth beads.
- Add stick-on magnets to the backs of old objects, such as playing cards, buttons, or pieces of costume jewelry, to create new magnets.
- Make new paper out of used paper: blend paper scraps and water in a blender to make a slurry, then pour the slurry onto mesh screens. Ask the children to use cardboard or newspaper to press the excess water out, then allow the slurry to dry. When it is fully dry, the children can peel away the slurry from the screen as a new sheet of heavy, thick paper. (Homemade paper makes a lovely cover for a journal.)

GARDENING

In our program, gardening has taken on many forms over the past twenty years. Different teachers have taken on our gardening projects during their tenure with the school, often with different visions and aims. This feels appropriate because most gardens, whether at school, home, or elsewhere, change over time.

For years, we focused on vegetable gardens. We felt strongly that connecting children to food and helping them understand planting, growing, and harvesting their own food were important. We still feel this way. However, those of us who have devoted hundreds of hours of time and energy to the process also understand the drawbacks.

In Wisconsin, the growing season is short. It is unwise, most years, to plant tomatoes before Memorial Day, and many vegetables need to be *hardened off* (prepared for the transition from a protected indoor environment) before moving them outside. As our school year generally concludes in May, we don't have much of a window to enjoy gardening with our students. The children leave for the summer when the gardens are planted, and usually an entirely new group joins us in the fall. Most of them miss the growing season completely. That does not mean that vegetable gardens are a lost cause. It does mean that we have to do more to help the children feel connected and invested in a garden they didn't help plant.

We have experimented with cold-weather crops—lots of greens can be grown in April, for instance. We have also experimented

with cold-frame gardening and starting seeds indoors, teaching gardening-themed summer camps, and inviting families to return regularly between June and August to help water and care for our growing gardens. These approaches work somewhat, but none addresses the biggest hindrance of all: the wildlife.

As a nature preserve, our trails and grounds are home to hundreds of wild turkeys, deer, rabbits, ground squirrels, and many other animals who view our gardens as their personal farmer's market. We have spent hundreds of dollars and invested days and weeks replacing plants gnawed down to the stalks. We have rigged together fences that did little to keep the rabbits away but made our gardens less accessible to children. We even sprayed synthetic fox urine around our raised beds, only to have our pumpkins, eggplants, bush cucumbers, pole beans, potatoes, and tomatoes dug up and devoured each evening.

We would encourage anyone who is determined, eager, and invested to grow fruits and vegetables with children. But we would also caution anyone who works where there is an abundance of wildlife to contact those who are knowledgeable about these matters and make some kind of management plan. It may be necessary to have one teacher take the lead for the entire gardening program, as during certain months it can be a full-time job.

Over the past five years, we have reimagined our gardens. Now, rather than vegetables, we invite each child to plant a single flower in our garden beds in the spring. (This works well in our school, as we have upwards of 150 children in our program.) Families can donate flowers, but we are also happy to purchase large flats of colorful annuals, such as marigolds and petunias.

CHAPTER SEVEN: THE NATURE-BASED CURRICULUM IN SPRING

The children spend a few weeks prepping the beds when it's still cool and rainy. They pull weeds, till the soil, and add fresh compost from our compost bins. In early May, we plant. Each child takes great pride in planting a flower and caring for it. They fill watering cans from the rain barrel, pull weeds, and get down close on their hands and knees to touch and smell each blossom.

Our gardens are a wonderful hodgepodge of color, shape, size, and texture. We only plant annuals, as we do not want to introduce nonnative perennials into our ecosystem. They give us much-needed bursts of pinks and purples when the landscape is still brown and grey. Because the flowers will bloom for months, we can enjoy the kaleidoscope of colors all the way through the end of October.

We also supplement the gardens with colorful polished rocks, homemade fairy houses, toad homes, plastic dinosaurs, and more. When dollhouse furniture pops up in the thrift stores, we buy it. The children delight in miniatures—tiny homes, tiny wheelbarrows, tiny wishing wells—and we have found that they play and interact with our gardens far more deeply and intensely than they did when these spaces comprised tomatillos and peppers.

We still plant tomatoes and herbs. We often give children scissors, and let them cut off pieces of mint, chive, or basil throughout the summer, allowing them to enjoy both the scents and flavors. Teachers will also plant beans indoors with the children when it's still cool out. But our primary beds are no longer for vegetables. Our flower gardens have now become places of play. For us, this is just perfect.

A FEW KEY CONCEPTS ABOUT GARDENING

- Vegetables and herbs are edible plants that grow from seeds. Most herbs have strong flavors and scents. It can be fun to rub their leaves and smell their unique fragrances.

- The food we eat depends on soil, sun, and rain.

- Gardens grow from healthy soil. We can make our own soil by composting our vegetable scraps. Compost is a mix of brown and green plant material that breaks down over time; brown can be old, dried leaves, and green can be fruit peels, grass clippings, and so on. Tiny microorganisms help this process.

- We can also add earthworms to garden beds! Earthworms help aerate the soil, keeping it from getting hard and compact.

- We can care for our growing plants by giving them space, keeping them watered, and not picking or pulling until it's time to harvest them.

- Many animals enjoy the same foods we do. Fresh garden greens are especially popular in early spring, when food is limited and the wildlife are hungry after the long, cold winter.

- Some flowers are called *annuals*. These bloom for months at a time but will not grow back the following year. Other plants are *perennials*, which return year after year but often bloom for a much shorter time.

- Some flowers have bright colors and fragrances. This attracts pollinators such as bees, butterflies, and even bats!

- Bees can see yellow and orange, blue-green, violet, blue, and a color called "bee's purple" that is a combination of yellow and ultraviolet light. (We can't see it at all.) Bees cannot see the color red. Purple, violet, and blue flowers are the most likely to attract bees (Riddle, 2016).

OUTDOOR EXPLORATION

Plant lettuce, kale, and cabbage during the cooler growing season. You can begin beans indoors or just wait and sow them outdoors when the weather warms. (They are fast growers.)

Plant or transplant beans, especially snow peas and climbing beans, outdoors beneath a garden trellis (you can make your own out of string) to encourage vertical growth. Plant oregano and mint in pots rather than garden beds, because they will quickly spread! Basil needs warmer days and nights to thrive. We enjoy making large batches of nut-free pesto with the children to enjoy over pasta.

When the weather is nice, bring out the painting supplies, and sit outside so the children can create *en plein air* still-life paintings of your garden.

IDEAS FOR GROUP-TIME OPPORTUNITIES

- Taste test different garden vegetables, and chart everyone's favorites.
- Ask the children to look at the edible parts of different plants and then lay them out on a large tray based on the parts of the plant from which they come. (For example, carrots are roots; celery is a stem; broccoli is a flower; cucumber is a fruit; lettuce is a leaf; beans are seeds; and cinnamon is bark.)
- Read books about gardening, such as *Up in the Garden and Down in the Dirt* by Kate Messner, *Growing Vegetable Soup and Planting a Rainbow* by Lois Ehlert, *Flower Garden* by Eve Bunting, *The Ugly Vegetables* and *Hasta Las Rodillas* by Grace Lin, and *One Little Lot: The 1-2-3s of an Urban Garden* by Diane C. Mullen.

IDEAS FOR SENSORY AND DISCOVERY TABLES

- Fill the sensory table with potting soil, containers, and fake flowers.
- Make a display on the discovery table using fresh flowers and herbs from the garden.

IDEAS FOR ART AND SCIENCE ACTIVITIES

- Have the children plant seeds and bulbs in the classroom: flower seeds and bulbs and beans are all fun choices.
- Provide the children with different seeds and flower petals to make a collage.
- Ask the children to paint pictures of soil, sun, and rain and then add cut-out pictures of gardens from magazines or empty seed packets.
- Encourage the children to draw still-life illustrations of vegetables, herbs, and spring flowers.
- Ask the children to help you make a salad, then eat it for a snack!

- Set up a flower shop in the dramatic play area. This can be as simple as adding baskets, bundles of fake flowers, and a plastic cash register.
- Have children build fairy houses and/or gnome homes and place them in the garden beds.
- Visit a local garden nursery, and ask for flower petals from the ground. Have the children scatter these around your garden beds like fairy dust or use them to make collages or in flower-petal pounding activities using hammers on cloth.
- Ask the children help you mix herbs with a mortar and pestle to make powerful scent combinations.

BIRDS, NESTS, FEATHERS, AND EGGS

As a general rule, we prefer to "discover" our seasonal topics through child-centered outdoor investigations rather than using teacher-driven, preplanned activities. In an ideal world, this would mean stumbling across nests and eggs, birds, and feathers by chance and then building a rich and meaningful curriculum around them.

In reality, we seldom stumble across nests and eggs by accident, although it is possible. We may come across a broken egg that has fallen from a tree or the remnants of a hatched egg in the prairie grasses. We have a good chance of finding robin and swallow nests in the eaves of our building. We may even spot a Canada goose sitting on her eggs across the water on Mystery Lake sometime in May. But, generally speaking, birds like to keep their nests and eggs hidden from us. Feathers are a nice surprise. So it tends to happen that every spring we dedicate a couple of weeks to birds, nests, feathers, and eggs, without ever knowing when or if we will find them in the wild.

Although we cannot always count on finding nests, eggs, and feathers in nature, we *can* count on hearing the birds all around us. Listening hikes in the springtime can sound like an outdoor symphony. We can also count on certain birds—chickadees in particular—visiting our bird feeders throughout the day without much concern for our presence. Ducks at the ponds, gulls at the lake, and wild turkeys in the woods are all-but-certain occurrences, if not daily then at least multiple times over the course of several weeks. We can therefore introduce the topic of birds by heading outside on a mild spring day or following a rain and walking to specific spots, such as near the bird feeders or near the eaves of the building, which may assure us of a successful sighting.

A FEW KEY CONCEPTS ABOUT BIRDS, NESTS, FEATHERS, AND EGGS

- Birds have feathers and wings, lay eggs, and are warm blooded.

- Birds have hollow bones, which help them fly.

- A nest is where a bird lays its eggs. Many birds make nests, and they use a range of materials to do so. They can be made of piles of twigs and leaves, a hole in the ground, or indentations in wild grasses.

- Some nests are as large and as heavy as a car; for example, the social weaver birds of Namibia, Botswana, and South Africa build nests that can pull down a tree if they become waterlogged (Simon, 2014). Bald eagles can make huge nests that weigh more than a ton (National Eagle Center, 2022)! An eagle will add to its nest year after year. An old eagle's nest might be large enough to hold a group of children (or an entire preschool class).

- The smallest nest belongs to the bee hummingbird. It is about the size of a quarter (BirdNote, 2018).

- Birds are the only animals alive on Earth today that have feathers. Birds evolved from reptiles, which means feathers evolved from scales.

- Birds shed their feathers at least once a year in a process called *molting*.

- Birds use their tail feathers to steer, balance, and brake. Stiff feathers allow birds to fly; soft, downy feathers keep birds from getting cold.

- Some feathers, such as those of ducks, have an oily coating to help keep birds dry.

- Baby birds cannot fly. Learning to fly happens once the chicks develop wing feathers that are large enough for flight. This is called *fledging*. Adult birds may become very aggressive when their young are learning to fly. Be careful around swallows and red-winged blackbirds, as they may fly at your head when their chicks are on the ground!

- All birds hatch out of eggs. Bird eggs are oblong in shape, which allows them to rest inside a nest or on the ground safely.

- Some birds recognize their own eggs. They may use color and speckled patterns to help with this.

But we can also use our discovery blanket to introduce birds. We place a variety of feathers, plush songbirds, eggs, nests, and field guides on the blanket and sit back, giving the children time to share. We may prompt them to share what they see on the blanket and to tell us what they know about birds and what they would like to know about birds. We may remain quiet and let their conversation flow without us. Either approach can provide a jumping-off place that may dictate the next several days or weeks.

Depending on your location, you may be able to take a guided bird hike with an expert bird watcher or accompany an ornithologist on a bird-banding expedition. You can also participate in live, virtual bird programs through raptor programs from around the country. Although less authentic, you can place life-sized laminated birds outside and give the children binoculars. Challenge them to find the birds by peering through large picture windows or as you head out hiking. Living birds often hide from us or fly away before we can really see them. But laminated birds will stay put, and finding them as we hike is still fun and highly satisfying for children.

OUTDOOR EXPLORATION

When hiking with children, look for swallow and robin nests on human-made structures, such as fences, rafters, beams, and alcoves, and goldfinch nests in meadows and prairies. The children can also look for feathers on the beach, in the woods, or around a pond. Look for signs of ducks, geese, grouse, and turkeys nesting on the ground.

Climb an observation tower (or visit a second-story window) to get a bird's eye view of the landscape. Set up bird feeders and visit them daily.

Play Robin's Nest Relay Race. Divide the children into two teams. Line them up at one end of an open area. Place a tub of mud in front of each team. Give the first person in each line a spoon. Each person must scoop a spoonful of mud, run to the other side of the space, and add the mud to a small bowl. Once everyone has had a turn, give each team a tub of dried grass and some plastic tweezers. Give each person a turn running to the bowl to add grass. In the end, look at the two bowls of mud and grass and compare them to a real robin's nest.

IDEAS FOR GROUP-TIME OPPORTUNITIES

- Read books about birds, feathers, nests, and eggs, such as *Bird, Egg, Feather, Nest* by Maryjo Koch, *Mama Built a Little Nest* by Jennifer Ward, and *Birds* by Carme Lemniscates. For a beautiful book about inclusivity, we recommend *Bird Boy* by Mathew Burgess, which features a nature-loving boy with a special connection to birds.

- Encourage the children to run and flap their wings like a songbird and then soar like a raptor.

- Pass around real feathers, nests, and eggs, or display them on a discovery table or blanket.

CHAPTER SEVEN: THE NATURE-BASED CURRICULUM IN SPRING

- Play the What's Missing? game with bird-related natural objects. Place feathers, eggs, nests, and bird figures on a tray and let the children see them. Then cover the items with a blanket. Remove one item, reveal the tray, and have the children guess what's missing.

- Paint cardboard eggs (available at craft stores) in sets of identical patterns and colors, and then ask the children to match the different eggs.

- Invite an ornithologist to visit the class and describe what they do.

- Participate in a community science bird count. You can contact a local nature center to see if they are leading any community science programs related to birds. You can also participate in Project Feeder Watch through the Cornell Lab of Ornithology, which collects and compiles data from across the country and provides detailed instructions and tally sheets (along with wonderful resources about birds).

- Even if you don't wish to participate in an official community science project, you can chart the songbirds you see on your hikes. If your school has more than one class, the children can share their findings across classes.

IDEAS FOR SENSORY AND DISCOVERY TABLES

- Add colored feathers (available at most craft stores) and colored bowls to your sensory table and ask the children to match the feathers and bowls.

- After putting water in your sensory table, add plastic eggs and tongs (to mimic bird beaks).

- Provide dried grass or ribbon for nest building in your sensory table.

- Make a bird display on your discovery table using real nests and feathers along with plush birds and plastic eggs.

IDEAS FOR ART AND SCIENCE ACTIVITIES

- Dye eggs. We like to use vegetable oil and natural dyes made from beets, onionskins, red cabbage, spinach leaves, blueberries, native plants, and coffee. (You can find instructions online for making natural dyes.)

- Invite the children to make playdough nests. Show them how to use garlic presses to turn the playdough into twigs.

- Ask the children to do still-life drawings of nests, eggs, and feathers.

- Help children use a magnifier or a microscope to examine different feathers up close.

- Measure the "wingspan" of each child and compare this to the wingspans of swans, turkeys, eagles, falcons, owls, and other birds.

- Encourage children learn different bird calls and sing these to each other outside.

PONDS

Picture the scene: sixteen children are lying on their bellies, spread out across a low, wooden boardwalk. They are dipping strainers into the pond before them. There are plastic tubs nearby, along with laminated pond identification sheets, so the children can catch, observe, and identify their findings.

The pond is full of life, from slimy duckweed to green frogs and turtles, from lily pads to the tiny invertebrates deep below the surface. There may be other visitors as well: a heron, goslings, or a pair of mallards. There may be raccoon tracks in the mud or deer hoofprints—indications of twilight or late-night passersby. The children embrace the soft feel of the water. Some may be unsure about the muck. A few may need reminders not to splash or run or lean over too far.

Exploring ponds is perhaps our most popular activity at nature preschool. It seldom disappoints, even if our nets yield no more than algae. Simply dipping our nets, scoops, or strainers into the water is an adventure. Besides the mud that we inevitably bring to the surface, we may discover fairy shrimp, salamander eggs, damselfly nymphs, and tadpoles in various stages of development.

As an activity, ponding simultaneously introduces children to the world of aquatic macroinvertebrates, food chains, and the overall health and vibrancy of the pond. It can also teach children how to use scientific tools, identification charts, and conservation practices. Additionally, it allows children to move in different ways, to lie on their bellies, and to learn water safety while literally getting their hands and feet wet. It is an activity that engages the body, heart, mind, and spirit.

When introducing ponding to children, we are careful not to begin with nets and identification charts; although, the goal is to add these once the children are ready. We begin by teaching children how to be safe and observant around our ponds. Our initial hikes are usually just opportunities to see the water for the first

CHAPTER SEVEN: THE NATURE-BASED CURRICULUM IN SPRING

time and to practice boardwalk safety, which in our case includes getting down on one's stomach to peer over the edge. We read books about ponds and enjoy the beauty of the landscape. We discuss what we see and hear and how the water feels, and we make guesses as to what we might find with deeper exploration. But we wait to add the equipment for at least a couple of weeks.

Once we feel our classes are ready to investigate the pond with nets or strainers, our teachers demonstrate pond-safety rules. We also demonstrate the correct use of pond tools such as strainers. We use aluminum strainers rather than nets because the children have much more control over strainers when they are first getting started. We attach floating key chains—the kind that are often attached to boat keys—to our strainer handles, which is useful when the strainers are dropped in the water.

We generally have a ratio of one adult per every eight children, but we may add extra adults for ponding, depending on the age of the group and their self-regulation skills. Generally, we have one teacher engaged with the children as they catch aquatic organisms and at least one, if not more, who is making sure everyone is safe. That means one teacher can be crouched over the tubs of water, helping children read the charts, identify their discoveries, and share their delight. The other teachers can document the activities with a camera but can also remain upright and attentive, making sure no one is about to fall in. In those rare instances that someone does fall in the pond, a teacher must be able and ready to pull the child from the water in seconds.

We adhere to the following rules whenever we are near the pond:

- Know the approximate depth of the water, and stay by the shallowest spots.
- Ensure that one adult is always standing upright, watching the children.
- Ensure that one adult is always just a few seconds away from the children.
- Ensure that at least one adult has the arm and body strength to remove a child, who may weigh more than fifty pounds due to wet clothing, from the water.
- Avoid wooden boardwalks on wet days; they become extremely slippery.
- While on a deck or boardwalk, have children remain on their bellies.
- On a sandy or muddy bank, be prepared for children to slip and potentially slide into the water. Have a rope, hiking stick, or other device to pull them back out and to prevent the teacher from falling in after them.
- Never take a group of young children ponding if you believe they are not yet ready to follow the safety rules.

A FEW KEY CONCEPTS ABOUT PONDING

- There is life in the ponds, but it is often so small that we cannot see it.

- Some common pond organisms include dragonfly nymphs, damselfly nymphs, water striders, whirligigs, water boatmen, fairy shrimp, mosquito larvae, tadpoles, predaceous diving beetles, toad spawn, water lilies, and duckweed.

- A tadpole is a young frog that lives and breathes entirely in water. Tadpoles hatch from small eggs in ponds and lakes. Frog eggs are round; whereas, toad eggs are laid in strings. A tadpole goes through metamorphosis by developing back legs, then front legs. As it grows, it loses its tail and develops lungs. Most tadpoles only eat pond plants.

- It takes some tadpoles about fourteen weeks to become frogs. Bullfrogs, however, typically remain tadpoles for two to three years, which means they must overwinter as tadpoles at the bottom of the pond.

- Some ponds are temporary. Vernal ponds and wetlands may dry up during the hottest months but often reappear seasonally. Temporary ponds do not have fish, but they may contain frog and salamander eggs.

- *Invertebrates* are animals without backbones. Many invertebrates are very small and live in ponds. They may live their entire lives in the water or may begin in the water and move onto land as they develop into adults.

- Many insects, such as dragonflies and mosquitoes, begin their lives in the water. Worms may live in the soft mud of the pond. Mollusks, such as freshwater snails, also live in ponds, as do crustaceans such as crayfish.

- Water spiders live in ponds. Many other spider species weave their webs near ponds to catch the insects that emerge.

- *Vertebrates* are animals with backbones. Pond vertebrates include fish, which live their whole lives in water; amphibians, such as frogs, toads, and newts; turtles; and water birds, such as ducks, geese, and herons, which move between water and land. Mammals, such as water voles, water shrews, muskrats, and beavers, build their homes near the edge of the pond or even in earthen lodges in the middle of the water.

In all the years that we have taken children ponding, we can count on one hand the number of times a child or teacher has gone in the water. However, the fact that we cannot count the number as zero is reason enough to take safety seriously. Ponding is a risk. As with anything that we do near water, it requires a heightened level of planning and attention. However, when done with the necessary safety parameters in place, it can be one of the most exciting and memorable activities we offer.

OUTDOOR EXPLORATION

Visit a pond, stream, or lake, and explore what lives in the water. Be sure to bring with you nets, tubs, and pond identification sheets. Spend as much time as you wish dipping nets, catching organisms, and placing what you find in tubs with pond water. Use laminated pond identification sheets to identify the organisms. (Tip: Have the children lie on their stomachs when they dip their nets from a boardwalk or pier.)

Ask the children to look for evidence, such as footprints in the mud near the water's edge, scat, and broken plants, of animals that have visited a pond, stream, or lake. Discuss with the children what they see and smell near the pond. Are the plants near or in the pond different from plants that grow in other places? What does the pond smell like? Does it smell different from other places? Ask the children to look for ducks and geese. How are they adapted for the water? Notice especially their feet, feathers, and bills.

IDEAS FOR GROUP-TIME OPPORTUNITIES

- Ask children what they might see at a pond. Talk about the differences between a lake and a pond.
- Put a big blue scarf in the middle of the circle to represent a pond. Give each child a plastic animal or a laminated picture featuring a species that lives in or around the water. Let each child place their animal where they think the animal should be in relation to the "pond" and talk about how the animal uses water.
- Make a felt pond and give each child a felt animal to place in or around the pond. Make felt sticks and stones (and maybe even some litter). What happens if too many sticks, stones, pieces of litter, and so on are thrown in the water? Is it still a good place for animals to live?
- Catch a live frog and put it, for a few minutes, into a large, clean parmesan-cheese container with the top lid open to allow air inside. Pass the container around for everyone to see, then release the frog where you found it.
- Make an aquarium. Add pond water, plants, and maybe even some tadpoles or snails, and bring it back to the class to study. After a week, return the water and contents to where you got them.

IDEAS FOR SENSORY AND DISCOVERY TABLES

- Create a pond in your sensory table with water, plastic frogs, fish, water lilies, nets, and scoops.
- Make a pond scene on your discovery table with all the different animals that depend on a pond.

- Place turtle shells, pond rocks, nets, and cattails on the discovery table.
- Display a water-insect chart on your discovery table, and include small plastic models of dragonflies, salamanders, frogs, and other pond animals.
- Make a frog life-cycle display.

IDEAS FOR ART AND SCIENCE ACTIVITIES

- Cut out different fish shapes, and ask the children to design a fish by painting it the colors they wish.
- Collect pond water, and encourage the children to look at the water under a microscope.
- Provide the children with blue, green, and brown fingerpaints so they can paint a water scene.
- Make a large mural of a pond on a large piece of butcher paper. Have children draw or cut out from magazines the plants and animals that live in the pond.

MAPS

Maps are not tied to any one season. Over the years, we have sometimes introduced them in fall as part of our quest to get to know our spaces. We have also waited until winter, when we began to work more on literacy and developing an understanding of symbols. We have waited until spring to introduce maps as a way of bringing these different skills together. Depending on the class, we may not study maps at all, besides looking at the maps we encounter on our trail signs or stash in various spots in our classrooms.

Generally, however, we enjoy maps. We enjoy trying to place ourselves on a map as part of a growing understanding about the larger community and our own place in it. On maps of the world, we may try to find North America, then Wisconsin, then Milwaukee. On maps of the state, we can see how interconnected things are—how one river connects to another, how the Milwaukee River begins north of us in Fond du Lac County before flowing our way and emptying into Lake Michigan. We even try to imagine ourselves as tiny figures on the map. Maps require us to translate the three-dimensional world into a two-dimensional representation, which invites a new, often challenging, way of thinking for preschoolers.

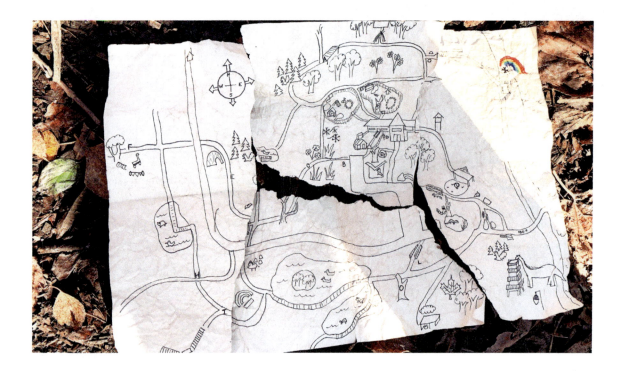

Maps are fun. We enjoy making maps of our rooms, houses, and neighborhoods; maps of our favorite hikes; and imaginary maps. We may also have children hide notes on the trail and then draw maps that lead to these secret messages for other classes to follow.

One of our teachers has developed an entire program using maps, which she has reimagined into something magical. She tells the children that a treasure map has been torn and scattered in four different areas of the nature-center grounds. Each day, the children must follow clues that lead either east, west, north, or south. Once they find all four pieces of the map, they can reassemble it. They then follow the complete map, which naturally leads to a buried treasure box on the beach.

There are some wonderful books that explore maps with young children. We often use the book *Me on the Map* by Joan Sweeney, as it not only explores the idea of place but also reiterates that every human on Earth has their own special place on the map. Other good books that introduce maps to children include *Follow that Map* by Scot Ritchie, *Mapping Penny's World* by Loreen Leedy, and *My Map Book* by Sara Fanelli.

Maps help us connect different areas in a visual way and can help us gain a better understanding of how maps, trails, and signs are all a part of wayfinding that allows us to get from place to place in a clear and consistent way.

At the beginning of each school year, we offer a family hike, during which families can come to the center, pick up a map, and hike the trails together. Our teachers are spread out at special spots along the trails so that they can meet and greet every family. The children are also given "passports" that the teachers can stamp. The true purpose of the hike is really to provide a fun opportunity for parents

A FEW KEY CONCEPTS ABOUT MAPS

- A map is a drawing of a specific location. It could range from the entire Earth (or even other planets) to a small area, such as a particular neighborhood. A map often depicts roads and bodies of water, as well as boundaries such as the borders between states and countries.

- Maps are usually flat, but the same information can also be displayed on a round surface, a globe. Globes are more accurate than flat maps, but flat maps allow us to see all of the information at once.

- Some maps will show you specific features of the Earth, such as the planet's temperature. Topographical maps show physical features, such as mountains and canyons, and historical maps show how boundaries, nations, and physical features such as mountains and rivers change over time.

- A map uses a *scale* that shows how much smaller the map is compared to the place it is depicting. For example, one inch on a map could represent one mile, ten miles, one hundred miles, or one thousand miles, depending on the scale of the map.

- To read a map, we need to understand direction. On a compass, there are four cardinal directions: north, south, east, and west. Maps usually feature a drawing of a compass showing us which way the map is oriented. Most maps in North America will have north at the top.

- Maps may feature special symbols that represent details such as roads, highways, lakes, trees, railroad tracks, and so on. Typically, a map will have a *key* or a *legend* that shows what these different symbols mean.

and children to hike together and for parents to feel more attuned to the school and to their child's experiences. A nice little side effect is getting to use a map in a meaningful and authentic way, which is always the best way to introduce any subject to a child.

OUTDOOR EXPLORATION

Choose a spot on a map, chart a route, and hike there. Pause on the hike, pull out your map, and ask the children to help you locate where you are. When you return from a hike, encourage the children to draw maps that highlight things they saw, such as a lake, a parking lot, or a special tree. Hide treasures nearby, and help the children use directions and maps to find them.

CHAPTER SEVEN: THE NATURE-BASED CURRICULUM IN SPRING

Make a map of your school grounds. Cut it into four pieces and hide these pieces outdoors, one piece in each direction. Over the next four days, hike to each piece, slowly reassembling the map. You can make these look like old pirate maps by writing in watercolor or India ink, then yellowing the paper over candle flames and burning the edges.

Create a black-and-white map of your outdoor space. Give copies of the map to each child, and have them stop and color each area as you hike: red for a sidewalk, green for grass, blue for water, and so on. If you hike in an area where trail maps are posted, pause to locate different spots on the trail map, including bridges, boardwalks, bathroom facilities, bodies of water, and more.

IDEAS FOR GROUP-TIME OPPORTUNITIES

- As a class, look at a range of different maps. Give children time to examine, observe, discuss, and ask questions about maps.

- Pass around maps of your own space (labeled or unlabeled), but do not tell the children what the maps represent. Allow children time to interpret them, and see if they can figure out what the maps are depicting.

- Make a group map. Decide what landmarks from your "beyond" spaces, outdoor play areas, or even your indoor classroom are important to include.

- As a class, make a nature map and come up with a legend together. What could symbolize the woods? What could symbolize ponds?

- Invite guests who work with maps to your class. At our nature center, the land-management team uses all kinds of maps, including some that use photographs taken from overhead drones.

- Use maps in other activities. For example, look at maps if you're talking about migration. Use maps to see what the land looked like two hundred years ago. Use maps before you take a hike to someplace new, so the children can help determine the best route.

IDEAS FOR SENSORY AND DISCOVERY TABLES

- Add playdough, snow, or soft clay to the sensory table, and invite children to sculpt it into mountains, rivers, canyons, lakes, and so on.

- Display a variety of maps and globes on the discovery table for the children to explore.

- Create a three-dimensional map by placing plastic animals, people, toy cars, houses, miniature trees, and other features onto a map of a city, neighborhood, state, or other familiar area. The map can be interactive, meaning that children can move the objects around. You can discuss with them where on the map they want these items placed, and why.

IDEAS FOR ART AND SCIENCE ACTIVITIES

- Create a giant map collage of your outdoor spaces. Ask the children to help paint it and add natural features, such as cattails, goldenrod, trees, and so on, from each area. Add photographs of the children taken at each spot to your finished map.

- Have children make maps of their favorite hikes, then invite family members to hike with their child using their map.

- Explore the four cardinal directions in your classroom, and add a special symbol on each of the four walls to denote north, south, east, and west.

- Include maps in your art, block, and construction areas.

- Provide the children with map puzzles.

- Cut older road maps or discontinued trail maps into different shapes for collages, ornaments, and journals.

ROCKS AND FOSSILS

Rocks and fossils are tremendously fun. Most children find them fascinating. We have found, however, that many teachers are intimidated by this topic, as they do not feel they have the necessary knowledge to do the subject justice. Fortunately, there is no need to have taken classes in either geology or paleontology to teach preschool children about rocks and fossils. (And once you see how fun it is, you'll wish you had time to learn more!) While knowing a little about rocks can be helpful when working with children, it is not necessary to be an expert. Simply providing space for them to explore, handle, and appreciate rocks can be valuable.

Rocks and fossils often go together in our school simply because the rocks we find are *sedimentary*, formed from sand, minerals, and other materials that settled from water. Sedimentary rocks often contain fossils from millions of years ago. (Our part of Wisconsin was submerged beneath the Silurian Sea.) We often spend time at the lakefront, looking along the beach for rocks containing ancient aquatic fossils. We sometimes find cross-sections of *arthropods* (invertebrates that have segmented bodies, jointed legs, and exoskeletons) that look like tiny Cheerios, as well as corals and mollusks. The fossils of *brachiopods* (an ancient shell-dwelling creature somewhat resembling a clam) and *crinoids* (creatures related to starfish and sea urchins) are especially exciting on those rare occasions when we find them.

However, most days we just find rocks. We enjoy looking for "wishing rocks," which are rocks with fully formed circles, usually made up of minerals in a contrasting color. We also enjoy "hag stones," which are rocks with naturally occurring holes in them that can be threaded and worn. We dip our rocks into the water and see what new colors appear. We sort rocks by size and shape. We discuss texture and weight. We test whether or not rocks have a scent. Sometimes, we'll find water-smoothed ceramic pieces and bricks, which leads to discussions about where these items came from, how they

CHAPTER SEVEN: THE NATURE-BASED CURRICULUM IN SPRING

were used, and why they ended up here. Some of our teachers know a lot about rocks and minerals; they are quick to identify granite, calcite, sandstone, and quartz.

But not everyone can do this. In our experience, the children don't necessarily require the name of a rock when they first pick it up. We can instead examine it. Does it feel smooth and hard or soft and crumbly? Does it look the same throughout, or are there lots of different textures and colors? Is it warm in the hand or cool? What does it make you think of when you look at it? What stories could the rock tell, if it could describe its own journey?

You can paint rocks with water. The temporary addition of water often highlights the different minerals, making the rocks change color, brighten, and even sparkle for a minute or two. We find the act of sitting down and painting rocks with water very soothing and calming.

We also prevent children from pocketing or collecting rocks for the entire school year—until the last day. On the last day of school, we take the children down to Lake Michigan and read the wonderful Byrd Baylor book *Everybody Needs a Rock.* This book encourages children to pay close attention to the size, shape, texture, color, and overall feel of a rock. They are told to find that one special rock that speaks to them above all others. It is a book that encourages a relationship with rocks and, thus, with the Earth. We allow the children to roam the beach in search of that one special rock. This is a serious, important activity, and the children treat it as such. They often begin with two, three, or four rocks and spend upwards of thirty or forty minutes trying to decide which one to keep. We are adamant that they can collect only one rock. We ask them to tell us why it is special, but they need not answer. Some teachers attach a small piece of tape to each child's rock and put the rocks in a special basket to carry back to school, thus avoiding the catastrophe of having a special rock fall out of someone's pocket during the long hike up our one-hundred-foot hill. Some children want to show everyone their rock. Others choose to keep their rock private. By saving this activity for the last day, we ensure the rock is something truly valuable.

For those who would like to spend some time really studying rocks and fossils, it is best to begin with rocks. Fossils and rocks taught simultaneously can be confusing for young children.

Rocks are nonliving objects that form naturally in the Earth. They are made from minerals. For preschool children, it is perhaps easiest to think of a mineral as something that is the same through and through, while a rock is a mix of more than one substance.

Besides looking at real rocks, which should be fairly easy to find, children can create their own versions of rocks by mixing polymer clays together in different swirls of colors. Each colored piece of polymer clay represents a mineral—the same through and through—and when we mix two or more minerals together, we get rocks. In other words, rocks are simply mixtures of minerals.

Another approach is to make cookies. Chocolate chips, butterscotch chips, or white chocolate chips can represent minerals. Mix them together, add a few other ingredients, bake them, and you end up with "rocks." It's not a perfect analogy, but it's fun. Make moon rocks by mixing a full box of baking soda with half a cup of water. Add black food coloring and biodegradable silver glitter. Mold the material into rock shapes, and allow them to dry overnight. (This is another good outdoor project.)

If you have time to explore rocks at length, over several days or weeks, you can introduce the three main types of rocks: igneous, metamorphic, and sedimentary.

- *Igneous rocks* are formed from lava and magma, which is the same thing as lava before it erupts. We generally think of magma and lava as melted, semiliquid rock. However, when they cool, they harden and become solid. *Igneous* literally means "from fire." Examples include pumice, which is light enough to float in water; obsidian, which was used for thousands of years to make knife blades; and crystals, such as geodes and rose quartz. You will not find fossils in igneous rocks because the heat would melt them.

- Some rocks are formed inside the Earth; these are called *metamorphic rocks*. The pressure and heat is so great that it actually rearranges the minerals and transforms one type of rock into another. Gneiss, for example, is metamorphosed granite. Marble is metamorphosed limestone. You will not find fossils in metamorphic rocks because of the heat and pressure that makes these rocks.

- *Sedimentary rocks* are formed at the Earth's surface and may or may not contain fossils. These are formed slowly over centuries, often under bodies of water. They are formed by the deposition of minerals mixed with organic particles, meaning minerals carried through water mixed with plant matter, animal bones, and so on, that accumulate and settling over time. Eventually, these materials harden, and what began as layers of loose particles gradually solidifies into rock.

CHAPTER SEVEN: THE NATURE-BASED CURRICULUM IN SPRING

We often use large, black felt circles when we want to showcase rocks and fossils. We cover the felt with rocks, minerals, and fossils so the children can examine them up close. We may also supply magnifying lenses and field guides.

Fossils, when it is time to introduce them, are formed in two basic ways (again, this is explained at a preschool level): through permineralization or through impressions. *Permineralization* is a process through which minerals slowly replace solid organic materials, as happens with petrified wood. This often occurs in water, over thousands of years. Animal bones buried in soft silt are slowly turned into rock as minerals seep into them while sediments surrounding the bone are also solidifying into rock. The result is a fossil. None of the original tissue exists, which means the bone is now rock, but the shape of the rock remains true to the living tissue it once was. We can therefore think of fossils as remnants of long-ago life recorded in rock form.

Sometimes, minerals do not replace the original material. Instead, the original organism decays, leaving only an imprint, called an *impression fossil*, behind. Think of a fern leaf pressed into clay. You can remove the fern, and the imprint remains. As the clay hardens or, in the case of fossils, the mud containing the leaf imprint slowly turns into rock, the imprint is captured and preserved.

People often broaden the definition of fossils to include other forms of preservation, such as ancient animals buried in ice or those preserved in peat bogs. But that gets complicated quickly. So for preschoolers, we leave the description of fossils as things preserved by minerals in stone.

OUTDOOR EXPLORATION

- Read *Everybody Needs a Rock* by Byrd Baylor, then let the children choose one special rock from a creek bed, riverbank, lakeshore, or even an outdoor playground that has been scattered with preplaced rocks. (You can buy rough or polished rocks in bulk online.) Other wonderful children's books about rocks include *A Rock Can Be...* by Laura Purdie Salas, *If You Find a Rock* by Peggy Christian, and *A Rock Is Lively* by Diana Hutts Aston.

- Make sand by rubbing sandstone with your hands or by placing sandstone inside old coffee cans with lids and shaking for a full minute. Encourage the children to look at sand under a microscope.

- Children can also make volcanoes from sand. Pour sand into a mountain shape. Add some baking soda at the top of the mountain shape, then add some vinegar. Watch the volcano "explode!"

- Go on a rock hunt. Take pictures of the rocks the children find. Ask the children to sort rocks by color, shape, size, and other attributes.

- Help the children dig up clay from the ground. Then mix the clay with water until it is pliable, and show the children how to make pinch pots. (You can find instructions online.)

- Go on a fossil hunt. Bring magnifying glasses and look carefully for fossils in the rocks you find. Look for fish skeletons or fern fossils, then encourage the children paint their own. They can also use clay or playdough to make leaf imprints.

A FEW KEY CONCEPTS ABOUT ROCKS AND FOSSILS

- Rocks are not alive; they are *inorganic*.

- All rocks are made of minerals. Minerals are solid substances that are present in nature. For children, it is probably easiest to describe them as pure substances that are the same through and through.

- Rocks differ in color, size, shape, hardness, and texture. Even the same kind of rock can vary in size and shape.

- Some rocks were formed billions of years ago; others form as soon as lava cools.

- The three rock types are igneous (from lava or magma), metamorphic (formed through heat and pressure inside the Earth), and sedimentary (formed from layers of sand and organic material; possibly containing fossils).

- Rocks and minerals can be used to make tools and parts of machines. Minerals such as zinc and iron can be used for medicines, and some, such as sodium, phosphorus, and magnesium, can be eaten. Rocks and minerals can be turned into paint. Rocks and minerals are used in buildings and roads. Graphite is the mineral in our pencils. Talc is used to make talcum powder. Salt is a mineral we eat. Chalk is made of limestone.

- The smallest rock at a beach is a single grain of sand.

- Rocks can build up over time as particles accumulate, and they can break down over time as wind and water cause erosion.

- Bone and wood can turn into rock over millions of years because water seeps in and fills them with minerals, changing them into a rock that still looks like wood or bone. But a fossilized bone is not the same as the actual bone, because the actual bone is not made of rock! Thus, bones and fossils are not the same.

- Fossils were once living things but are now changed. Besides fossils that have turned into rock (petrified), there are imprint fossils, which look like pictures.

IDEAS FOR GROUP-TIME OPPORTUNITIES

- Invite a geologist or someone who knows about rocks to talk with the class.
- Let each child bring a rock to circle time. Have them study their rock carefully and think up different words to describe their rock. List all the words.
- Let the children bring rocks to circle time. Give them time to carefully study their rocks, then put all the rocks in the middle. Can they pick out their own rock?
- Make up a group story called "The Life of a Rock" telling about what the rock has seen and experienced. Was it inside a volcano? buried deep in the Earth? underwater in a river?
- Go on a fossil dig. Bury plaster animal parts in a sandbox, then dig them up and put them back together.

IDEAS FOR SENSORY AND DISCOVERY TABLES

- Fill the sensory table with sand and rocks, adding water if you want, and then have a rock and fossil excavation.
- Make a display on the discovery table of different kinds of rocks, including fossils. Add a laminated identification chart or a field guide, along with magnifying glasses.

IDEAS FOR ART AND SCIENCE ACTIVITIES

- Start a classroom rock museum, with rocks brought in from every child. Display them with labels that include the child's name, the rock type, and where the rock came from.
- Invite the children to make designs or patterns with little pebbles on black felt.
- Weigh rocks on a scale. Let children predict which will weigh the most and the least.
- Invite children to make conglomerate rocks with small pebbles and playdough. Have examples of real conglomerate rocks for them to study. (A *conglomerate* rock is a sedimentary rock that contains pieces of rocks within it.)
- Encourage the children to press fern leaves into clay. They can also make fern paintings by rolling them with gold and bronze paint and leaving an imprint on black paper.
- Have the children create art with colored chalk, which is a kind of rock.
- Order bulk fossils such as brachiopods online, then let the children turn them into necklaces or use them in collages.

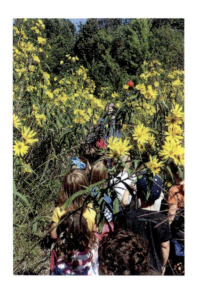  

PHENOLOGY

Phenology refers to the seasonal timing of life-cycle events within the natural world. (It should not be confused with *phrenology*, which is the long-ago debunked belief that the size and shape of one's skull indicates intelligence or moral character.) When we pay close attention to what is happening in nature—when a particular summer flower blooms, a particular insect hatches, or a particular tree bud appears—and note how these occurrences are tied to certain seasons, certain temperatures, and degrees of rainfall or drought, then we are studying phenology. Phenology is, at its essence, the study of the signs of the seasons.

Although we have included phenology as a topic of study, we do not necessarily pause once a year to discuss it. Instead, phenology as a concept underlines our entire curriculum. For example, in September, our prairies are ablaze with goldenrod. Not by accident, they are also full of butterflies, bumblebees, and goldfinches, all of whom use goldenrod as a primary food source. About fifty insect species also feed on goldenrod when they are still in their larval stage. This is why so many goldenrod stems contain galls. These larvae will in turn attract predatory insects such as the praying mantis.

Even if we never focus on the prairie as a topic of in-depth study with the preschool children, we will certainly hike through it or walk around its edges, pausing to observe and listen. We measure the height of the plants, get down low to see it from the ground, collect its seeds, and sweep it with nets. Or we may just sit and watch in silence, listening to the cacophony of insects while the goldenrod, asters, grasses, and sunflowers wave and dance in the breeze. We can hear how alive the prairie is in the fall, even if at that point we are more focused on getting to know each other. If all we do is read a book or two as we rest in the prairie or learn the difference between a prairie and a forest, we are still experiencing the prairie in fall.

CHAPTER SEVEN: THE NATURE-BASED CURRICULUM IN SPRING

By winter, in contrast, much of the prairie is sleeping. There is a blanket of snow over most of the plants, and the prairie as a whole has grown silent. We may see vole tunnels leading from the packed trails to little hollows down at the ground. We may find deer beds and turkey, rabbit, and fox tracks, indicating to us that these mammals are still awake and active. But the birds that feed on the seeds have now left. The insects have died off or are asleep, waiting for their eggs to hatch the following spring. We can remember how noisy and busy the prairie was just a few months earlier. Back then, we likely could not see above the plants. Now, we are the tallest things around, and we can even see across the mounds of snow to the forest beyond.

When spring arrives, the snow melts, and the very first plants to start growing back will be those that thrive in wet, loamy soil. These are often easy to spot, as they are the only drops of color in a mostly brown and damp landscape. Many spring prairie plants are small, not yet overgrown by the taller plants yet to come. Spring prairie plants include the gentle pasque flower, spiderwort, penstemon, and blue false indigo.

Our conservation team may deliberately burn a section of the prairie in spring to encourage new growth and decomposition. These small, controlled fires make it easier for seeds to take root while burning off tree seedlings that can encroach on and crowd out the native grasses. The fire also adds much-needed nitrogen back into the soil. The children will watch these burns from a distance, seeing the prairie go within seconds from brown and spiky to blazing orange, then flat, black, and charred. Over the next few weeks, they see firsthand how the scorched earth turns green with new life, as tiny grasses grow and as birds suddenly arrive and eat fresh new seeds and newly hatched insects. By the time the end of the school year arrives, the prairie is once more fresh, green, growing, and thriving but not yet at the towering heights it will reach by late August.

In this way, the children experience a pattern of growth and life that is tied directly to the seasons. They may not understand in depth the concept of phenology. But they do see, perhaps for the first time, an interconnectedness between season, temperature, plant life, and animal life from which a deeper understanding can grow.

We may never use the term *phenology* with the children. However, over the course of nine or ten months, we introduce them to the concept of phenology simply by visiting the same trails and hiking spots again and again, noting the changes. Some teachers consider phenology little more than a wonderful by-product of a year spent at nature preschool, while others may make it a deliberate part of the curriculum. To do this, they will often focus on one spot in particular. Perhaps they choose a single tree to adopt or a favorite little spot in the woods. They will then make a point of visiting this spot at least once every four weeks. They may take photographs and compare the tree, the clearing, or the pond on each monthly visit. They may do the same activity, such as painting what they see or comparing color swatches, each time. They may even create a visual display in their classroom with drawings and photographs that shows the same tree every month, so that parents and others can see the changes. They may keep a specific journal devoted exclusively to that spot, which they can also use to document evidence of other things the children find on their hikes. Did they see tracks? chewed pine cones? a nest? a den? What other plants are present? What birds are they hearing? What is the weather? What is the air temperature?

The children are, in essence, creating a phenology journal, through which they can look back, month after month, as well as use it to make predictions about what may come next. They can include themselves, if they wish: What were they wearing when they last took this hike? How tall were they? What book did they read? What songs did they sing? In noting how much the land around us changes, it is always fun to bring it back to the children and to remember how much we too are always growing and changing.

OUTDOOR EXPLORATION

Select one spot to visit repeatedly and deliberately as a class. You can also have individual children select a "sit spot" to visit regularly. Take color swatches from local paint stores each time you visit the spot. Provide the children with paints or markers to capture the surrounding colors on paper. Photograph the same area with the children. Give the children embroidery hoops and magnifiers, and have them examine that same area inside their hoop. Record in a special journal everything the children see and hear: birds, insects, plants, colors, temperature, clothing, weather, even their own moods. Repeat every three to six weeks.

IDEAS FOR GROUP TIME EXPLORATIONS

- Have the children read books, write in journals, play music, do yoga, paint, or just sit in silence in their specially selected spot.

- Each time you and the children visit the spot, read aloud the journal entries from your previous visits, and pull out photographs from prior visits. Compare the changes with the children. Ask the children to describe what they were feeling, or ask them what they remember about the last visit. What are they feeling and thinking today?

- Document the sounds the children hear as they sit in silence in their special spot. Make a list, read it back, show the children the written words, and use this as a starting place for emerging literacy development.

- Measure each child beside a particular plant or tree on each visit. Document their heights, along with any changes to the tree or plant.

IDEAS FOR SENSORY AND DISCOVERY TABLES

- Change your sensory-table contents to match the corresponding seasons, such as filling it with water in fall and spring and with ice and snow in winter.

- Create a color palette in your sensory table. Fill the table with a range of items that match the colors of the class's seasonal hikes.

- Collect materials from the class's hikes, such as prairie seeds and flowers in fall (not too many, as the animals depend on them), and make a seasonal landscape on your discovery table with corresponding plastic animals.

CHAPTER SEVEN: THE NATURE-BASED CURRICULUM IN SPRING

- Make a table display featuring images, taken every six weeks, of the children at their special nature spot to show how it changes from visit to visit.

IDEAS FOR ART AND SCIENCE ACTIVITIES

- Create a museum exhibit featuring one or two special items from nature collected from the hikes you take each month.
- Ask the children to make paintings using dot markers that show what they have observed in nature—yellows and oranges in autumn, for example—and include the date on each painting. Compare the paintings every six weeks.
- Create a black-and-white outline of a tree. (You can base this on an actual tree that your class can visit.) Have the children collage a new version of the tree every eight weeks, based on what they observe.
- Provide the children with homemade playdough that corresponds to the colors in nature that season. (Playdough should be replaced every four weeks, if not sooner, which means you can easily keep up with the changing dominant colors outside.)
- Help the children press wildflowers in spring, summer, and autumn. They can use them to decorate journals, make bookmarks, or create collages.
- Create a phenology-themed photo exhibit (in person or online) that can either be replaced or, ideally, added to, every month throughout the year. The exhibit can feature the children, the landscape, your adopted nature spot, animal tracks, plants, the sky, temperatures, hours of daylight, and so on.

JUST FOR FUN

Certain activities at nature preschool are beloved but do not necessarily align with the seasons or even with nature topics. They fall into a category we call Just for Fun. One of the most effective ways we can encourage children to form lasting relationships with nature is to give them happy experiences. Children who are having fun while playing outdoors are far more likely than those who don't to look on nature as a friend and a companion, as a place where they have positive experiences, and as a place that makes them feel their best.

It is important not to dismiss activities that are just for fun. Joyful, playful experiences should be a part of every childhood. Besides, Just for Fun is a bit of a misnomer. These activities provide cognitively rich experiences that support large and fine motor movement, social interactions, creative expression, and much, much more. We have chosen four of our favorites to highlight here: water play, mud play, adventure play, and fairy houses. Our teachers would agree that hardly a week goes by when we are not engaged in at least one, if not all, of these activities.

Rather than breaking these four activities down into different areas of exploration, we simply summarize what they look like in action and offer a few ideas for your own program should you wish to try something similar.

WATER PLAY

Not every program has access to a lake, stream, river, or pond. Nor are those bodies of water necessarily safe for the kind of open play that children require. Providing watering cans, sprinklers, bubbles, outdoor water tables, and even simple tubs of water makes for wonderfully joyful and creative play that is also safe and can take place far away from open water, within fenced-in spaces.

Outdoor water play is a large part of our program, so much so that we have developed a handful of summer camps that only play with water. Children in our water-themed camps may visit the different ponds on the property, but just as often they will remain in our outdoor classrooms and experiment with blocks of ice or with waterfalls they create themselves by pouring water down a rocky hill. They will collect water from cisterns and rain barrels and create art with water.

We do not introduce water play in any formal way; we simply incorporate it into our outdoor spaces on an almost daily basis. If it rains, we may add small wooden boats to our puddles. We may watch the water as it flows from the downspouts into our barrels. We may collect, measure, and document rainfall in our rain gauges.

On hot, dry days, we may turn on a sprinkler, toss ice cubes into our outdoor sensory tables, carefully water our flowers and herbs, and even create misting zones using different settings on our hoses. Although we could sit down to discuss scientific concepts such as the water cycle or the physical properties of water, we honestly prefer to just play. The water cycle can wait until the children are older. For us, it is enough that they experience rain, see the puddles, and watch as they dry up. As for the physical properties of water, by seeing how water changes from liquid to solid as the air gets cooler, looking at drifting clouds overhead, and watching the evaporation process during maple-sugaring season, children can experience water in its various states without adults stopping to draw a line under it. That feels appropriate for preschool. That is why this section remains short and sweet. Water play does not require a great deal of planning. As long as you go about it safely, it can be a part of your daily experience. Safety guidelines include ensuring a watchful adult is present at all times, even with something as small as a shallow plastic tub. Be mindful of the temperature, and do not offer outdoor water play on days when getting wet could mean getting dangerously cold. Be prepared to change wet clothing, and have plenty of extra socks and waterproof bags on hand. Give caregivers and parents fair warning so they are prepared to pick up wet children and belongings or else have a plan to mitigate this.

Water play, although different in its approach depending on the season, is as much a part of our program as sticks, bark, pebbles, and other natural loose parts have come to be. Here are just a few examples of how to incorporate water play into your nature-based program:

- Make a rainbow with a garden hose on a warm, sunny day.

- Plants need the right amount of water. Experiment with several very similar plants, watering some and not others. Ask the children to observe what happens.

- Have the children make water-cycle bracelets using blue beads for water, white beads for snow, and clear beads for water vapor.

- Ask the children to lie down on their backs and look up at the clouds. What shapes do they see?

- In a sandbox or at the beach, let the children explore erosion by making mountains and rivers. What happens when a pailful of water gets added to the sand?

- Encourage the children to look for any water in the environment. Do they notice dew early in the morning? Are there clouds in the sky? Are there puddles after it rains?

- Take watercolors outdoors, and if it's not too muddy, the children can use the puddle water to paint.

- Set up a bubble area with large bubble wands. Ask the children to make bubbles on cold days as well as warm days, and then note the difference. Do the cold-temperature bubbles freeze?

- On warm days, fill tubs with water and biodegradable soap, and then let the children wash their outdoor tools and equipment. Washing these things not only preserves the life and quality of the tools, it's also wonderfully soothing for the children.

- Create an old-fashioned wash station with large basins, environmentally friendly soap, and washboards. Provide children with soft strips of fabric, wooden safety pins, and a clothesline. Let them play with the wash station on warm, dry days.

- Provide the children with water so they can create rivers and dams in the sandbox.

- Create "nature soup" recipes with old bowls, spoons, water, and natural materials that the children collect. Record their recipes for an added literacy component.

- Follow the path of the water after it rains. Have the children get down low and explore the path of the runoff up close. Can they find tiny waterfalls and rivers?

- Erect a pop-up tent, hang a tarp, or create some other waterproof shelter. Gather beneath and read books about the rain. Do this while it's raining for an extra cozy experience!

PARTNERING WITH *Nature* IN EARLY CHILDHOOD EDUCATION

- Mix watercolor paints with snow and ice painting.

- Go sledding, make snow angels, build snow forts, and make snow people.

- Boot-skate across frozen puddles.

- Let children find sticks to crack thin sheets of ice and listen to the sound it makes. They can also toss pebbles across frozen water for a different kind of sound effect.

- Provide children with water tables, buckets, scoops, basins, small strainers, toy boats, ice-cube trays, access to rain barrels, and watering cans. See what their imaginations create!

MUD PLAY

Picture a Wisconsin puddle in March: It is filled with a thick, silty mud similar to potter's clay. The water has pieces of ice floating in it, as the puddle likely froze overnight. For some children, this is something to avoid, but for many, it is an invitation. They see a puddle, they want to splash. Perhaps they want to go fishing for the individual pieces of ice, curious whether they feel like glass. They want to know how deep the puddle is and whether the mud is sticky, solid, or like chocolate pudding. Some children want to experiment with mud. Can they create mud balls? use it as glue? Can they sculpt tiny bowls or coil it into worms and snakes? Some children may wish to use a ladle to slowly pour the mud over their arms and legs, watching intently as the water spills off in rivulets. Mud play can be lively and cooperative, but it can also be quiet and personal.

Some of our favorite mud activities include the following:

- Painting with mud on paper, fabric, wood, or even our own faces

- Adding baskets of daisies, leaves, petals, acorns, pebbles, and so on to our mud play

- Adding molds for making mud bricks, mud cakes, mud tiles, and so on (You can make your own molds from household objects, such as bread pans or gelatin molds, or buy ready-made snow and sand.)

- Creating mud-kitchen recipes, including upside-down cakes, soups, puddings, ice cream, salads, and more

- Composing and singing songs about mud

- Making mud prints on snow, paper, or painted boards

- Mixing mud with snow to create new colors and textures

- Burying items, such as gemstones and other special rocks, in mud and letting the mud dry and harden, then setting up an archeological dig to excavate the buried items months later

- Celebrating International Mud Day (https://worldforumfoundation.org/workinggroups/nature/mud-day/)

Playing in mud engages the senses while also engaging critical thinking. Children learn about force and resistance. They learn about viscosity and what happens to mud when it dries and solidifies. Mud

CHAPTER SEVEN: THE NATURE-BASED CURRICULUM IN SPRING

play strengthens their tactile skills along with their balancing skills as they learn how to navigate slippery terrain. It even helps children develop emerging engineering prowess as they fashion bridges over widening puddles or figure out how to make bricks and dams. Finally, according to "In the Loop: Let Them Eat Dirt (or at Least Play in It)" by Dana Sparks (2016), playing in mud can help strengthen children's immune systems, exposing them to small doses of germs in the soil that encourage a more robust immunity to illness.

If you don't have access to a naturally occurring mud hole, a large plastic tub filled with water and dirt can easily suffice. Add a few metal bowls, spoons, eggbeaters, muffin tins, and Bundt pans, and you've got a delightful mud kitchen. Add wheelbarrows, shovels, planks, and molds for bricks, and you've got a construction site. Add tin cups, plates, and ice-cream scoops, and you've got a sidewalk cafe, a coffee shop, or an ice-cream parlor. The possibilities of mud play are almost endless.

 We do want to add a caveat. As much as mud can be a joyful, messy, full-body, and sensory-rich experience for young children, it can also be a caregiver's nightmare. We hear of adults who are almost in tears when a child is handed over to them covered head-to-toe in mud. While allowing a child to take a bath in mud can be a wonderful experience for the child, it is not always considerate of the adult who needs to somehow transport them home. This is why mud play also comes with a public service announcement: Please allow children to play in mud. But please also do whatever you can to help their caregivers when it's time to depart. Remember that they must get the children home again, or perhaps they need to stop off at the grocery store, and they would like to do so without ruining their car seats or dripping mud all over a clean, indoor space. Please don't ruin the children's clothes. Make sure they are completely covered in waterproof outer gear before letting them play in mud. If possible, provide a place at school where muddy gear can drip-dry or be washed. Build time into the day to clean the worst of the mud from the child as well. Mud play should be inclusive, but programs need to take thoughtful steps to make sure the negative side effects of mud play are carefully addressed.

We address the mud issue in these ways:

- Provide large, waterproof bags for families. The bags must be large enough to contain snow pants, rain pants, boots, hats, mittens, and a winter coat. This gives adults a very practical way to transport their child's muddy gear home.

- Change the child's clothes when possible. If your program is entirely outdoors, this may be harder to manage. In that case, hose off the children as best you can. We have literally lined up entire classes and started at their shoulders, using a hose set to the lightest setting. This is very doable if the children are wearing waterproof gear. We stand outside near a large drain in a corner of our asphalt parking lot. Starting from the muddiest spot on their upper bodies, we hose them off all the way down to their boots about 15 minutes before pickup time. If necessary, we even towel them off, using large towels that can go straight into the wash as soon as the last child departs.

- Prepare families in advance for the mud. We show videos of previous years so they know what's coming. We also explain how and why children benefit from mud so they can remember this when mud season arrives.

- Do not assume families can afford multiple pairs of boots, rain pants, and other gear or that doing laundry daily is possible. Provide extra gear when you can.

- Share tips for managing muddy gear at home. Our best tips come directly from parents and include the following:

  » Drip-dry the muddy outer gear in the shower, above a utility sink, or even just over a towel. It is better not to run rain pants through the washing machine too often, as this can make them less waterproof overtime. We recommend waiting until the mud season is over before washing them.

  » After drip-drying, brush the mud off with a heavy scrub brush, available at most general stores, or a horse brush, available at pet-supply stores.

  » Soak boots in a tub of water or hose them off, then stuff them with paper towels or newspapers. (This is only necessary if the insides have become wet.)

  » Invest in boot and mitten dryers. (Either purchase them for your school or suggest them to families.) This can help ensure that children returning to school later in the week have warm, dry boots and mittens to put on. Although some are very expensive, mid-range versions cost around fifty dollars. Simpler options include homemade pegs on which boots and mittens can be placed upside down near a heater.

The benefits of mud play far outweigh the inconveniences. But it is also incumbent on us as educators to impart these benefits to families and to help them manage the mess to the best of our ability. We don't want to make parents and caregivers miserable. Fair warning in advance is not only thoughtful, it can make the experience better for everyone. And sharing the wonderful photographs and videos of children engaged in mud play, along with explanations of both the spiritual joy and the cognitive growth taking place, helps put everyone on the same side.

ADVENTURE PLAY

Adventure play can be defined as almost everything we do at our nature preschool, particularly outdoors. Digging in sand, exploring tiny, hidden paths, and chasing the waves on Lake Michigan fall under adventure play. But it is also possible to create deliberate areas with very specific kinds of adventure play in mind, areas that promote climbing, balancing, swinging, and leaping through different terrains.

There is one such spot at our school where a new trail was added. It includes a pile of fallen logs, a high tree stump, and twisting pine roots that invite fairy homes. There is a nearby bridge, a ravine, and several low-hanging branches that create a permanent canopy. The children refer to this spot as the "Ninja Warrior Adventure Course." It is one of their favorite destinations. They climb, jump, balance, and teeter. Those who may at first be hesitant to clamber up a stump and leap into the air may push themselves to try it after weeks of watching others do so, and they feel exhilarated when they succeed. Children who may not be in the mood to climb or swing also have plenty of smaller stumps on which to rest, read books, or stare up at the trees overhead. Children learn to take turns and to give each other time and space. They understand that the Ninja Warrior Adventure Course is more serious and challenging than the average playground, and with that come rules and expectations that they themselves help craft.

Even before this magical spot existed, we had areas in our outdoor classrooms that we deliberately left undeveloped. Over time, children blazed trails through brush and branches, creating special pathways largely inaccessible to adults. It is important for children to have these, as it provides them with a perceived sense of adult-free play and develops independence and self-reliance within a wilderness setting. From these experiences grow confidence and a powerful sense of self-efficacy, two qualities that will help them so much as they encounter new challenges. When we can provide these areas in ways that still ensure everyone's overall safety, we are giving children what they need while maintaining structure and protection.

To create an adventure play area, do the following:

- Create boundaries, either real or perceived. For example, while we have fences surrounding our outdoor classrooms, we do not have a fence at our Ninja Warrior Adventure Course. One boundary here is a bridge. Children could conceivably cross it, but that would be clearly out of bounds. Children feel safer, and indeed are safer, when their adventure space is clearly defined.

- If there are trees for climbing, make sure that an adult is always near enough to watch and, depending on the height of the branches, physically spot the climber.

- If there are boulders and stumps for jumping, make sure that there are no jagged roots, rocks, or other hazards in the landing zone.

- Check first and often for wasp nests, stinging plants, active animal dens, and other things to avoid.

- Consider different heights and different styles of movement. Is there an area that requires children to get down low and crawl or slither? Are there spots where children can be taller than the teachers? Are there uneven surfaces or spaces where they have to determine just where to put their feet? Are there opportunities to develop overhead strength and swinging arm movements?

- Try to find a spot that balances the adventure play with a quiet resting area for children who may need a break or prefer to watch. You also may need a quiet spot in the unlikely but still possible case of injury.

- Be mindful that if injuries occur on a regular basis, the adventure play area is too advanced and dangerous. We accept that an occasional bump, scratch, or even a twisted ankle can sometimes occur with this kind of play. As long as these injuries are rare, we feel that they are manageable. More serious injuries, such as those to the head, or injuries that occur almost weekly are signs that things have crossed from risky play into hazardous play. Stricter safety measures are required.

- Take advantage of your resources: Do you have access to logs? Can these be bolted together so they don't topple out from beneath a group of scampering children? Do you have access to a couple of trees with a few climbing branches? If not, can you design a climbing area that mimics the uneven spacing of tree limbs rather than the consistent rungs on commercially made jungle gyms? Do you have parent volunteers, community volunteers, church volunteers, or even corporate volunteers who would build you an outdoor adventure area? Can you add new features to an existing space that allow children to balance, climb, swing, hide, navigate, and leap?

- Remember that any off-trail adventure area you create could affect the health of the land. If you work at a nature preserve, talk with your land and conservation team about what you want to create and why. These conversations are important, as is the compromise between children's play and protecting the land.

CHAPTER SEVEN: THE NATURE-BASED CURRICULUM IN SPRING

- Remember to discuss your adventure play area with parents and administrators, highlighting the benefits and the importance of managed risk. Many adults are alarmed by deliberately created risky-play areas. Yet there is so much evidence that supports the benefits of reasonable, controlled risk, one could even argue that, by avoiding risky play, we do children greater harm than a bumped shoulder or skinned knee ever could.

When children are denied the opportunity to assess risk for themselves, they fail to develop what is essentially a survival skill. This can lead to them putting themselves into greater danger, not less, as they grow older. We also deny them their feelings of accomplishment and pride when they pull off the physical and mental feats that go hand in hand with adventure play.

NAEYC offers several important articles about the benefits of risk, including Heather Taylor's 2019 essay on risk and learning in a forest school; Ron Grady's 2020 article, "Climbing Trees, Risk, and Relationships"; and Larissa Hsia-Wong's touching 2021 essay, "Learning Joy and Resilience Through Kindergartners."

Adventure play is a part of our daily experience at nature preschool. Depending on the child, it may involve as much running, climbing, and movement as possible. It may involve climbing onto a tree branch to consider the world from a new perspective. It could also be as simple as rolling down a hill. We never force a child who doesn't wish to climb a high branch or leap from a boulder to go beyond their comfort zone. We do try to provide opportunities where they can watch and consider whether they wish to try for themselves.

Over the years, we have filled our spaces with wobbly stumps, a homemade teeter-totter, an elevated stage, a concrete tunnel, and balance beams, all of which promote the kind of adventure play we wish to support. On the other hand, an inviting adventure-play area doesn't need to be chock full of structures. Nor does it need to mimic a full-on obstacle course. It just needs to provide an element of risk for children, opportunities for solving these risks, and a feeling of adventure. Everything else can and will be provided by the children.

FAIRY HOUSES

Building fairy houses has become a staple activity at our nature preschool. We build them deep in the woods near the bases of trees, where we often find moss, roots, and entrance tunnels. We build them at the beach using beach glass, driftwood, pebbles, and flowering dame's rocket (an invasive yet attractive plant). And we build them in our children's gardens, often adding plastic animals, gemstones, tiny signs, and biodegradable glitter. Whether we call them fairy houses, gnome homes, nature dwellings, or something else, the purpose is always the same: to create tiny, semi-familiar structures (as they generally include bedrooms, kitchens, pathways, tables, and food) using natural materials.

While fairy houses can be, and often are, a delightful part of the nature-play curriculum, fairies themselves can be problematic. For a start, just about every children's book or predesigned kit features exclusively White fairies. This also goes for gnomes. This isn't necessarily surprising, as fairies and gnomes are European in origin. Nonetheless, it is disappointing. A quick search on Wikipedia reveals that many cultures, including several throughout Asia, Africa, and the Middle East, have fairy equivalents, such as the African Aziza, the Chinese mogwai, and the Malaysian pari-pari. In Hindu and Buddhist mythology, there are nature fairies called yaksha, which dwell in forests and mountains. There are also many Native American cultures that feature supernatural, fairy-like creatures. However, we would caution against introducing an unfamiliar and appropriated mythology into your

nature-based classroom. Many of these supernatural beings, for example, are tied to religious practices and protected rituals that are not intended for children. Using their names and likenesses could be highly disrespectful. It is also too easy to make mistakes. The yaksha, for example, are not just benevolent nature fairies; in some traditions, they are cannibalistic demons that haunt the wilderness and consume lost travelers. Whatever the original intention, it is never a good idea to incorporate intercultural traditions into a program without the knowledge and understanding that should go with them.

It is also worth noting that while we assume that all children enjoy fairies, some are genuinely frightened by the idea of tiny, winged creatures with supernatural powers. For all these reasons, we prefer to take the emphasis off the fairies themselves and to focus instead on making miniature dwellings, restaurants, and villages out of natural materials. Although we still call them fairy houses, you can call them anything you like. If you prefer to remove the fairies entirely, that's fine. It is truly the act of creating miniatures that is our focus. In the process of building, we are not only stimulating the imagination, we are problem solving (how do I fashion a staircase using the parts of a pine cone?) while strengthening fine motor skills, communicating ideas, and creating magical experiences. Whatever you may choose to call them, designing tiny nature houses allows children to invent new worlds and create stories about those worlds. The children become narrators, sharing their invented worlds with others. In addition, a fairy house (or better yet, an entire neighborhood of fairy houses) can function almost as a map: it allows children to see an entire world at once, with all its details, directions, walkways, and landmarks visible. Given that very young children are often unable to realize how different locations are connected, this new way of seeing connected spaces can give children a sense of both order and reassurance.

At our nature preschool, we sometimes introduce fairy houses as a directed activity, particularly during our weeklong summer camp devoted to fairy homes. We spread out multiple baskets of inviting materials, such as plain or dyed strands of raffia, dried moss, polished rocks, birch bark, twigs, pods, and even seed fluff. We may also provide glue, scissors, and colored tape (but not necessarily). We read books about fairy houses and may share photographs for inspiration. We often help the children write tiny signs, which might say anything: "Welcome to the Fairy Village," "Gnome Home for Sale," or (because this is Wisconsin) "Farm Stand Ahead: Fresh, Local Produce!"

Sometimes, the children opt to build fairy houses during their free play. In these instances, we have not necessarily stocked baskets in advance. No matter. The children find what they need for themselves, simply by scouring the forest and prairies. Fairy houses in autumn will look different from fairy houses in winter and spring. We love it when children construct tiny dwellings unprompted, using only the materials that nature provides.

To create a place for tiny nature dwellings, simply:

- Select one or more magical-looking locations. We are partial to areas that feature a variety of natural materials and interesting shapes and cavities. Good options include the bases of trees, root systems, fallen logs, and decaying stumps.

- Set out baskets of inviting materials. These might include shells, pine cones, acorns, seeds, dried sunflowers, locust pods, milkweed fluff, goldenrod, dandelions, dame's rocket, buttercups, pebbles, twigs, sticks, ribbons (we use biodegradable paper ribbon), scissors, twine, raffia, moss, and paper flowers.

- Add little signs or messages for the fairies, if you wish. These can be secured to tiny sticks or sketched in ink and chalk on pebbles.

- Leave little notes of thanks from the fairies and gnomes, if you wish.

- Add biodegradable glitter, either as part of your design or, later, to indicate that the fairies have visited. We also sometimes sprinkle colored sugar on each fairy house to suggest that the fairies visited during the night.

If you wish to build more permanent structures, you can use a hot-glue gun to create an initial frame; either a box or tipi shape with sticks is an easy place to begin. Children can then add materials, including fabric, to this frame:

- You can enhance the play by creating a water area where you can mix "fairy potions" using colored water in an outdoor water table. (Tip: Add colored ice in contrasting colors, and watch the colors change as they melt!) Add a few drops of essential oils, flower petals, bubbles, and so on to your potions, and either leave them in the water table or put them in tiny bottles for every child to take home.

- Decorate long sticks with ribbons, bells, leaves, dried flowers, and seed pods to make fairy wands (or just "nature wands"). Create nature crowns using strips of paper, ribbons, dried flowers, paper flowers, autumn leaves, and so on, secured with either hot glue or staples.

- Take photographs of each child's fairy house in detail, and then print these out as a display or create a class photo book. Include text for each picture, highlighting the materials the children used and explaining the different features.

- Experiment with new materials and with a range of locations and habitats. Build tiny nature homes in every season and see how different they become!

CHAPTER SEVEN: THE NATURE-BASED CURRICULUM IN SPRING

- CHAPTER EIGHT -

Challenges and Inspiration

Our challenge isn't so much to teach children about the natural world but to find a way to sustain the instinctive connections they already carry.

— *Terry Krautwurst* | **AUTHOR AND HISTORIAN**

In this chapter, we discuss some of the challenges you might encounter in a nature-based preschool. These include the smaller, constant challenges that teachers face on a daily basis as well as the larger issues of health and safety. We include a discussion about how one of the greatest recent challenges in our lifetimes enabled us to create new opportunities and strengthened our commitment to nature-based education. Finally, we address the need to make early childhood nature-based experiences more inclusive across demographics, including income levels, race, ethnicity, and those with physical and neurological differences.

COMMON CHALLENGES TEACHERS FACE IN A NATURE-BASED PROGRAM

On a cold and blustery afternoon, our teaching staff sat down to compile a list of challenges we often encounter in a nature-based program and to brainstorm solutions. Issues that came to mind immediately included dressing appropriately for the weather, navigating bathroom visits in a mostly outdoor program, managing wet and muddy gear, and remaining safe around bodies of water. Equally challenging for many teachers is how to lead joyful and meaningful hikes when three children want to race ahead, four want to linger at the back, and one just lies down in the middle of the trail and steadfastly refuses to budge. Some challenges can be quite serious, particularly in an outdoor setting. These include emergencies and behavioral issues that often feel amplified if your classroom includes open, fence-free areas.

At our preschool, we regularly renew our training in child abuse and neglect, abusive head trauma, first aid, and CPR. In this way, we are no different from any other licensed program. However, we also have to discuss what to do in case of wild animals, cracking ice, lightning storms, and aggressive wasps. We have to pay close attention to weather reports, beach hazard warnings, and even local air-quality alerts and mosquito infestations. Some programs have to be mindful of venomous creatures, wildfires, dangerous winds, and hurricanes.

Over the years, our teachers have discussed, strategized, and problem solved both the daily hiccups that pop up in any given week and the bigger and more serious challenges that can sometimes arise in early childhood education. By doing this consistently, and by thinking ahead and having carefully considered plans in place, we are prepared for most of the typical challenges we encounter.

Unfortunately, nature-preschool teachers do not always get the full credit they deserve, especially when it comes to the daily small challenges we encounter. People frequently describe our job as "playing outdoors with children," which sounds delightful but can feel dismissive. Remember that playing outdoors with children also includes keeping children safe, healthy, and happy in single-digit temperatures (possibly while wearing facemasks during a global pandemic). It means showing up in person, managing hazards, and receiving less pay—and sometimes less respect—than is warranted. There is a learning curve to what we do. Gifted teachers make it look easy, but this does require both effort and practice.

We aim to provide a program that allows for freedom, play, stillness, conflict, experimentation, and trust. We do not use time-outs, punishments, sticker charts, or other short-term approaches to classroom management. Eschewing quick fixes in favor of long-term goals means we have to confront challenges head-on rather than simply diverting attention. It means we have to consider the needs of both the individual and the group while also considering the outdoor landscape. It is one thing to have a child struggling with self-regulation in a four-walled classroom. It is another to have the same child out of control alongside a deep, cold lake. Even the most experienced teachers can have difficult moments and hard conversations or find that they need additional support. But by being aware of the possible struggles and by having thought through several possible responses, we are far better able to succeed.

RUNNERS AND SEED COUNTERS

Runners and *seed counters* are terms we use to describe children who prefer to move fast, releasing their energy through movement, versus children who prefer to move slowly, investigating their surroundings in detail. The same child could very well be both a runner and a seed counter, depending on the day or their mood. The challenge, however, is the same: How do we hike with children who walk at different paces? How do we ensure that everyone is involved and interested? Sometimes, it feels as though all

we're doing is telling children to either speed up or slow down, which is frustrating both for the children and the teachers.

Some nature-based preschools manage this by dividing their students into two or three groups. One group may not hike, particularly if they are very young. Another may hike only very short distances. Only the third, most experienced group may venture into the beyond. Which child goes on which hike is determined as teachers observe and get to know their students.

We have experimented with dividing our groups into smaller cohorts, allowing the children to take the hikes best suited to their personalities. Doing this regularly, however, does not always serve our long-term goal of creating community through shared experiences. Teachers also do not always like leading hikes without a second adult, so whether or not this is possible may come down to ratios. At our preschool, separating into smaller groups is something we may do initially, with the goal of reuniting the class and spending most of our hikes together as soon as all of the children are ready.

More often, we allow the children to spread out on the trails, keeping one teacher up front with those who move quickly and allowing the others to fall back and walk slowly. If we are lucky, we will have a third adult, often a volunteer, who covers the middle. We always hike with walkie-talkies so that the

CHAPTER EIGHT: CHALLENGES AND INSPIRATION

front and back of the group can communicate with one another. (Note: some programs may prefer cell phones to walkie-talkies. We don't rely on cell phones where we teach for a handful of reasons. First, our program has been around since before cell phones were in common usage; hence, we developed our communication protocols without them. We also do not want to make it a requirement of employment that teachers use their personal phones for work. Over the years, more than one cell phone has fallen in a pond. It is far easier and certainly more equitable to supply the same communications devices to the entire staff. Finally, our cell phone service is unpredictable, and it is essential to have a reliable means of contacting another person while down at the beach or in some distant locale. Although they require upkeep and care, we prefer our walkie-talkies.)

We also try to mix up our hikes. This means that we do not always have preplanned destinations. Instead, we simply allow the interests and pace of the group to dictate where we go. Our hike may end up being about the sky overhead or about the earth underfoot. We might provide tools, such as bug boxes, and encourage everyone to see the world from a grasshopper's point of view. We may simply lie on our backs and look up at the clouds.

On the other hand, we sometimes have destination hikes, where the purpose is to get to a particular spot on the grounds. On these days, we may have to encourage the slower children to walk, if not at a fast pace then at least at a steady one. We reward them for their efforts with plenty of time to play and explore once we arrive. We would never hike all the way to the beach, observe the waves for two minutes, and promptly turn around. We make sure there is time once we've made it to our destination for the children to spread out, hunt for sea glass, build in the sand, and capture pieces of floating driftwood. In this way, we try to meet the needs of all the children in our group while also giving each child a chance to see things from the point of view of another. Perhaps one day the child who likes to run ahead will see the value in slowing down, pausing to investigate a seed up close. Perhaps one day the child who likes to move slowly will experience the rush of joy that comes from chasing every wave that comes crashing on the sand.

We may not meet each child's specific needs at every moment of every day, especially when those needs are in opposition to each other. But by being aware of the differences in how children hike and interact with nature, we acknowledge each mindset and provide positive experiences for all.

HAVING THE RIGHT OUTDOOR CLOTHING

We cannot overstate the importance of having the right gear. Being dressed for the weather allows children to play comfortably outdoors in every season. Helping children develop the skills they need to manage their outdoor clothing—zipping and unzipping jackets, getting mittens on and off, and keeping track of their own hats, scarves, water bottles, and sunglasses—not only strengthens children's fine motor skills but also gives them control over their own comfort. A child whose hands and feet are bitterly cold, or who is wilting from the summer heat, cannot play in comfort. Without the right gear, this child may grow to dread extended time in the natural world.

Some practical advice we offer new parents includes sizing up. A slightly too big rainsuit accommodates a growing child and allows for extra layers underneath. A waterproof outer layer is essential for Wisconsin weather and can even go over a snowsuit when fluffy snow turns into wet, heavy slush. Winter boots, too, should not be too tight. A slightly roomy toe box paired with a thick pair of wool socks (never cotton) and perhaps a stick-on foot warmer on a bitterly cold morning will keep feet warm and comfortable, a must when the temperatures are in the teens or below.

Other advice we offer includes bringing your outer gear *every day*. Just because there is no rain in the forecast doesn't mean the forecast is accurate. We have seen the weather radar showing clear skies while we're in the midst of a pop-up thunderstorm more than once. Besides, rain gear protects against more than rain. It protects against stinging nettles, biting insects, cool damp ground, and puddle play.

CHAPTER EIGHT: CHALLENGES AND INSPIRATION

DRESSING APPROPRIATELY FOR WEATHER

HOW TO DRESS IN WARM WEATHER (70 DEGREES FAHRENHEIT AND HIGHER)

- Light-colored clothing is best.

- We recommend lightweight pants tucked into socks to protect against ticks. (In our part of the country, Lyme disease is a serious concern.)

- We suggest purchasing a head net, which is best worn over a hat with a visor. (This is an optional but worthwhile purchase during mosquito season.)

- Children should bring a windbreaker in their outdoor gear bag.

- Children should wear sunglasses and comfortable outdoor shoes (no flip-flops).

- Children should carry a full water bottle.

- All clothing and accessories should be labeled with the child's name.

HOW TO DRESS IN COOL OR WET WEATHER (45-60 DEGREES FAHRENHEIT)

- Have waterproof outdoor gear—rain pants and rain jacket or an all-in-one combination—and waterproof boots. These items should come to nature preschool even when it isn't raining.

- Layers are best. For example, you can pair a long-sleeved flannel shirt over a t-shirt and then add a fleece or rain jacket on top. We can adjust these layers if needed.

- Wool or wool-blend socks are better than cotton. Wool will remain warm even if it gets wet. Cotton pulls warmth away from the feet, making them colder.

- Footies and ankle socks often come off inside boots, resulting in blisters. Longer socks perform better inside rain boots.

- Have waterproof mittens. Waterproof is a step up from, and preferable to, water resistant. We like the waterproof mittens made of rainsuit material that fasten around the wrist and fit over sleeves to keep out water. Some are fleece-lined, which is more comfortable over bare hands. You can even pair these over wool or fleece mittens as it gets colder.

HOW TO DRESS IN COLD WEATHER
(45 DEGREES FAHRENHEIT OR LOWER)

- As soon as the temperature drops below 50 degrees, we suggest switching from rubber rain boots to insulated rain or winter boots.

- Wool-blend socks will keep feet warm in cold weather, even if they get damp.

- Stick-on foot warmers can be a game changer. Just remember that these go on the outside of socks, never against bare skin. (A note about disposable warmers for hands and feet: Some people find these problematic. However, most contain nontoxic activated charcoal, which can be poured directly onto a garden bed or a compost bin once the warmer stops working.)

- Base layers made of silk, wool, or synthetic fibers are all good options; avoid cotton as a base layer in winter.

- Snow pants, a snow coat, a warm hat, warm and waterproof mittens, and a neck warmer are important for cold-weather play, even when there is no snow.

TIPS REGARDING OUTDOOR GEAR
IN COLD AND SLOPPY WEATHER

- *Waterproof* is not the same as *water resistant*. We strongly prefer waterproof mittens made of rainsuit material over water-resistant "ski gloves" that may be fine for powdery snow but are no match for our mud puddles.

- In our experience, a good-quality rain suit is more valuable than a snowsuit, as multiple base layers can provide adequate warmth underneath a truly waterproof top layer.

- Consider a one-piece, oversized rainsuit that can fit over a snowsuit or several base layers.

- Remember that regular rubber rain boots are not warm enough when the temperature is below 50 degrees Fahrenheit, unless they are insulated. Do not trust temperature ratings on boots, as they are overly optimistic.

- Buy insulated rain or winter boots one size up. The added space at the toe box, combined with foot warmers and wool socks, will keep feet much warmer.

- Although layering clothes is usually a benefit, layering socks may actually make feet colder when toes become cramped inside boots. The only time we suggest layering socks is when the layer closest to the skin is made of a very thin fabric designed to wick away moisture.

- When the core body temperature falls, it can be hard to warm back up. Provide children with warm drinks, hand and foot warmers, and even microwavable rice packs during the cold winter months.

- Having a warm, dry head does wonders for one's enjoyment of nature. Our teachers have been known to dry their heads off with a hair-dryer between morning and afternoon classes!

CHAPTER EIGHT: CHALLENGES AND INSPIRATION

Finally: layer, layer, layer. We can always remove a layer if a child gets too warm. If they get too cold, however, we cannot add what isn't there. Air trapped between layers is a benefit, as this provides additional insulation. Layering is one of the best ways to ensure a child remains comfortable no matter what the changing weather may bring.

It can be very frustrating—and extremely time-consuming—to ask children to navigate zippers, heavy mittens, scarves, and other gear without help. The typical adult inclination is to jump in to assist so that they can get outdoors more quickly. But it can be just as detrimental to allow children to sit back helplessly while their parents or caregivers do everything for them. Dressing and undressing are essential daily-living skills that lead to greater confidence and independence. We make managing outdoor gear a deliberate part of the curriculum. Teachers sing songs that help children remember the order in which to put their gear on and take it off. They take the time to work one-on-one with every child, showing them how to hang up damp rain pants so they can dry and how to place boots at the base of their cubby. As with so much of what we do, this process requires a lot of "front-loading" at the beginning of the school year. But the effort is worth it. Teachers who take the time to develop these skills with their students may find that, by the time winter rolls around, the children have become so capable in managing their own clothing that adults can often stand aside while the children manage unassisted. When this happens, we have set them up for success. When parents ask us what we're doing to get their children ready for kindergarten, an unexpected but honest answer is "We're teaching them to put on their own boots and mittens."

Communicating clothing needs to families is easy enough, but teachers must be prepared to do it more than once. There is a difference between hearing, "We go outside even when it rains" and experiencing this firsthand. We have communicated our outdoor gear needs to families through Zoom, through videos, on our website, in person, and in newsletters. When the seasons change, we send out reminders. We offer suggestions on how to transport it all, knowing that parents prefer to keep the inside of their cars as dry as possible. We have hosted gently used outdoor-gear sales and have created private chat groups in which families can share suggestions, tips, reviews, and information about local sales. This information needs to be repeated and updated year after year. Brands change, quality changes, new versions come out, and new families come in. Conversations about gear happen often.

During the peak of the COVID-19 pandemic, our program took place entirely outdoors. This meant that children did not have the daily practice of getting their gear on and off but came and left again fully outfitted for whatever that day's weather called for. Knowing this, we had to put time aside to work on clothing skills. This was possible mostly because changes in temperature throughout the day often called for adding and removing layers. It was especially important to us that children learn how to put on, replace, or adjust their own facemasks.

Our ultimate takeaway from this experience was that, even if putting on or removing all of one's outer gear is not a part of the daily experience, it is still possible to make the basic management of clothing a thoughtful and intentional part of the program. Ultimately, learning how to put on mittens is just as interesting and worthwhile to the children as whatever activity is on the lesson plan. We encourage teachers and parents not to rush through this part of the day to get to the "fun" stuff but to stick with the process, no matter how long it takes.

PARTNERING WITH *Nature* IN EARLY CHILDHOOD EDUCATION

INSPIRING CHILDREN TO HIKE IN UNCOMFORTABLE WEATHER WHEN THEY FEEL TIRED, HUNGRY, COLD, OR SAD

When children are tired, hungry, homesick, or in the process of getting sick (at which point they should *not* be at preschool), going on a nature hike may not be one of their preferred activities. This can be especially true when the weather is wet and chilly. Some children have a difficult time adjusting to the change of season and the need to wear heavier layers. Others may wake up in a contrary mood. Perhaps the child has not yet learned how to be comfortable outdoors. Perhaps the child is bored or has been awake since 5 a.m. Perhaps an older sibling has the day off and is going to spend fun time one-on-one with a parent. There are several reasons why a child may not be in the mood to come to school, let alone go hiking. Add to that a dismal-looking, cold, damp day, and the child may look upon the approaching activities with dread.

Some children overcome their reluctance through time and gentle persuasion. A fellow classmate may extend the hand of friendship, and suddenly all woe is forgotten. Sometimes, the teachers can push the child a little beyond their comfort zone with the hope that they will eventually cheer up. Sometimes, a child just needs a rest. It takes time to get to know each child and to determine what works and what doesn't.

One year, we had a child who simply ran out of gas while hiking. She would indicate her exhaustion by lying down in the middle of the trail. We developed a game in which we would pretend to wind a giant spring in her back, as though she were a wind-up toy. Once wound-up, she would find the energy she needed to continue walking. This became a silly but effective way for her to keep going while creating a nice little bond between child and teacher. In fact, reassurance of that bond may have been the true motivation she needed.

We have several hiking games we play to encourage children up to the top of steep hills. These include stop-and-go games; games in which we fly, hop, race, or crawl; and games in which the children pretend to be mice or rabbits, freezing in place whenever the hawk (their teacher) turns around unexpectedly. They enjoy the games so much that they often forget they are walking uphill.

We frequently sing songs as we hike, making up silly lyrics as we go. We are also thoughtful about our hikes, increasing our stamina over time. We would never think of leading a two-hour endurance hike with three-year-olds during the first month of school!

INSPIRING CHILDREN TO HIKE WHEN THE ADULT FEELS COLD, TIRED, AND HUNGRY

Sometimes, it is not the students who are tired, cold, or run down. Teachers will often push themselves into states of discomfort and even sickness for their students. This may mean coming to school feeling exhausted, heading outside in icy sleet, and trying to be cheerful even when it feels forced. It should be understood that a teacher who is truly sick must stay home. But if teachers stayed home every time they felt tired, there would be no one left to teach! Being a nature-preschool teacher can be a wonderful job, especially on days when the sun is shining, the children are happy, and there are no conflicts or concerns to manage. On days when it is pouring rain or bitterly cold or when the children are testing their boundaries in the myriad ways children do, teachers may require deep wells of effort and energy to remain motivated.

There is no easy fix for a teacher who is not feeling well, but in general, it helps when teachers have a good support system in place. When teaching partners genuinely care about one another, when the atmosphere at the school is kind and nurturing, and when teachers know themselves well enough to have their own self-comforts (music, hot baths, close friends, pets, spouses, family), normal life stressors can lessen. It also helps when teachers have a genuine love of children and nature and a good sense of humor, as this can keep them laughing even when they feel like crying.

PARTNERING WITH *Nature* IN EARLY CHILDHOOD EDUCATION

All teachers will experience bad days. Balance the need to vent frustration with reminders about what drew us to the profession. People who do not want to work with young children should not teach in a preschool. People who do not want to go outside in damp weather should not teach outdoors. People who genuinely enjoy both can give themselves a break now and then by remembering that if we are willing to change the plan when the children are cold, tired, or just plain miserable, we can also do the same for ourselves.

Make hot chocolate. Light a campfire. Set up a heater inside a shelter, and gather around it with blankets and books. While it is not a great idea to complain excessively in front of the children, there is also nothing wrong with letting them know that you feel tired and that looking up at the fluttering leaves or sitting by the pond might help. This can prompt wonderful conversations about how adults and children both get tired and cranky. It can help promote empathy. It can also help create a teachable moment about the different ways we take care of ourselves. Other ways to quietly but effectively support teachers include the following:

- Providing them with a reasonable stipend to purchase quality outdoor gear
- Providing a catered lunch or even take-out on occasion
- Creating a wish list for teachers that parents and others can contribute to (This can be a monetary fund or a list of teaching supplies or preferred shops from which parents can purchase gift cards.)
- Providing field trips, seminars, and social outings that encourage community building and professional development

If possible, keep the following on hand for communal use:

- Ibuprofen and migraine medication
- Cough drops
- Benadryl
- Feminine-hygiene products
- Packets of Emergen-C
- Hand and foot warmers
- Extra rain pants and boots in various adult sizes
- Hand lotion
- Sting wipes

CHAPTER EIGHT: CHALLENGES AND INSPIRATION

- A hair dryer
- Electric boot and mitten dryers
- Tea, cocoa, and coffee
- A coffee maker
- A hot-water kettle
- Chocolate

Sometimes, the little things can make all the difference.

MAINTAINING RATIOS

Maintaining ratios outdoors can be tricky. Our nature preschool has two teachers in a group of sixteen, or a one-to-eight ratio. Other schools may have eighteen in a class with three teachers or one teacher in a class of six. Different states, countries, and programs will have their own approaches. What is important to remember is that what may feel comfortable in an indoor classroom can sometimes feel inadequate outside. While a one-to-eight ratio is fine for our play spaces, a trip to the top of our sixty-foot tower often warrants an additional adult.

There are any number of emergencies that could require a teacher to step away, leaving the group out of ratio. What if a child needs to go to the bathroom? What if there is a medical concern? How do we maintain ratios and still attend to the sudden and unexpected needs of one or two children at a time? The answer will vary. We depend heavily on volunteers, and we have several volunteers who are retired teachers. We often have parents who volunteer for a day and teachers with office hours who may assist with a particular group if we are hiking to a more challenging spot. Having additional adults does a lot to keep everyone safe.

At the same time, it is important to remember that under licensing guidelines, most of these adult volunteers will not be counted toward ratio without additional training. We make a point of providing

this training (which includes fingerprinting), but it is not an easy process and requires a significant commitment on the volunteer's part. During our first COVID-19 year, we had a grand total of two volunteers in our entire preschool, and yet somehow, we got by. The fact is, when you have to meet ratios, teachers will do what needs to be done. It may not always be ideal bringing six to eight children to the bathroom at once, but sometimes it is necessary.

A big part of managing ratios is knowing what to do in an emergency. We carry first-aid kits with us, so that if a child needs a bandage for a small cut out on the trail, it can be given immediately. We also carry walkie-talkies so that, in a more serious situation, any adult from the building can be summoned at once. Finally, we arrange our teaching schedules so that there is always a member of our preschool staff with "office hours" who is available to jump in and help if needed. Having additional staff with enough nonteaching hours per week goes a long way to support mandated ratios.

DEALING WITH THE SIDE EFFECTS OF JOYFUL NATURE PLAY

The messy side effects of nature play may roll off the backs of more experienced teachers, but new teachers, and certainly parents, can find it overwhelming. We are referring to the wet socks, sopping mittens, and scattered boots strewn across hallways and outdoor classrooms. We are referring to the puddles and the salt residue and to the piles of sand poured out of boots following a trip to the beach. Such moments are integral to our daily experiences, yet they seldom make the marketing photos.

Over the years, we have perfected a variety of ways to manage (but not minimize) the aftereffects of joyful nature play. We block off the carpeted areas of our classroom with chairs as a gentle reminder to families not to walk with wet and muddy boots across the rugs on which we sit. We teach children how to hang their gear on their hooks, allowing coats and pants to drip dry. We mop down the hallways between classes when necessary. We encourage families to come to school with large, waterproof bags, or we sell them as part of our fundraisers or even give them away. We keep hundreds of extra socks on hand. We may carry extra towels in our backpacks. We have even lined up sixteen children in a long row outdoors and hosed them off, car-wash style, during a particularly spectacular mud season.

But more important than any of this is the fact that we communicate to parents regularly how mud and water play nurtures the cognitive, physical, and spiritual health of their children. We remind parents that childhood is fleeting and that sending them home messy means we've done our job. In other words, we do our best to make the accompanying chaos feel like a gift rather than a burden. Mess is in the eye of the beholder.

CHAPTER EIGHT: CHALLENGES AND INSPIRATION

LAUNDRY TIPS

- Try not to wash outdoor gear, especially rain gear, too often, as machine washing can make the waterproofing less effective.

- Drip-dry soggy clothing and take a brush to the mud once the clothing is fully dry. (A horse brush or scouring brush works well.)

- If outer gear requires deeper cleaning, soak it in a tub of tepid water, or wash it on a gentle cycle using a plant-based detergent. Rinse and, if possible, let it drip dry.

- Consider investing in a boot or mitten dryer to thoroughly dry the insides of boots and mittens following wet and slushy weather.

BATHROOM NEEDS

Toileting in a nature-based setting is one topic that people outside our field may consider briefly but that those within the field often discuss at length whenever we convene. While our stories are often lighthearted, it is also true that bathroom issues take up quite a lot of our time and attention, especially during the initial weeks of school. We often find ourselves outdoors, far from any kind of bathroom, with young children who are not yet used to thinking ahead. We go to school on very cold days, and the children may be dressed in multiple layers. Taking care of bathroom needs is more than an amusing anecdote. It is a central part of our day.

Unfortunately, there are not a lot of solutions to emergency bathroom needs beyond having an outdoor potty or basic plans and preparations. Sometimes this means knowing the children's toileting habits better than they do themselves. If the same child has to use the toilet twenty minutes after lunch every day, it is easier to be proactive and make sure that child is near a bathroom twenty minutes after lunch every day. Some children are predictable in this way. Some are not.

Our policy is that, because we spend most of our time outdoors, children must visit the bathroom just before nature school starts. This decreases but does not entirely eliminate the need for potty breaks outside. Some preschools are licensed to change diapers, which means they may have different approaches to emergency bathroom concerns. Ours is not, which means children must be potty-trained before attending our program.

Rarely have we used the surrounding trees or bushes to conceal a child who simply cannot wait. We share our center with bird watchers, painters, and visiting school groups, among others. We do not wish to detract from their experiences by treating the trails as our personal outhouse. Nor do we wish to convey the message to newly toilet-trained children that the trails and grounds are there for their toileting needs whenever they wish. However, we will admit to taking advantage of the great outdoors when there were no other options.

Other outdoor bathroom ideas we have seen in action include establishing an outdoor composting toilet (either building a permanent one or creating a portable version that can be moved from place to place); renting seasonal portable toilets; or creating a designated "pee tree" so that there is one agreed-upon outdoor area where it may be acceptable to urinate.

We find that the best approach to bathroom needs is to keep it understated. We do our best to build in toilet breaks before emergencies arise. We also reiterate to parents and caregivers the importance of bathroom visits before school starts. But when prevention isn't possible, we encourage teachers to minimize the situation to the best of their ability, to escort the child inside when there are enough adults to maintain ratios, and to treat the entire situation with as little fuss as possible. On colder days, a visit to the indoor bathroom can be paired with an indoor story or activity, thus creating some much-needed warm-up time. Calling on extra teachers or staff with available office hours to assist with bathroom visits is also a tremendous help. We do our best to keep toileting low-key. If we treat it like a disruption, children may not wish to tell us when they need to go. If we make it too exciting, they may want to go often, even if they don't need to. Keeping it matter-of-fact and perhaps even a little dull is the goal.

CALMING CHILDREN WHO ARE UNHAPPY, FEARFUL, OR STRUGGLING IN NATURE

Not every child feels at home in nature. For many children, preschool may be their first experience away from home. Being in an unfamiliar group surrounded by an unfamiliar landscape can be a frightening experience. Add to that an outdoor landscape, and some children grow quite overwhelmed.

Although we would like to believe that nature is soothing, for some, at least initially, the absence of four walls can be stressful. Some children may find the sensory overload of the outdoors particularly difficult to process. Other children, who may have adapted perfectly well to preschool when temperatures were seventy degrees, may suddenly feel very different when they are bundled into multiple layers and sent outside in the wind and rain.

Although we find that most children grow to love being in nature, we must not ignore their initial fears. Teachers need to spend time with the children, getting to know what works best for each. There is no such thing as a single approach that will calm the fears of every child. There are, however, several things teachers can do at the start of the year to help children overcome their discomfort.

- Invite children to visit the preschool before the first day of school to let them get to know the outdoor spaces. We know of parents who brought their children in a few weeks before school solely to use and familiarize themselves with the bathrooms. This is an excellent idea, but we also suggest going outside and getting to know the mud kitchen.

- Invite families to a weekend hike at the start of every school year. This allows the entire family to enjoy the outdoor spaces together.

- Do not rush to get the class out on the trails before they are ready. Spend time getting to know one or two spots, and allow the children to build up a comfort level in nature and with each other before pushing them further.

- Make transitions a focus at the start of the year. Many children struggle with these, not just the children who are fearful. By emphasizing the transition times, the children have time to practice them rather than seeing them as disruptions. What do we mean by emphasizing transitions? We mean slowing down so that putting materials away, handwashing, and standing in line become deliberate, mindful parts of the day rather than segues between events. Putting this into a nature-based context, this means we try not to focus on having destinations at the beginning of the year. The focus is on experiencing the hike.

- Provide comforting and cozy materials, especially familiar books and beloved toys, to children who are new to nature. We know that some outdoor educators are not necessarily fans of bringing indoor objects outside. But we have found that stuffed animals and baby dolls will often provide wonderful security for anxious children and will help give them something familiar to hold onto while they adjust.

- Be patient. We have never yet had a child at our preschool who did not eventually overcome their fear of nature, animals, or going to school.

INAPPROPRIATE BEHAVIOR IN NATURE

As we have established, on days when the weather is glorious, when the children are happy and everyone is having fun, being a nature-preschool teacher is one of the best jobs in the world. But when a child refuses to follow the rules, acts in an aggressive manner, or runs away from the group, being a nature-preschool teacher can be highly stressful. It's one thing if a child slips out of the classroom and runs along an interior hallway. It's another if that "hallway" is a slippery boardwalk over a pond. Certain inappropriate behaviors we might encounter outdoors are tied directly to nature: stepping on ants, chasing turkeys, or swinging sticks in an unsafe way. Other behavior issues could exist in any early childhood classroom but feel especially challenging in a nature-based setting.

It is always upsetting, for example, when one child willfully hurts another. This is true whether the program is nature-based or not. In a more traditional setting, this kind of behavior might be handled by sending an aggressive child to the director's office or by giving the child a time-out until they are back in control. But how do you remove an aggressive child from your outdoor space, even temporarily, when you are standing on the edge of Lake Michigan a good twenty minutes away from the building? How do you keep an eye on every child at once when you have to stand guard beside a tree that a group of children want to climb?

Thankfully, serious injuries are extremely rare in a nature-based classroom. This is in part because we are always watching, engaged, and alert to our surroundings. Interestingly, we have also found that our gear protects us from more than the weather: the addition of mittens, rain boots, and so on also protect children from cuts and scrapes. Having said this, we cannot take the relatively peaceful classroom that nature provides for granted. It is impossible to manage inappropriate behaviors by ignoring them. Part of self-regulation is learning how to behave in nature. This includes being respectful of all living things. It means not throwing rocks at paper-wasp nests or intentionally peeling bark from live trees. It means we may sometimes have to cancel a hike or a nature activity if the children are struggling with behavior expectations. It may feel as though we're tossing our curriculum aside because we need to talk about basic school rules. But that is not actually the case; we're just taking our curriculum in a different direction for now.

Learning to care for other living things helps to develop a child's more nurturing characteristics. Teachers can encourage this in their daily actions. For example, they may rescue a toad from a half-frozen pond or an earthworm from a deep puddle. They may plant a tree or grow a garden. There are many ways to make kindness and empathy a daily part of the nature curriculum.

In chapter 2, we discuss how a well-designed classroom can support a constructive, cooperative atmosphere. The same can be said for the outdoor space. If a child is fearful in nature or does not understand how to play appropriately in it, having a variety of options can help. Create a safe, quiet area with

CHAPTER EIGHT: CHALLENGES AND INSPIRATION

blankets, puppets, and books. Have an area with water, which soothes. Have an area where children can run. Creating inviting spaces can mitigate negative behaviors, especially when children are genuinely excited and delighted by their environment.

One question that comes up year after year is how to manage stick play. It is not hard to convince educators of the benefits of playing with sticks. Sticks can become fishing rods, digging tools, fairy homes, forts, and so on. However, it is no fun being in charge of children who are waving long sticks around one another's faces or pointing sticks perilously close to their eyes. The simplest solution would be to announce, "No stick play," and leave it at that. But the result is a lost opportunity for imaginative and enriching play. Therefore, we believe in setting careful boundaries around stick play. For some classes, this may mean guidelines such as the following:

- One end of the stick needs to remain on the ground at all times.

- Sticks may not be taller than the child.

- Sticks may not come to our outdoor circle time.

- Sticks may need to be shaved down if they have thorns or sharp points.

However, these are general guidelines. They do not necessarily apply to every class. Our older classes, for example, may have shown themselves to have the motor skills needed to keep their sticks in control. They may benefit from the challenge of maneuvering long sticks and branches, especially if we know they can do this without injury to themselves or others. They may also suggest on their own that a few sharp branches or edges be removed to make the stick safer.

We apply the same rules to stick play that we apply to rock play, sand play, and water play: We model how to do so safely. We discuss what is and isn't appropriate. We help children understand the best way to handle these materials in a way that is safe and respectful of others. We also reserve the right to halt the play if we feel the children are not playing appropriately. But our goal is always to earn the play back.

A note about pretend guns in a nature-based environment: This is an issue that comes up year after year, particularly during stick play. Children often pick up small sticks and turn them into make-believe guns. They happily pretend to shoot one another, shouting things like, "You're dead!" However, in the context of the wider world, this kind of play is no longer shrugged away by teachers or parents. Some people are deeply concerned by gunplay, even as others explain that this is a normal part of childhood expression and we should not read too much into it. We also understand that some children are raised in families that hunt, which means they are familiar with guns and do not necessarily see them as weapons.

At our program, we have determined that gunplay, while not necessarily intentionally harmful, does often result in hurt feelings. It can also create anxiety, especially for some children. While we do not criticize the child who may wish to engage in imaginary gunplay, we do redirect the play toward something that is not so frightening to many. We explain that as part of a nature sanctuary, there are no guns allowed at our school. There is a "no weapons" sign posted at the entrance. No hunting is allowed, which means the animals are protected. We request that the child find an alternative: Can their stick become a magic wand or a firehose? We understand that other programs may have their own policies about imaginary gunplay. This is a decision that each program must make. Having the discussion is important.

THE LANDSCAPE

One of the biggest challenges that programs face when they take children outdoors is finding the appropriate space. Nature is not evenly divided across communities, a subject we address in more detail later in this chapter. For now, we need to acknowledge that in some neighborhoods taking children outdoors means making the most of asphalt pavements or thin strips of grass beside plastic playgrounds. You may have to share your local parks with members of the public, affecting your activities and adding an element of uncertainty. In other cases, the closest available land may be undeveloped and perhaps covered in thorns or litter. Even if the landscape is inviting, trees can still topple, bees can still sting, and uneven terrain can cause twisted ankles. While these hindrances can feel overwhelming, most of the risks and potential dangers associated with the landscape can be managed with caution and common sense.

When we are near water, we make sure there are enough adults to keep watch over the proceedings, that the children are walking or sitting still, and that whenever possible they either crouch down near the shallow edge or lie down (if there is a deck) on their stomachs. We allow children to handle rocks but do not allow them to hurl rocks willy-nilly when we are gathered in groups. Teachers get down at a child's eye level and read the landscape from

their perspective, making sure there are no tripping hazards or sharp branches poking out at the height of a child.

It takes awareness, foresight, and constant vigilance, but managing a challenging landscape can be done. Nature is always changing, and not only will seasonal adjustments, such as adding an outdoor fire pit in cold weather or laying down extra wood chips in the muddy season, have to be made, but outdoor natural play space will look different every few years. Materials decay. Branches break. Water diverts. We look back on photographs of our first outdoor classroom from twenty years ago and can barely recognize it.

Our spaces may flood when the snow melts, filling up with water and mud. They may turn into ice rinks when the temperature drops, requiring a new way of walking. We have had trees come down, fences replaced, and slides break, and once we had an overly curious raccoon wander over while we were sitting in our gathering circle, which was concerning to see at 9 o'clock in the morning. These incidents, however, are not reasons to stay indoors. Wildlife can be livetrapped and relocated to more remote spots. Fallen trees can be turned into outdoor climbing structures. Challenges can actually be fun, resulting in new designs and structures every couple of years.

We should also consider the skills that children develop when they learn how to study the surrounding landscape. Scanning the sky for storms, interpreting winter tracks in the snow, listening for the sound of cracking ice while venturing onto a frozen pond—these are highly useful abilities that involve prediction, evaluating evidence, and deduction. Consider the child's growing vestibular sense in learning to balance on uneven terrain. Consider their ability to make intelligent decisions, such as whether or not to set foot on a partially frozen pond, and how this translates into common sense and personal risk assessment.

Yes, if you share your nature-school grounds with venomous snakes, stinging insects, poisonous mushrooms, or rushing water, you must be mindful. We embrace risk management. We do not put ourselves in deliberate danger. No matter the landscape or climate, it is imperative that the adults leading the program are familiar with the trails and paths. They should know where to go and how to return. They should know what areas to avoid. They should walk the land before the children and know how to get to shelter if necessary. They should have a sense of how long it may take to move from point A to point B, not just at an adult pace but also with a group of slow-moving three-year-olds. It will likely be necessary to have systems in place and to work with a local parks department, a facilities team, or perhaps a private landowner to make decisions and to address concerns regarding the upkeep and management of the land.

SITE ASSESSMENTS

We strongly recommend that programs conduct annual or even biannual site assessments. This includes walking through every space to check for overall safety and making proactive decisions about decaying structures. Test the trees in the outdoor classrooms by literally pushing on the trunks. If they do not feel firmly rooted in the ground, they may need to come out before they fall over. Make sure

SUGGESTIONS FOR MANAGING THE LAND SAFELY AND EFFECTIVELY

- Be proactive. Walk the trails in advance.

- Get to know the flora and fauna.

- Pay attention to tripping hazards, slippery surfaces, bridges with loose boards, fences that children may wish to climb, sudden inclines, gravel, mud, open water, and so on.

- Conduct a formal site assessment at least once a year.

- Determine which areas may need to be secured. Should you block access to certain spots? build a fence? Fasten a gate?

- Is there a steeply leaning tree about to come down?

- If a child investigates an unexplored space, such as a newly formed ice ledge or a rocky ravine, is it possible for that child to climb back out?

- Determine which areas should remain untouched and how you can best navigate and adjust your own teaching methods to remain safe in these unaltered spaces.

- Establish procedures for managing fallen trees, sinkholes, stinging insects, poisonous plants, wild animals, and so on. Sometimes, you may call on a land manager to assist you. In other cases, you may need to teach the children how to safely and comfortably share their school with hornets, snakes, and coyotes.

- Accept that change is inevitable. You can mourn the loss of beloved trees, bid farewell to old paths and trails, and reminisce about shorelines and beaches that have been reshaped or even lost over time. But you cannot keep nature still. Embrace your changing classroom.

there are fall zones around climbing boulders, tree houses, and raised platforms. Make sure gates have latches. Do your outdoor classrooms have more than one way in and one way out? This may not be mandatory, but there may be a benefit to having two gates if one is suddenly inaccessible.

Look up. Tree branches often break in storms but remain in trees, balancing precariously until a strong wind knocks them down. We have had members of our facilities teams outside with long rope lassos pulling broken limbs out of trees so they don't come crashing down on the children.

Look down. Are there wasp nests under your slides or beneath eaves and bridges? Do you have steep hills in your outdoor spaces? Do you have wooden boardwalks? How do you safely navigate these when they are covered in snow, water, or ice?

Document your plans to address any safety issues you find, and then follow through. Having written documentation of every change you make to your outdoor spaces may not seem necessary in the moment but will be invaluable in the years to come. You will be able to understand which items need constant care and upkeep and which can be left alone. You will be able to create a seasonal maintenance plan. Most important, you will be able to guide children into nature knowing you have done everything possible to ensure a hazard-free environment.

Over the years, we have seen trails close, pathways change, and beloved spots become inaccessible. We have seen new ponds dug, found new trees to climb, and discovered new adventure spots. There is a constant balance between adapting the land to one's program and adapting one's program to the land.

PREPARING FOR POTENTIAL EMERGENCIES

Safety is of paramount concern to anyone who works in early childhood. It takes on a completely new dimension when the program is based outdoors. We have already addressed ways to hike safely, to assess the landscape, and to encourage risk while eliminating hazards. What we have not addressed are the extreme emergencies, those that require additional training or a call to emergency services. Obviously, when an emergency occurs in an outdoor environment, one of the biggest concerns is location. How does an ambulance get to us when we're in the middle of the woods? What if a child ingests a poisonous plant? What if a teacher is stung by a wasp and has an allergic reaction?

ALLERGIES AND EPINEPHRINE

Over the years, we have seen the number of severe allergies rise dramatically, particularly those related to wasp stings, tree nuts, peanuts and other legumes, and dairy. We have made some of our classrooms dairy-free in response, and our entire school has been nut-free for years. But we still encounter acorns, walnuts, and hickory nuts on the trails. Occasionally, a family may show up with granola bars or homemade treats without realizing they contain restricted ingredients. We do our best to control the

risk of exposure to allergens by posting "nut-free" signs, but there is little we can do to control the wasp population.

As more children began entering our program with their own prescribed epinephrine injectors, we decided we needed more in-depth training. We contacted a local hospital and arranged, at no charge, for formal training for our staff. We learned how to keep the injectors working outdoors in extreme weather conditions. Most epinephrine injectors become far less effective when stored in cold temperatures. We now keep ours in insulated carrying cases. We learned to recognize the signs of anaphylactic shock. We learned what laws are in place to protect us should we need to administer an emergency shot. We have had honest conversations with parents about how severe their child's allergy may be. As diligent as we are, we cannot promise that no child will ever be stung by a bee, rub up against poison ivy, or accidentally pluck a black walnut from the ground.

CHAPTER EIGHT: CHALLENGES AND INSPIRATION

In recent years, we have obtained our own preschool-prescribed epinephrine injectors. We encourage other programs to do this as well, if possible. It is important to first familiarize yourself with your state laws and licensing requirements regarding prescription medications in schools and child-care centers. In many cases, medication prescribed to an organization, rather than to an individual, can only be dispensed if there is a licensed medical professional on site or if the rest of the staff undergoes special training. Legal guardians must agree (in writing) that in case of life-threatening anaphylaxis, the school may use its own epinephrine injector on their child. Unfortunately, these injectors also come with a hefty price tag. We have had to specially budget for ours, and that has meant spending less in other areas. For some, the expense may simply be too high. However, having a program-prescribed epinephrine injector that can be used on any child or teacher in an emergency can literally be a lifesaver, buying you much-needed time while paramedics are on the way. It is our hope that acquiring these injectors for early childhood programs will become less expensive and far easier over time.

DANGEROUS INTRUDERS AND MISSING CHILDREN

It is a sad and terrible reality that many, if not all, schools must now consider the possibility that a dangerous intruder could enter their premises intending to do harm. Although our nature-based setting allows us to spread out in spaces where, statistically, we are less likely to be targeted, we would be naive and even reckless if we assumed all nature-based programs are automatically safe from the dangers of the wider world. At our school, we have conducted walk-through tours with the local chief of police, examining our teaching spaces both indoors and out.

We asked the police chief to help us address a long list of terrible questions: Where is the best place to reconvene away from the building? What happens if we have to run outside in the winter without coats? As frightening as it was to have to state these questions aloud, working through the answers was remarkably empowering.

Note: We recognize that we are not necessarily providing clear-cut answers to these questions here, and that is deliberate. One thing we learned was that it actually works against a program to have a single plan or to even practice an emergency drill without allowing for flexibility. You don't want to limit yourself to one emergency-response plan. Circumstances are unique and can change so quickly that trying to learn a single set of procedures hinders making the best possible choice in the moment.

Having a plan for an armed intruder in some ways is no different from having a plan in case of a fire, flood, tornado, hurricane, or any other natural disaster. It is, however, far more disturbing on an emotional level. It is also, statistically speaking, less likely. What is far more likely is having a child go missing outdoors. We once had a potential teacher cut an interview short when we asked her how she might respond if she counted the children in her group and found that someone wasn't there. She was so alarmed by the question that she decided an outdoor program was not for her.

Being unable to locate a child outdoors is truly terrifying for teachers. The best way to manage this is to prevent it from happening. This is why having set procedures for hiking, regularly counting the children in the group, and carrying communication devices is important. However, in the slim chance that a child suddenly cannot be found, there are a few ways to respond. First, alert your team. Other adults need to be summoned at once. If possible, you will need to determine whether the child has wandered away or has possibly been abducted. The police response to these two scenarios will be different. If there is any reason to believe a child was abducted, and if you teach in a place where it is possible to barricade an exit, then closing the gates and sealing off the grounds is one of the first things that needs to happen. This can be done even as someone else is calling 911.

In all the years our preschool has been open, we have never had a child abducted or even been at risk of this happening. However, children do suddenly step behind trees, duck behind bushes, or opt to hide in our outdoor play spaces. It is indeed possible not to know *exactly* where they are at all times, however briefly, and in those moments, ten seconds can feel like ten minutes.

Make counting heads a regular part of your day. Make sure your group remains together as you hike, or if you prefer to spread out, make certain each splintered group has an adult to oversee it. Stop at crosswalks, parking lots, and forks in the trail, and wait for those at the end to catch up. Teachers should check in with each other: "I've got eight children with me. How about you?"

One reason we do not always rush to get on the trails during the initial weeks of school is because if we have a group full of runners, it may not be safe to take them hiking until they have mastered self-regulation. If a child believes it is fun to run off on the trail, they are not ready to hike. They may not fully understand the dangers of racing off toward a steep ravine or dashing into the forest. For them, this is a game. But going to school outside differs from going to school in a building. Running off is a serious issue and needs to be treated as such.

Just as we teach children to treat plants and animals with respect, we also teach them to be cautious. Wild turkeys may take umbrage if we try to chase them. Many plants are highly toxic. We do not want children to head into nature trembling in fear, but we do want them to understand that nature requires us to tread lightly and to treat it as an equal and that existing in harmony with nature means being careful. We are grateful that true emergencies are unlikely in a nature-based classroom, but it is not because they could never happen. It is because a thoughtful, intentional staff and curriculum also considers the possible worst-case scenarios and does everything it can to prevent them.

THE CHALLENGE OF A GLOBAL PANDEMIC: NEW INSPIRATIONS

In the spring of 2020, our program, like so many across North America, closed its doors from March through May in response to the COVID-19 pandemic. When we reopened our program in June, learning to manage a highly contagious illness while also resuming our regular programming presented new and previously unforeseen challenges.

As a nature-based program, we were uniquely situated to manage the COVID-19 pandemic. We had the infrastructure in place that easily allowed us to take children outside, which also enabled us to convert our program into a 100-percent outdoor preschool. Some solutions were mandated for us:

wear facemasks, be outside as much as possible, and quarantine classes when exposures occur. Other challenges had solutions, but we still had to figure out the logistics for ourselves: How do we install outdoor sinks with running water in each of our outdoor play spaces? How do we heat our outdoor classrooms when we don't feel safe going indoors in the winter? Is it safe to serve snacks? What about hot drinks?

The biggest challenge, it turned out, was managing our own emotions. Some teachers felt the risk of returning to teach was too great, which meant their fears needed to be addressed or we might lose very valuable staff. Some parents felt that the fear was overrated and that we should be running programs with no change, which included letting the children play indoors. Some wanted reassurances that everything would be back to normal by fall, by winter, or by the following spring.

One of the biggest struggles with COVID-19 was that it was an unknown entity. Nobody could predict how bad it would be, how long it would last, or when we would get it under control. We were trying to create a plan of action in the face of the unknown. What we learned throughout those first twelve months was that the best way to counter fear, stress, anger, and anxiety was to get excited. We had to acknowledge that we were in a hard situation, but then we had to focus on new opportunities that the situation afforded. Each loss could bring with it some new gain, as long as we opened our hearts to it.

Teachers are at their best when they are passionate about an idea. Several of our teachers had long wanted us to adopt a forest kindergarten model, and in 2020, we did just that. We also replaced our annual harvest soup parties with an outdoor wood-burning stove that we used to make fry bread, dandelion fritters, apple cider, and hot maple tea.

We discovered new children's books, purchased new puppets, and created a new outdoor classroom that featured a beautiful gathering tipi. We exchanged ideas with teachers from other nature-based programs across the United States and Canada. We expanded aspects of the curriculum to include discussions about anti-racism and gender identity, albeit at a preschool level. We learned how to use Zoom to communicate with parents, and while we missed our in-person family activities, using an online platform for parent workshops allowed us to reach about 90 percent of our parent body. (This was a noticeable improvement over the usual 40 percent when workshops took place in person at night.) We held fewer staff meetings. This sometimes made us feel disconnected, but there was no denying teachers had far more time to get other work accomplished and that they could sometimes leave earlier on a Friday, giving them just a little more downtime during a particularly stressful year.

Every adjustment we made in the name of COVID-19 resulted in a new discovery. Creating new curricula and learning new skills not only took our minds off what we were losing, they also reminded us of our deeper mission. In focusing on what we could do, we nurtured the best in ourselves. In creating a space where others could thrive, our teachers managed to thrive as well.

We learned that as long as the teachers were excited, our school remained exciting. The teachers might take their inspiration from the children, from the land, and from one another. But it was the new ideas and energy that grew from this that truly made the program shine.

MAKING A NATURE PRESCHOOL FOR ALL

If you scroll through the website of almost any private nature preschool in North America, you will see a largely White, middle-class, able-bodied group of children wearing high-quality (i.e., expensive) outdoor gear. However well-intentioned our programs may be, when it comes to diversity, equity, access, and inclusion (DEAI), there are still far too many children left out. In this, the final section of the book, we attempt to address the current shortcomings in the field of nature-based early childhood education. We discuss what is known as the *nature gap* and highlight a small but growing number of programs across the country taking steps to close it.

Perhaps one of the greatest struggles right now in nature-based education is making it available and accessible to a truly diverse population of children and families. How do we ensure that children living in neighborhoods where nature is all but absent, those with specific physical or cognitive disabilities, and those who feel culturally unwelcomed are included? Although it is easy to make the case that nature itself is not exclusive—after all, the natural world cares nothing about ethnicity or income—it is a sad reality that nature-based experiences have become increasingly unequal not just in early childhood but across all of society.

In 2020, the Center for American Progress released a report fittingly entitled "The Nature Gap." The authors report that throughout the United States, people of color are disproportionately more likely to live in areas deprived of nature: "In twenty-six states, Black communities experienced the highest levels of nature deprivation. In sixteen states, Asian communities experienced the most nature deprivation. Hispanic and Latino people experienced the most nature deprivation out of all racial and ethnic groups in eight states. Natural area loss is particularly acute for Hispanic and Latino communities along the U. S.–Mexico border in South Texas, around El Paso, Texas, and in other border communities in New Mexico and Arizona" (Rowland-Shea, Doshi, Edberg, and Fanger, 2020).

This report brings to light three very alarming trends across the nation today. First, that communities of color are three times more likely than White communities to live in areas deprived of nature. Second, that 70 percent of low-income communities throughout the United States live in areas deprived of nature. Third, that low-income communities of color are more likely to live in areas that have experienced nature destruction (Rowland-Shea, Doshi, Edberg, and Fanger, 2020).

Let us now look at another report. In 2022, Dale Farran, a research professor in early childhood education at Vanderbilt University, published the findings of a study on early development competencies that took more than a decade to complete. In the study, Farran and her team compared the long-term academic outcomes of children from lower-income families enrolled in public pre-K programs with those of children of similar ages and backgrounds not enrolled in these programs. The pre-K programs were taught by licensed teachers and featured an academically focused approach to instruction that included worksheets, numeracy, and letter tracing.

The outcomes were surprising to many. While the children in the pre-K programs experienced an earlier academic push and initially outscored their peers on standardized tests, by the third grade they were performing worse than their peers who had not attended public pre-K, and by sixth grade, they were performing *significantly worse* than their counterparts. These same children were also more likely to experience behavior-related school suspensions by sixth grade. In other words, according to Farran, academic-oriented pre-K programs developed with the goal of improving student performance in reality have a statistically *negative* effect (Farran, 2022).

In searching for an explanation, Farran realized that, she, like many others, had approached the study with preconceived ideas about what actually constitutes a high-quality early childhood program. As she explained in an interview with Anya Kamenetz on National Public Radio, "One of the biases that I hadn't examined in myself is the idea that poor children need a different sort of preparation from children of higher-income families" (Kamenetz, 2022). Higher-income families, she found, do not tend to opt for didactic, academic programs when selecting preschools for their children. Instead, they choose play-based programs with plenty of art, movement, and access to nature (Kamenetz, 2022).

While one study cannot be said to be definitive, Farran's work is perhaps one of the catalysts we need to rethink our approach to equity in early childhood education. If we know that children from affluent families are thriving in play-based, nature-infused classrooms, then surely the answer is not to sit children from lower-income families down in front of worksheets. They need the same sorts of playful, engaging experiences as those from higher-income groups.

So how do we go about making our own programs more accessible and inclusive to all? We know that the majority of nature-based early childhood programs in North America, at least at the time of this writing, depend heavily on private tuition (Sneideman, 2013). Decreasing tuition costs could certainly make many programs more affordable; however, without tuition, many of these

programs would cease to exist. In most cases, this would also mean paying early childhood teachers—who are already underpaid—an even *lower* wage. We have mentioned throughout this book the importance of outdoor gear. Good-quality outdoor gear is expensive, and while there are grants that will allow programs to purchase outdoor clothing, even the best outdoor gear may not always keep the clothes underneath spotlessly clean or dry. For some families, this is significant. Not everyone owns or has ready access to a washer and dryer.

Even if every nature-based early childhood program could feasibly lower tuition, supply outdoor gear, and take care of laundry needs, these actions would still not be enough by themselves to level the playing field. Scholarships, passes, free busing, and other measures may help address certain issues of access. However, as long as nature and nature-based schools are perceived as the domain of upper- and middle-class White America, these spaces will never feel truly welcoming to those who live outside that demographic.

As Rowland-Shea, Doshi, Edberg, and Fanger so clearly demonstrate, many children from lower-income families today live in nature-deprived areas. They are unfamiliar with wilderness. This can make them uncomfortable, even anxious, when stepping into areas beyond their own neighborhoods. Added to this is the reality that when people from marginalized groups do venture into parks and preserves, they often do not feel welcomed. There have been many documented instances of people of color treated as trespassers when visiting natural spaces seen as culturally beyond "their own" neighborhoods (Nir, 2020).

CHAPTER EIGHT: CHALLENGES AND INSPIRATION

There is also another factor to consider. A 2019 study by the Economic Policy Institute found that children living in low-income communities are far more likely to have experienced toxic stress than children from affluent communities. *Toxic stress* is a heightened hormonal response to frightening situations, which include income and housing instability. It also has a direct impact on a child's ability to self-regulate and adapt to new and unknown situations (Morsy and Rothstein, 2019). In these situations, it is especially necessary to be willing to adjust activities based on the individual children in your program. By taking time and considering the perspectives and needs of the children before leading them into nature, we can better foster the development of a positive relationship with nature.

Our nature preschool is part of a longstanding partnership with two neighborhood organizations, Malaika Early Learning Center and The Next Door Foundation, which serve mostly Black and Latino families in the city of Milwaukee. Many of the families in these programs live below the federal poverty line. Each year, about 100 children from these two organizations each year visit the nature center multiple times between September and May. The children who attend at age four return for a second year at age five. Over time, they develop a connection and sense of belonging both at the nature center and in nature. Because the program is supported through grants, the families of the participating children pay nothing. One school provides its own bus. The other comes on a bus paid for by an outsider funder.

In addition to these visits to us, at least once a month teachers from our nature preschool visit the Malaika and Next Door centers, bringing with them an assortment of natural artifacts and live teaching animals. This gives the children an opportunity to act as hosts, which also allows the dynamic to shift. Our teachers have the chance to experience the neighborhood, the school setting, and the spaces that the children inhabit on a daily basis. Our teachers are also able to work in partnership more fully with the Next Door and Malaika teachers by visiting them in their classrooms.

Team teaching across these three schools is a core part of this program. Teachers from all three centers work together to ensure that the children are dressed for the elements, that their families understand what these visits entail, and that the children are given time to develop their own relationships with nature. All of this teamwork pays off. Once the children feel comfortable in nature, their curiosity shines. They climb trees, balance on logs, leap into leaves, run, and find endless ways to have fun. Before long, the teachers are leading them farther afield, letting them experience "the beyond" in spots that may include lakes and shorelines, quiet woods, and winding boardwalks around bodies of water. In the end, children are children. Regardless of race or income, we see no difference in how they play in nature, assuming they have been given time to develop a strong sense of place and to build loving bonds of trust with their teachers.

As the voices around DEAI grow stronger and these conversations continue to spread, many nature preschools have begun to redouble their efforts to actively serve children from communities that have traditionally been left out of nature experiences. We highlight a few below, although we recognize that we are leaving out a great many others. The handful that we mention represent a range of approaches. We hope they serve as inspirations and models for everyone hoping to do more.

Tiny Trees Preschool in Seattle (https://tinytrees.org) is an all-outdoor forest school that operates within the county park system. The absence of a physical building allows them to keep tuition costs low. Recent changes in the Washington state licensing laws also mean that outdoor programs like Tiny Trees, which were formerly not allowed to be licensed, are now eligible to become so. This opens the door to government tuition assistance that directly supports low-income families. In 2019, Tiny Trees received funding to develop an anti-racist initiative called re-Defining the Outdoors (rDTO), which seeks to create space for families of color, including immigrants and refugees, in nature-based, outdoor experiences.

Not far from Seattle, in Bellevue, Washington, is the My World Mandarin Nature School (https://myworldedu.com), a 100-percent outdoor, nature-based, Mandarin-language immersion school. Its students are predominantly Asian American. My World is, as far as we know, the only nature-based Mandarin-language preschool in the country.

About a thousand miles south, in the city of Los Angeles, is Aventuras Forest School (https://aventurasforestschool.org), a nature-based Spanish-immersion preschool located in a public park known as Fern Dell. Aventuras features a play-based, emergent curriculum where 90 percent of the spoken language is Spanish.

The Aullwood Nature Center (https://www.audubon.org/conservation/aullwood-nature-center-and-farm-preschool) in Dayton, Ohio, is a member of the National Audubon Society and is the site of a farm-based preschool run by the Miami Valley Child Development Centers (MVCDC). As a Head Start program, there are no tuition fees, and participating children and families have access to a range of Head Start resources. The nature center provides the space, along with visiting farmers and

CHAPTER EIGHT: CHALLENGES AND INSPIRATION

naturalists, while MVCDC hires the Head Start teachers and manages the preschool's day-to-day operations.

There is a growing number of nature-based early childhood programs across the country that have developed partnerships with their local school districts, often using a model that includes one fully certified teacher and one naturalist teaching in conjunction. There are tremendous advantages to nature-based preschools collaborating with their local school districts, including free tuition, assistance with gear, and access to early intervention programs such as speech and language support. Teachers in these programs are often employed by the district, which tends to result in higher salaries. The downside, unfortunately, is that in most cases the curriculum is predetermined and does not take the unique location of the school or its campus into account. Ironically, the need for the curriculum to be consistent across the entire school district often means that a school in a nature-based setting may not necessarily offer a nature-based curriculum. We have seen programs in truly beautiful spaces, spaces that invite ample opportunities for outdoor exploration and play, where the children are kept indoors learning phonics because the curriculum is set by an outside entity. There should not be a choice between offering children an equitable curriculum and providing fair and equitable access to nature. What is needed, we feel, is an entire school district that embraces nature-based education.

This brings us to the Camden/Rockport Elementary School, part of the Five Town Community School District (https://www.fivetowns.net) in Maine. In 2021, the district opened the state's first public, nature-based pre-K program for four-year-olds. The school district has made nature-based experiences and education a priority. There are newly designed outdoor classrooms on all campuses, as well as secondary-level coursework in sustainability and outdoor leadership. Children who attend the district's nature-based preschool at age four now have opportunities to continue experiencing nature-based education, tuition-free, all the way through high school.

There are a number of other exciting programs springing up around the country with the shared goal of making nature experiences more inclusive. While not all are centered on early childhood, they are still worthy of a mention.

Outdoor Afro (https://outdoorafro.com) is a national nonprofit network working in partnership with diverse organizations across the country to connect Black communities to nature while simultaneously training Black people in the field of outdoor leadership. Unearthing Joy (https://unearthingjoytogether.com) provides programs to largely Black, Brown, and Indigenous communities in the Nashville, Tennessee, area with the goal of sparking joy, connection, and pride of ancestry through nature-based experiences.

Back in Milwaukee, Cream City Conservation and Consulting (https://www.creamcityconservation.org/) is an organization that works with environmental groups throughout the state, doing the difficult but necessary work to address internal work cultures, policies, and practices in an effort to encourage inclusivity in the fields of conservation and environmental education. They also work to train and employ the next generation of environmental educators, conservationists, and green industrialists, intentionally pulling from communities that have long been underrepresented in these fields.

It is important to remember that there are other barriers to access and inclusion in nature besides income level, ethnicity, or zip code. Children with physical disabilities are often left out despite the best of intentions. Although Title III of the American with Disabilities Act specifically prohibits child-care centers from excluding children with disabilities, parents often decide that the physical nature of many outdoor schools simply cannot meet the needs of their children.

Thankfully, there is a growing number of nature-based programs not only set up to support children with specific needs but also able to model, train, and instruct others on how to do so as well. We specifically want to acknowledge the wonderful Forest Day Learning program created by Sally Anderson at the New Mexico School for the Deaf (https://www.nmsd.k12.nm.us/), which was the first school in the nation to offer an outdoor-based forest school program for deaf and hard-of-hearing students.

The Starting Early Preschool (https://certified.natureexplore.org/developmental-disabilities-institute/) in Huntington, New York, is an integrated early childhood program that serves children with and without disabilities. In 2015, the school developed an outdoor nature classroom, working with an outdoor-classroom designer in consultation with a special education teacher, education behavior specialist, physical therapist, and occupational therapist, to create a place for children of all abilities.

Of course, not all needs are immediately visible. Some children have cognitive delays or intellectual disabilities. Some children have autism spectrum disorder. Imua Inclusion Preschool (https://imuafamily.org/the-benefits-of-inclusion-preschool/) in Hawaii is a nature-infused early childhood program in which 25 percent of the children have an identified developmental delay. In addition to the school's own outdoor spaces and gardens, they have access to nearby city parks and make outdoor nature excursions an extensive part of their curriculum.

Just a few miles down the road from our preschool is St. Francis Children's Center (https://sfcckids.org/), which employs a staff of professional educators, social workers, therapists, and administrators to meet the needs of more than nine hundred children, including those who are typically developing and those with special needs. St. Francis has recently redesigned its outdoor play areas to be more open ended and nature based, proving that a program doesn't need to be organized specifically around nature to make nature a part of its program.

SO MUCH MORE WORK TO DO

So far, we have highlighted a small number of centers, educators, and community leaders doing what they can to bring more children with a range of backgrounds and experiences into nature. What we want to address now is the other side of this coin: finding new and innovative ways to bring more nature to children, especially in urban communities. Simply stated, children shouldn't have to take a bus or get on a highway to experience nature. It should be possible to step outside and teach children about the trees in their own neighborhoods. If we need to trade pelicans for pigeons, we can make that trade. We can still explore squirrels and insects in cities. We can still explore wildflowers and weeds.

CHAPTER EIGHT: CHALLENGES AND INSPIRATION

In their article "From Puddles to Pigeons: Learning About Nature In Cities," authors Goldstein, Famularo, and Kynn discuss the misperception that cities are devoid of nature and of nature-based learning experiences. "Parents, educators, and other primary caregivers might not realize that a small patch of grass, a single tree, and a walk to the store are opportunities to observe nature, generate questions, and conduct experiments to find answers—all critical science practices. Taking advantage of these opportunities provides children with ways to engage with important environmental science concepts, connect science with the real world, and build their understandings of everyday phenomena, such as why leaves fall from trees, where rain goes in a city, and how city animals find shelter" (Goldstein, Famularo, and Kynn, 2018).

The authors, all researchers at Massachusetts's Education Development Center, describe a series of community science activities they developed through a grant from the National Science Foundation. The activities were designed specifically for families and educators living and working in urban neighborhoods and made use of playgrounds, parks, and neighborhood sidewalks. Topics include water, wind, plants, and animals. The authors note, "[B]eing able to conduct outdoor science activities with little preparation, in a short period of time, and within walking distance of home was highly motivating to parents and educators" (Goldstein, Famularo, and Kynn, 2018).

There need to be more opportunities for children and families in urban communities to explore nature in their immediate neighborhoods. The Urban Ecology Center (https://urbanecologycenter.org/) in Milwaukee excels at this, providing a vast assortment of educational and community science experiences for low-income families of color within their own neighborhoods. While inviting people of all backgrounds and experiences into nature is important, conserving natural spaces in the places where people actually live is equally essential.

Organizations that promote green and healthy curricula often work with schools to redesign indoor and outdoor spaces, providing natural play areas on what was formerly barren asphalt. Milwaukee has seen several urban elementary schools work in partnership with groups such as Green and Healthy Schools to develop internal composting systems, put up hothouses, install new outdoor prairies and rain gardens, and otherwise transform their tot-lots into areas with canopies, plants, and even logs for balancing, jumping, or as a place to hold lessons.

Federal programs such as the U.S. Department of Education Green Ribbon Award provide tools and recognition for schools that develop innovative green infrastructure. State departments of public instruction, in-state universities, and statewide environmental education associations can work together to develop curricula that allow teachers to take children outdoors. Schools can do more to collaborate with cities and counties to explore their local watersheds, care for parks, adopt trees, and plant gardens. It is possible to write grants, solicit donations, establish scholarships, and even contact companies for discounted outdoor equipment and gear.

We celebrate the growing number of organizations that have developed nature-based classrooms and curricula in urban spaces. We celebrate those that have made it part of their mission to include children of all races, ethnicities, and abilities. We celebrate every program that is striving to be more inclusive, as well as those that blend nature-based education with other early childhood disciplines. There is a strong push underway to reshape environmental education, including nature-based early childhood education, into a field that is inclusive of all. It is exciting to see, and even more exciting to participate. While change does not happen overnight, we have seldom seen a group of educators more eager to make their programs more understanding and welcoming than those who work in nature-based education. Spending time in nature can and should be a right for all children. While it requires energy, time, creativity, and financial investment to make our programs stronger and better, as long as we agree it is necessary, doing so becomes possible.

CHAPTER EIGHT: CHALLENGES AND INSPIRATION

- EPILOGUE -

Partnering with Nature

In August 2021, our team of nature preschool teachers sat on a deck overlooking Lake Michigan, discussing the upcoming school year. After an extensive review of licensing policies, COVID-19 safety protocols, and emergency first aid, the conversation landed on our goals for the initial weeks of school. We did not talk about lesson plans, sensory tables, or art and science activities. Rather, we talked about the importance of creating experiences. In thinking back on the previous year, one teacher recalled floating little nature boats in puddles with a group of children. The boats featured tiny clothespin sailors and giant oak-leaf sails. She loved the stories that came from this experience and the layers of play that grew from it over the course of several days. Another teacher shared her experience of playing a gathering drum near the water, while the children accompanied her with wooden shakers. They played music that incorporated the sounds of the waves. They talked about how the drumbeats made them feel. These experiences captured the imagination and honored the children while honoring nature.

The teachers concluded that this, far more than a lesson plan with every box filled in, was how they wanted to start the year. They wanted an outdoor classroom that drew each child in and invited different kinds of play. They wanted to ensure that their hikes and activities were less about literacy and math and more about those rare and fleeting feelings of spiritual connection. Literacy and math would follow, of course, but the children would grow from these deeper experiences.

When pandemic stress and exhaustion seemed to reach an all-time high, we talked about the value of slowing down, of not packing our days too full of transitions, and of embracing the in-between moments. If a child needs ten minutes to find a dry pair of socks and another ten minutes to wiggle them onto wet feet before pulling on a pair of rain boots, could that potentially be just as important—and possibly even more important—than ushering the child over to an activity table?

Remember, nature is not only *what* we teach. Nature is also *how* we teach.

A quality nature-based curriculum is not product driven. It does not measure its worth in how many craft activities or journal pages go home. As long as the days are full of wonder and excitement, as long as we are building trust and creating meaningful experiences, the nature preschool curriculum is doing what it should.

APPENDIX A:
RECOMMENDED BOOKS TO SHARE WITH CHILDREN

Anthony, Joseph. 1997. *The Dandelion Seed*. Nevada City, CA: Dawn Publications.

Appelhof, Mary, and Joanne Olszewski. 2017. *Worms Eat My Garbage: How to Set Up and Maintain a Worm Composting System*. North Adams, MA: Storey Publishing.

Asch, Frank. 2008. *The Earth and I*. New York: Harcourt Brace and Company.

Aston, Diana Hutts. 2015. *A Rock Is Lively*. San Francisco, CA: Chronicle Books.

Bauer, Marion Dane. 2009. *The Longest Night*. New York: Holiday House.

Baylor, Byrd. 1985. *Everybody Needs a Rock*. New York: Aladdin.

Brett, Jan. 2009. *The Mitten*. New York: G. P. Putnam's Sons.

Bunting, Eve. 1991. *Night Tree*. New York: Voyager Books.

Bunting, Eve. 2000. *Flower Garden*. New York: Voyager Books.

Burgess, Matthew. 2021. *Bird Boy.* New York: Alfred A. Knopf.

Carney, Margaret. 1997. *At Grandpa's Sugar Bush*. Toronto, ON: Kids Can Press.

Chamberlin, Mary, and Rich Chamberlin. 2006. *Mama Panya's Pancakes: A Village Tale from Kenya*. Cambridge, MA: Barefoot Books.

Christian, Peggy. 2008. *If You Find a Rock*. Orlando, FL: Clarion Books.

Cooper, Susan. 2019. *The Shortest Day*. Somerville, MA: Candlewick Press.

DiSalvo-Ryan, Dyanne. 2019. *City Green*. New York: HarperCollins.

Edwards, Carolyn McVickar. 2005. *The Return of the Light: Twelve Tales from Around the World for the Winter Solstice*. New York: Marlowe and Company.

Ehlert, Lois. 1987. *Growing Vegetable Soup*. New York: Voyager Books.

Ehlert, Lois. 1988. *Planting a Rainbow*. Orlando, FL: Harcourt.

Ehlert, Lois. 1995. *Leaf Man*. New York: Harcourt.

Fanelli, Sara. 2019. *My Map Book*. New York: HarperCollins.

Fleming, Denise. 2001. *Time to Sleep*. New York: Henry Holt and Company.

Fredericks, Anthony. 2001. *Under One Rock: Slugs, Bugs, and Other Ughs*. Nevada City, CA: Dawn Publications.

Fries, Hannah. 2021. *Thank You, Tree*. North Adams, MA: Storey Publishing.

Gallo, Frank. 2001. *Bird Calls*. Norwalk, CT: Innovative Kids.

George, Lindsay Barrett. 1998. *In the Woods: Who's Been Here?* New York: Greenwillow Books.

Gershator, Phillis. 2008. *Listen, Listen*. Concord, MA: Barefoot Books.

Gianferrari, Maria. 2021. *Be a Tree!* New York: Harry N. Abrams.

Glaser, Linda. 2001. *It's Fall!* Minneapolis, MN: Millbrook Press.

Hoose, Phillip, and Hannah Hoose. 1998. *Hey, Little Ant*. Berkeley, CA: Tricycle Press.

Kelley, Marty. 1998. *Fall Is Not Easy*. Middleton, WI: Zino Press.

Koch, Maryjo. 1999. *Bird, Egg, Feather, Nest*. New York: Smithmark Publishers.

Kudlinski, Kathleen. 2005. *The Sunset Switch*. Minnetonka, MN: NorthWord Books for Young Readers.

Lee, Herbert Wong. 2022. *Who Likes Rain?* New York: Square Fish Books.

Leedy, Loreen. 2003. *Mapping Penny's World.* New York: Henry Holt and Company.

Lemniscates, Carme. 2019. *Birds.* Somerville, MA: Candlewick Press.

Lin, Grace. 2001. *The Ugly Vegetables.* Watertown, MA: Charlesbridge.

Lin, Grace. 2021. *¡Hasta Las Rodillas!/Up to My Knees!* Watertown, MA: Charlesbridge.

Lindstrom, Carole. 2020. *We Are Water Protectors.* New York: Roaring Brook Press.

MacLachlan, Patricia. 2020. *My Friend Earth.* San Francisco, CA: Chronicle Books.

Maillard, Kevin Noble. 2019. *Fry Bread: A Native American Family Story*. New York: Roaring Brook Press.

Messner, Kate. 2014. *Over and Under the Snow*. San Francisco, CA: Chronicle Books.

Messner, Kate. 2017. *Over and Under the Pond*. San Francisco, CA: Chronicle Books.

Messner, Kate, 2017. *Up in the Garden and Down in the Dirt*. San Francisco, CA: Chronicle Books.

Messner, Kate. 2020. *Over and Under the Rainforest*. San Francisco, CA: Chronicle Books.

Messner, Kate. 2021. *Over and Under the Canyon*. San Francisco, CA: Chronicle Books.

Metzger, Steve. 2005. *We're Going on a Leaf Hunt*. New York: Scholastic.

Minor, Wendell. 2015. *Daylight Starlight Wildlife*. New York: Nancy Paulsen Books.

Mullen, Diane C. 2020. *One Little Lot: The 1-2-3s of an Urban Garden*. Watertown, MA: Charlesbridge.

Nail, Jim. 1996. *Whose Tracks Are These? A Clue Book of Familiar Forest Animals*. Lanham, MD: Roberts Rinehart.

Pak, Kenard. 2016. *Goodbye Summer, Hello Autumn*. New York: Henry Holt and Co.

Pasquier, Roger F. 2019. *Birds in Winter: Surviving the Most Challenging Season*. Princeton, NJ: Princeton University Press.

Pfeffer, Wendy. 2016. *A New Beginning: Celebrating the Spring Equinox*. New York: Puffin.

Raymond-Duvernell, Laureanna. 2020. *Under in the Mud*. Waukesha, WI: Orange Hat Publishing.

Repchuk, Caroline. 1997. *The Snow Tree*. New York: Dutton Juvenile.

Ritchie, Scot. 2009. *Follow That Map! A First Book of Mapping Skills*. Toronto, ON: Kids Can Press.

Salas, Laura Purdie. 2015. *A Rock Can Be...* Minneapolis, MN: Millbrook Press.

Sehgal, Surishtha. 2018. *Festival of Colors*. San Diego, CA: Beach Lane Books.

Snyder, Inez. 2005. *Sap to Syrup*. New York: Scholastic.

Sweeney, Joan. 2018. *Me on the Map*. New York: Dragonfly Books.

Thompson, Mya. 2020. *Ruby's Birds*. Ithaca, NY: Cornell Lab Publishing Group.

Tyers, Jenny. 1996. *When It Is Night, When It Is Day*. New York: Houghton Mifflin Harcourt.

Udry, Janice May. 1987. *A Tree Is Nice*. New York: HarperCollins.

Ward, Jennifer. 2014. *Mama Built a Little Nest*. San Diego, CA: Beach Lane Books.

Wilder, Laura Ingalls. 1999. *Sugar Snow*. New York: HarperCollins.

Willems, Mo. 2008. *Are You Ready to Play Outside?* New York: Hyperion Books for Children.

Wilson, Karma. 2002. *Bear Snores On*. New York: Margaret McElderry Books.

Wilson, Karma. 2008. *Bear Wants More*. New York: Little Simon.

Wittstock, Laura Waterman. 1993. *Ininatig's Gift of Sugar: Traditional Native Sugarmaking*. Minneapolis, MN: First Avenue Editions.

Yuly, Toni. 2022. *Some Questions About Trees*. New York: Atheneum Books for Young Readers.

The following is a list of topics included in several series of field guides for children.

- **About Animals Guides for Children** by Cathryn and John Sill: birds, mammals, reptiles, insects, amphibians, fish, arachnids, crustaceans, mollusks, marsupials, rodents, penguins, and raptors
- **About Habitats** series by Cathryn and John Sill: deserts, wetlands, mountains, grasslands, oceans, seashores, tundras, forests, rivers and streams, and polar regions
- **All About** series by Jim Arnosky: alligators, sharks, deer, turkeys, owls, frogs, rattlesnakes, lizards, turkeys, turtles, and manatees
- **National Audubon Society First Field Guides**: birds, reptiles, mammals, insects, trees, wildflowers, weather, rocks and minerals, night sky, amphibians, shells, and fishes
- **Peterson First Guides**: mammals, insects, fishes, birds, caterpillars, urban wildlife, wildflowers, butterflies and moths, reptiles and amphibians, clouds and weather, and trees
- **Take-Along Guides**: birds, nests, and eggs; berries, nuts, and seeds; caterpillars, bugs, and butterflies; frogs, toads, and turtles; planets, moons, and stars; rabbits, squirrels, and chipmunks; rocks, fossils, and arrowheads; seashells, crabs, and sea stars; snakes, salamanders, and lizards; tracks, scat, and signs; trees, leaves, and bark; wildflowers, blooms, and blossoms

APPENDIX B:
ASSESSMENT TOOL FOR A NATURE-BASED EARLY CHILDHOOD CURRICULUM

CLASS: _____

FALL / WINTER / SPRING

SCHOOL YEAR: _____

ENVIRONMENTAL CONNECTION

ASSESSMENT TOOL FOR
A NATURE-BASED EARLY
CHILDHOOD CURRICULUM

Child	Shows little interest in the natural world or in other living things	Takes an interest in the natural world and the living things in it	Shows respect and empathy for the natural world	Cares about the natural world and is motivated to take action to protect it

PARTNERING WITH *Nature* IN EARLY CHILDHOOD EDUCATION

ENVIRONMENTAL LITERACY

ASSESSMENT TOOL FOR
A NATURE-BASED EARLY
CHILDHOOD CURRICULUM

Child	Shows little interest in or understanding of environmental concepts	Shows a beginning understanding of environmental concepts such as camouflage and metamorphosis	Indicates a desire to learn more about the natural world and initiates investigations	Is developing a sense of personal responsibility within the environment

APPENDIX B: ASSESSMENT TOOL FOR A NATURE-BASED EARLY CHILDHOOD CURRICULUM

APPROACHES TO LEARNING: CURIOSITY

ASSESSMENT TOOL FOR A NATURE-BASED EARLY CHILDHOOD CURRICULUM

Child	Uses a variety of senses to explore the environment	Engages in imaginary play and offers new ideas while playing with others	Experiments and tinkers using tools and other materials	Demonstrates an eagerness to learn by asking questions and pondering answers

PARTNERING WITH *Nature* IN EARLY CHILDHOOD EDUCATION

APPROACHES TO LEARNING: ENGAGEMENT

ASSESSMENT TOOL FOR A NATURE-BASED EARLY CHILDHOOD CURRICULUM

Child	Pays attention to sights and sounds	Sustains interest in age-appropriate tasks for short periods	Sustains attention during group gathering times	Shows flexibility and persistence during activities, even after interruptions

APPENDIX B: ASSESSMENT TOOL FOR A NATURE-BASED EARLY CHILDHOOD CURRICULUM

EMOTIONAL DEVELOPMENT

ASSESSMENT TOOL FOR A NATURE-BASED EARLY CHILDHOOD CURRICULUM

Child	Needs adult help to regulate emotions	Is able to regulate emotions without adult intervention	Is usually able to find solutions to emotional conflicts	Controls emotions in an appropriate and constructive manner (most of the time)

PARTNERING WITH *Nature* IN EARLY CHILDHOOD EDUCATION

SOCIAL DEVELOPMENT

ASSESSMENT TOOL FOR
A NATURE-BASED EARLY
CHILDHOOD CURRICULUM

Child	Parallel: plays near other children using similar materials or actions	Is able to join a group successfully	Joins in and sustains positive cooperative play in small groups	Initiates cooperative, complex, and imaginative play

APPENDIX B: ASSESSMENT TOOL FOR A NATURE-BASED EARLY CHILDHOOD CURRICULUM

INDEPENDENCE

ASSESSMENT TOOL FOR A NATURE-BASED EARLY CHILDHOOD CURRICULUM

Child	Is unable to care for own needs	Asks for help when unable to care for own needs	Tries to take care of personal needs even when it is hard	Demonstrates confidence in meeting own needs

PARTNERING WITH Nature IN EARLY CHILDHOOD EDUCATION

RULES AND ROUTINES

ASSESSMENT TOOL FOR
A NATURE-BASED EARLY
CHILDHOOD CURRICULUM

Child	Listens to directions	Accepts redirection from adults	Follows classroom rules with few reminders	Follows rules and can apply them to new situations

APPENDIX B: ASSESSMENT TOOL FOR A NATURE-BASED EARLY CHILDHOOD CURRICULUM

COMMUNICATION

**ASSESSMENT TOOL FOR
A NATURE-BASED EARLY
CHILDHOOD CURRICULUM**

Child	Uses words to communicate	Names familiar people, animals, and objects so that most people can understand	Communicates clearly about experiences and knowledge	Incorporates new, less familiar, or scientific words in everyday conversations

PARTNERING WITH *Nature* IN EARLY CHILDHOOD EDUCATION

EMERGING LITERACY (READING)

ASSESSMENT TOOL FOR A NATURE-BASED EARLY CHILDHOOD CURRICULUM

Child	Narrates stories	Connects print with oral language and shows interest in books and letters	Associates letters with sounds and can read some words	Matches oral language with words on the page

APPENDIX B: ASSESSMENT TOOL FOR A NATURE-BASED EARLY CHILDHOOD CURRICULUM

EMERGING LITERACY (WRITING)

ASSESSMENT TOOL FOR A NATURE-BASED EARLY CHILDHOOD CURRICULUM

Child	Scribbles	Writes some letters and some letter-like shapes	Writes name but not quite accurately yet	Writes name accurately

PARTNERING WITH *Nature* IN EARLY CHILDHOOD EDUCATION

MATHEMATICAL THINKING

ASSESSMENT TOOL FOR
A NATURE-BASED EARLY
CHILDHOOD CURRICULUM

Child	Understands concept of quantity and concepts of one, two, or more	Counts up to five objects (rocks, sticks) accurately	Makes sets of objects and can identify which has more, fewer, or the same amount	Uses a variety of strategies (such as counting objects or using objects) to solve word problems

APPENDIX B: ASSESSMENT TOOL FOR A NATURE-BASED EARLY CHILDHOOD CURRICULUM

SCIENTIFIC THINKING

ASSESSMENT TOOL FOR
A NATURE-BASED EARLY
CHILDHOOD CURRICULUM

Child	Uses senses to explore the natural environment	Manipulates natural objects to understand their properties and to make comparisons	Demonstrates an ability to sort and classify	Makes predictions, thinks of ways to solve problems

PARTNERING WITH *Nature* IN EARLY CHILDHOOD EDUCATION

LARGE MOTOR SKILLS

ASSESSMENT TOOL FOR A NATURE-BASED EARLY CHILDHOOD CURRICULUM

Child	Can maintain short hike on flat terrain without falling	Sustains balance during movement experiences (such as jumping or spinning)	Can hike in a controlled manner in a variety of terrains (such as hills, sand, rocks)	Maintains balance while walking along a log or ice

APPENDIX B: ASSESSMENT TOOL FOR A NATURE-BASED EARLY CHILDHOOD CURRICULUM

FINE MOTOR SKILLS

ASSESSMENT TOOL FOR
A NATURE-BASED EARLY
CHILDHOOD CURRICULUM

Child	Grasps pencil but may jab at paper	Exhibits eye-hand coordination in manipulation of objects	Uses fingers to manipulate tiny objects	Uses writing and drawing tools with control

PARTNERING WITH *Nature* IN EARLY CHILDHOOD EDUCATION

AESTHETIC DEVELOPMENT

ASSESSMENT TOOL FOR
A NATURE-BASED EARLY
CHILDHOOD CURRICULUM

Child	Is willing to try art projects	Shows interest in using a variety of art materials	Shows interest in using classroom art table to produce their own creations	Uses imagination to create with a variety of materials to make designs and projects

APPENDIX B: ASSESSMENT TOOL FOR A NATURE-BASED EARLY CHILDHOOD CURRICULUM

SENSE OF COMMUNITY

ASSESSMENT TOOL FOR
A NATURE-BASED EARLY
CHILDHOOD CURRICULUM

Child	Does not yet consider the needs of the group	Is developing an understanding of the needs and feelings of classmates and friends	Shows an understanding of sharing the environment with people and animals	Shows an understanding of neighborhood, place, and social justice for others

PARTNERING WITH *Nature* IN EARLY CHILDHOOD EDUCATION

SENSE OF PLACE

ASSESSMENT TOOL FOR A NATURE-BASED EARLY CHILDHOOD CURRICULUM

Child	Feels a personal connection to the classroom and outdoor spaces	Is developing an interest in maps and in understanding our location in the world	Is expanding their understanding of community to include local flora and fauna	Shows an interest in other human groups (past and present) and how we are connected

APPENDIX B: ASSESSMENT TOOL FOR A NATURE-BASED EARLY CHILDHOOD CURRICULUM

PEACE

ASSESSMENT TOOL FOR A NATURE-BASED EARLY CHILDHOOD CURRICULUM

Child	Exhibits a peaceful approach to life	Shows empathy and respect for living things	Engages in meaningful conversation about what is fair and right	Shows an interest in resolving conflicts and encouraging peaceful play among others

PARTNERING WITH *Nature* IN EARLY CHILDHOOD EDUCATION

SPIRITUAL DEVELOPMENT

ASSESSMENT TOOL FOR
A NATURE-BASED EARLY
CHILDHOOD CURRICULUM

Child	Expresses awe and wonder at the natural world	Derives comfort and meaning from nature	Asks big questions about how things came to be	Shows awareness of having an individual spirituality

APPENDIX B: ASSESSMENT TOOL FOR A NATURE-BASED EARLY CHILDHOOD CURRICULUM

REFERENCES

Associated Press. 2006. "'Rescuing Recess' Campaign Launched to Let Kids Play at School." May 17. Fox News. http://www.foxnews.com/printer_friendly_story/0,3566,195821,00.html

Bailie, Patti E. 2016. "Nature Preschools: The Cross Fertilization of Early Childhood and Environmental Education." In *Nature Preschools and Forest Kindergartens: The Handbook for Outdoor Learning*. St. Paul, MN: Redleaf Press.

BirdNote. 2018. "Get to Know the Bee Hummingbird, the World's Smallest Bird." Podcast. Audubon. https://www.audubon.org/news/get-know-bee-hummingbird-worlds-smallest-bird

Burgess, Eva, and Julie Ernst. 2020. "Beyond Traditional School Readiness: How Nature Preschools Help Prepare Children for Academic Success." *The International Journal of Early Childhood Environmental Education* 7(2): 17–33.

Child Development Centre. 2018. "What Is Crossing the Midline and Why Is It Important?" Child Development Centre. https://www.cdchk.org/parent-tips/what-is-crossing-the-midline/#:~: text=Crossing%20the%20midline%20is%20vital,right%20hemispheres%20of%20the%20brain

Dalskov, Stine-Mathilde, et al. 2016. "Seasonal Variations in Growth and Body Composition of 8–11-Year-Old Danish Children." *Pediatric Research* 79: 358–363.

Di Carmine, Francesca, and Rita Berto. 2021. "Contact with Nature Can Help ADHD Children to Cope with Their Symptoms: A State of the Evidence and Future Directions for Research." *Visions for Sustainability* 15. http://dx.doi.org/10.13135/2384-8677/4883

Edwards, Carolyn, Lella Gandini, and George Forman, eds. 1998. *The Hundred Languages of Children: The Reggio Emilia Approach—Advanced Reflections*. 2nd ed. Greenwich, CT: Ablex Publishing.

Earth Charter International. 2021. *The Earth Charter*. Earth Charter. https://earthcharter.org/read-the-earth-charter/

Elkind, David. 1986. "Formal Education and Early Childhood Education: An Essential Difference." *Phi Delta Kappan* 67(9): 631–636.

Encyclopedia Britannica. 2020. "Winter Solstice." Britannica.com. https://www.britannica.com/science/winter-solstice

Ernst, Julie, and Firdevs Burcak. 2019. "Young Children's Contributions to Sustainability: The Influence of Nature Play on Curiosity, Executive Function Skills, Creative Thinking, and Resilience." *Sustainability* 11(15): 4212.

Ernst, Julie, Hannah Juckett, and David Sobel. 2021. "Comparing the Impact of Nature, Blended, and Traditional Preschools on Children's Resilience: Some Nature May Be Better Than None." *Frontiers in Psychology* 12: 724340.

Evans, Debbie. 2018. "Importance of Crossing the Midline." Therapies for Kids. https://therapiesforkids.com.au/importance-of-crossing-the-midline/

Faber Taylor, Andrea, and Frances E. M. Kuo. 2011. "Could Exposure to Everyday Green Spaces Help Treat ADHD? Evidence from Children's Play Settings." *Applied Psychology: Health and Well Being* 3(3): 281–303.

Farran, Dale. 2022. "Early Developmental Competencies: Or Why Pre-K Does Not Have Lasting Effects." Defending the Early Years. https://dey.org/early-developmental-competencies-or-why-pre-k-does-not-have-lasting-effects/?fbclid=IwAR3EWuD0Kd5wqYQ1vkF8Fy_Nu7c0LwoNifQVP6Ysejc3N_eeJdveB0Znw8Q

Fjørtoft, Ingunn. 2001. "The Natural Environment as a Playground for Children: The Impact of Outdoor Play Activities in Pre-Primary School Children." *Early Childhood Education Journal* 29(3): 111–117.

Friedman, Susan, et al., eds. 2022. *Developmentally Appropriate Practice in Early Childhood Programs Serving Children from Birth through Age 8*. 4th ed. Washington, DC: NAEYC.

Ginsburg, Kenneth R, the Committee on Communications, and the Committee on Psychosocial Aspects of Child and Family Health. 2006. "The Importance of Play in Promoting Healthy Child Development and Maintaining Strong Parent-Child Bonds." *Pediatrics* 119(1): 182–191.

Goldstein, Marion, Lisa Famularo, and Jamie Kynn. 2018. "From Puddles to Pigeons: Learning about Nature in Cities." *Young Children* 73(5): 42–50.

Grady, Ron. 2021. "Climbing Trees, Risk, and Relationships: Using Nature to Empower Children." *Teaching Young Children* 15(1).

Gray, Peter. 2013. *Free to Learn: Why Unleashing the Instinct to Play Will Make Our Children Happier, More Self-Reliant, and Better Students for Life*. New York: Basic Books.

Hanscom, Angela. 2016. *Balanced and Barefoot: How Unrestricted Outdoor Play Makes for Strong, Confident, and Capable Children*. Oakland, CA: New Harbinger Publications.

Hsia-Wong, Larissa. 2021. "Learning Joy and Resilience through Kindergartners." NAEYC. https://www.naeyc.org/resources/pubs/vop/dec2021/learning-joy-resilience

Jensen, Eric. 2008. *Brain-Based Learning: The New Paradigm of Teaching.* Thousand Oaks, CA: Corwin Press.

Jensen, Eric. 2013. "Guiding Principles for Brain-Based Education: Building Common Ground Between Neuroscientists and Educators." brainbasedlearning. https://www.brainbasedlearning. net/guiding-principles-for-brain-based-education/

Kamenetz, Anya. 2022. "A Top Researcher Says It's Time to Rethink Our Entire Approach to Preschool." NPR. https://www.npr.org/2022/02/10/1079406041/ researcher-says-rethink-prek-preschool-prekindergarten

Kellert, Stephen R. 2005. *Building for Life: Designing and Understanding the Human-Nature Connection.* Washington DC: Island Press.

Lentini, Rochelle, Lindsay Giroux, and Mary Louise Hemmeter. 2008. *Tucker Turtle Takes Time to Tuck and Think: A Scripted Story to Assist with Teaching the "Turtle Technique."* https://challengingbehavior.cbcs.usf.edu/docs/TuckerTurtle_Story.pdf

Louv, Richard. 2005. *Last Child in the Woods: Saving Our Children from Nature-Deficit Disorder.* Chapel Hill, NC: Algonquin Books.

Marselas, Kimberly. 2015. "Losing Our Grip: More Students Entering School without Fine Motor Skills." LancasterOnline. https://lancasteronline.com/features/losing-our-grip-more-students-entering-school-without-fine-motor/article_c0f235d0-7ba2-11e5-bf0d-5745f74f9717.html

Medina, John. 2014. *Brain Rules: 12 Principles for Surviving and Thriving at Work, Home, and School.* Updated and expanded ed. Seattle, WA: Pear Press.

Merriam-Webster. 2022. "Stand." Merriam-Webster.com Dictionary. https://www.merriam-webster.com/dictionary/stand

Miller, Lisa. 2015. *The Spiritual Child: The New Science on Parenting for Health and Lifelong Thriving.* New York: Picador.

Montessori, Maria. 1912. *The Montessori Method.* Translated by Anne E. George. New York: Frederick A. Stokes Company.

Montessori, Maria. 1967. *The Discovery of the Child.* Translated by M. Joseph Costelloe. New York: Ballentine Books.

Morrison, George S. 2001. *Early Childhood Education Today.* 8th ed. Upper Saddle River, NJ: Prentice-Hall.

Morsy, Leila, and Richard Rothstein. 2019. "Toxic Stress and Children's Outcomes." *Economic Policy Institute*. https://www.epi.org/publication/toxic-stress-and-childrens-outcomes-african-american-children-growing-up-poor-are-at-greater-risk-of-disrupted-physiological-functioning-and-depressed-academic-achievement/

National Eagle Center. 2022. "Eagle Nesting and Young." National Eagle Center. https://www.nationaleaglecenter.org/eagle-nesting-young/

Nir, Sarah M. 2020. "How 2 Lives Collided in Central Park, Rattling the Nation." June 14. *The New York Times*. https://www.nytimes.com/2020/06/14/nyregion/central-park-amy-cooper-christian-racism.html

Norris, Jeff. 2016. "Crosstalk between Left and Right Brain Is Key to Language Development." University of California San Francisco. https://www.ucsf.edu/news/2016/04/402731/crosstalk-between-left-and-right-brain-key-language-development

Page, James. n.d. "Philosophy of Peace." Internet Encyclopedia of Philosophy. https://iep.utm.edu/peace/

PBS. 2015. *E. O. Wilson: Of Ants and Men*. Documentary. https://www.pbs.org/show/eo-wilson-ants-and-men/

Pelo, Ann. 2013. *The Goodness of Rain: Developing an Ecological Identity in Young Children*. Redmond, WA: Exchange Press.

Peterson, Amber. 2020. "Literacy Is More Than Just Reading and Writing." NCTE. https://ncte.org/blog/2020/03/literacy-just-reading-writing/

Riddle, Sharla. 2016. "How Bees See and Why It Matters." *Bee Culture*, May 20. https://www.beeculture.com/bees-see-matters/#:~:text=They%20can%20also%20see%20blue,color%20much%20faster%20than%20humans

Rowland-Shea, Jenny, et al. 2020. "The Nature Gap: Confronting Racial and Economic Disparities in the Destruction and Protection of Nature in America." Center for American Progress. https://www.americanprogress.org/article/the-nature-gap/

Schein, Deborah. 2018. *Inspiring Wonder, Awe, and Empathy: Spiritual Development in Young Children*. St. Paul, MN: Redleaf Press.

Schwartz, Eugene. 2009. "Anthroposophy and Waldorf Education: The Kindergarten Years." *Millennial Child*. http://knol.google.com/k/eugene-schwartz/anthroposophy-and-waldorf-education-the/110mw7eus832b/9#

Simon, Matt. 2014. "Absurd Creature of the Week: The Bird that Builds Nests So Huge They Pull Down Trees." *Wired*, August 22, https://www.wired.com/2014/08/absurd-creature-of-the-week-the-bird-that-builds-nests-so-huge-they-pull-down-trees/

Skibbe, Lori, et al. 2017. "Nature-Based Educational Programming in Relation to Literacy and Mathematics Development in Kindergarten and First Grade." Poster presentation. 24th Annual Meeting of Society for the Scientific Study of Reading, Halifax, Nova Scotia.

Sneideman, Joshua M. 2013. "Engaging Children in STEM Education Early!" Natural Start Alliance. https://naturalstart.org/feature-stories/engaging-children-stem-education-early

Sparks, Dana. 2016. "In the Loop: Let Them Eat Dirt (or at Least Play in It)." Mayo Clinic. https://newsnetwork.mayoclinic.org/discussion/in-the-loop-let-them-eat-dirt-or-at-least-play-in-it/

Spinoza, Baruch. 1670/1951. *A Theologico-Political Treatise*. Translated by R. H. M. Elwes. Mineola, NY: Dover Publications.

Taylor, Heather. 2019. "From Fear to Freedom: Risk and Learning in a Forest School." *Young Children* 74(2). https://www.naeyc.org/resources/pubs/yc/may2019/forest-school

US Department of Justice, Civil Rights Division. 2020. "Commonly Asked Questions about Child Care Centers and the Americans with Disabilities Act." ADA. https://www.ada.gov/childqanda.htm

Vaughn, Bobbie, et al. 2009. *Creating Teaching Tools for Young Children with Challenging Behavior: User's Manual*. Tampa, FL: University of South Florida. https://challengingbehavior.cbcs.usf.edu/Pyramid/pbs/TTYC/tools.html

Walinga, Jennifer, and Charles Stangor. 2021. "10.3 Communicating with Others: The Development and Use of Language." *Introduction to Psychology*. 1st Canadian edition. Creative Commons. https://opentextbc.ca/introductiontopsychology/chapter/9-3-communicating-with-others-the-development-and-use-of-language/

Washington State Department of Children, Youth, and Families. 2020. *Outdoor Preschool Pilot: Legislative Report*. Washington State Department of Children, Youth, and Families. https://dcyf.wa.gov/sites/default/files/pdf/reports/OutdoorPreschoolPilot2020.pdf

Wisconsin Department of Public Instruction. 2017. *Wisconsin Model Early Learning Standards*. 5th ed. Madison, WI: Wisconsin Child Care Information Center.

YoungStar. 2017. "Making Your Playground Accessible." Wisconsin Department of Children and Families. https://dcf.wisconsin.gov/files/youngstar/pdf/eci/makingyourplaygroundaccessible.pdf

INDEX

A

Academic readiness, 9–10

Active learning, 6–7

Adding nature to your classroom, 25–33

The Adventures of Captain Rainbowbeard, 43

Aesthetic development, 73–75, 295

Allergies, 258–260

All-terrain wagons, 36

American Sign Language, 119

Americans with Disabilities Act, 269

Animal tracks, 172–174

Animals, 31–32

    bird migration, 135–139

    birds, nests, feathers, and eggs, 203–206

    handling techniques, 40–41

    hibernation and dens, 160, 168–171

    hibernation and dens, 168–171

    nocturnal and crepuscular, 153–156

    owls, 180–183

    squirrels and chipmunks, 139–143

    turtles, 54–56

    winter birds, 178–180

Arrival, 94

Art and science activities

    animal tracks, 174

    bird migration, 139

    birds, nests, feathers, and eggs, 206

    Earth Day, 198

    evergreen trees, 153

    friendship, 178

    gardening, 202–203

    harvest time, 147

    hibernation and animal dens, 171

    insects, 112–113

    leaves, 130–131

    maple sugaring, 191

    maps, 215

    monarch butterflies, 124

    nature's palette, 127

    new life and growth, 194–195

    nocturnal and crepuscular animals, 156

    owls, 183

    ponds, 211

    rocks and fossils, 220

    seeds, 134–135

    snow and ice, 166

    spiders and webs, 116

    squirrels and chipmunks, 143

    winter adaptations, 162

    winter birds, 180

    winter solstice, 159

    worms and slugs, 119

Art area, 25–26

Arthropods, 215

Assessment, 82–83, 279–299

Attention deficit disorder, 3, 70

Autism spectrum disorder, 269

Autumn, 88, 91

    bird migration, 135–139

    harvest time, 143–147

    insects, 108–113

    leaves, 127–131

monarch butterflies, 120–124

nature's palette, 124–127

nature-based curriculum, 107–147

seeds, 131–135

spiders and webs, 113–116

squirrels and chipmunks, 139–143

worms and slugs, 116–119

B

Backpacks, 98–100

Bathroom needs, 250–251

The Beyond, 45

Bird migration, 135–139

Birds, 178–180

Birds, nests, feathers, and eggs, 203–206

Blocks and building area, 27–28

Book area, 30–31

Boundaries, 8, 231

Brachiopods, 215

Brain-derived neurotrophic factor (BDNF), 15

Butterflies. *See* Monarch butterflies

C

Calming children, 251–252

Camouflage, 125

Cayuga people, 186

Challenges, xi, 237–271

bathroom needs, 250–251

calming children, 251–252

clothing, 240–244

COVID-19 pandemic, 261–263

inappropriate behavior, 253–255

inclusivity, 263–269

inspiring children to hike when the adult is uncomfortable, 246–248

inspiring children to hike when they are uncomfortable, 245–246

the landscape, 255–257

maintaining ratios, 248–249

more work to do, 269–271

preparing for emergencies, 257–261

runners and seed counters, 238–240

side effects of nature play, 249–250

site assessments, 256–257

Children with disabilities, 269

Chipmunk Bridge, 51–53

Chipmunks. *See* Squirrels and chipmunks

Chlorophyll Game, 130

Cleanup, 95

Clothing, 240–244, 250

Communicating with families, 10, 262–263

Communication skills, 5, 62–65, 288

COVID-19 pandemic, 39, 46, 60–61, 71, 94–96, 244, 261–263, 273

CPR certification, 40

Creativity, 24

Crepuscular animals. *See* Nocturnal and crepuscular animals

Critical-thinking skills, 4, 24

Crossing the midline, 14

Curiosity, 3, 24, 51–53, 282

D

Dangerous intruders, 260–261

Departure, 97

Depression, 16

Divergent thinking, 24

Diversity, equity, access, and inclusion (DEAI), 263–269

Dramatic play area, 31

E

Early brain development, 10–12

Earth Charter, 78

Earth Day, 195–198

Ecoliteracy, 3–4

Ecological identity, 4

Emergencies, 258–261

Emerging literacy skills, 62–65, 289–290

Emotional development, 54–56, 284

En plein air, 74, 107, 202

Engagement, 51–53, 283

Enriched environment, 14

Environmental connection, 46–49, 280

Environmental literacy, 49–51, 281
Epinephrine, 40, 258–260
Essential teaching intentions, 46–82
    aesthetic development, 73–75
    communication and emerging literacy, 62–65
    curiosity and engagement, 51–53
    emotional development, 54–56
    environmental connection, 46–49
    environmental literacy, 49–51
    large and fine motor development, 70–72
    mathematical thinking, 66–67
    peace, 77–78
    risk assessment and self–efficacy, 75–77
    scientific thinking, 68–69
    sense of community and place, 59–62
    social development, 56–59
    spiritual development, 79–82
Ethnobotanical histories, 186
Evergreen trees, 92, 150–153
Evidence-based practices, 19
Experimentation, 4

F
Fairy gardens, 38
Fairy houses, 232–235
Fall. *See* Autumn
Families
    communicating with, 10, 244, 262–263
    hiking with, 212, 252
    involving, 24, 197
    preparing for mud play, 229
Fine motor skills, 2, 6, 15, 70–72, 294
Flexibility, 102
Fossils. *See* Rocks and fossils
Fostering community, 23
Free play, 15, 94–95
Friendship, 175–178

G
Gardening, 74, 198–203
Getting started, 20–24
    fostering community, 23
    involving families, 24
    natural materials, 20
    nature exploration and engagement, 22–23
    playing to learn, 24
    sensory experiences, 21
Grandpa Tree, 175–176
Green and Healthy School, 271
Group time, 95
Grouping children, 238–240
Group-time activities
    animal tracks, 174
    bird migration, 138
    birds, nests, feathers, and eggs, 205–206
    Earth Day, 197
    evergreen trees, 152
    friendship, 176–177
    gardening, 202
    harvest time, 146
    hibernation and animal dens, 170–171
    insects, 111–112
    leaves, 129–130
    maple sugaring, 189–190
    maps, 214
    monarch butterflies, 123
    nature's palette, 126
    new life and growth, 194
    nocturnal and crepuscular animals, 154–155
    owls, 182
    ponds, 210
    rocks and fossils, 220,
    seeds, 134
    snow and ice, 166
    spiders and webs, 115
    squirrels and chipmunks, 142
    winter birds, 179
    winter solstice, 159
    worms and slugs, 119
Gunplay, 254–255

H
Hand strength, 2
Harvest time, 143–147

Haudenosaunee people, 186
Head Start, 267–268
Hibernation and animal dens, 160, 168–171
Hiking, 96–105
    backpacks, 98–100
    before, 100
    during, 101–103
    essentials, 247–248
    inspiring children when the adult is uncomfortable, 246–247
    inspiring children when they are uncomfortable, 245–246
    preparation, 95–96
    snack time, 97
    with families, 212, 252

I

Ice. See Snow and ice
IdentiFlyers, 99, 178
Inappropriate behavior, 253–255
Inclusion, 70–72, 263–269
Independence, 286
Individual success, 8
Insects, 108–110
International Mud Day, 227
Invertebrates, 209
Iroquois people, 186

J

Jello-Baby Game, 168–170

K

Key concepts
    animal tracks, 173
    bird migration, 137
    birds, nests, feathers, and eggs, 204
    Earth Day, 196
    evergreen trees, 151
    friendship, 177
    gardening, 201
    harvest time, 145
    hibernation and animal dens, 169
    insects, 110
    leaves, 129
    maple sugaring, 188
    maps, 213
    monarch butterflies, 121
    nature's palette, 125
    new life and growth, 192
    nocturnal and crepuscular animals, 155
    owls, 182
    ponds, 208
    rocks and fossils, 219
    seeds, 133
    spiders and webs, 114
    squirrels and chipmunks, 141
    winter adaptations, 161
    winter birds, 179
    winter solstice, 157
    worms and slugs, 117

L

Landscape, 255–258
Language development, 15, 86
Large motor skills, 5, 15–16, 70–72, 293
Leaves, 127–131
Licensing, 40–41
Literacy. *See* Emerging literacy skills
Low-income communities, 263–269

M

Maintaining ratios, 248–249
Maple sugaring, 186–191
Mapping skills, 43–45, 123, 211–215
Math and manipulative area, 28–29
Mathematical thinking, 9, 66–67, 86–87, 291
Memory, 14
Metamorphosis, 110
Migrate, Activate, and Hibernate trail game, 138
Migration, 120–124, 135–139, 160
Mimicry, 125
Mindfulness, 13
Minority students, 263–269
Missing children, 260–261
Mohawk people, 186

Monarch butterflies, 120–124
Moving entirely outdoors, 39
Mud play, 227–230
Music and movement area, 33
Musical instruments, 177

N

National Association for the Education of Young Children (NAEYC), 6, 232
National Audubon Society, 267
National Center for Pyramid Model Innovations, 54
National Council of Teachers of English, 64
National Eagle Center, 204
National Public Radio, 264
National Science Foundation, 270
Native Americans, 189, 233
Nature and play
    academic readiness, 9–10
    case for, x, 1–17
    dealing with side effects, 249–250
    early brain development, 10–12
    history, 2–3
    learning through, 6–8
    nature–spirit connection, 12–15
    new education landscape, 16–17
    skills and dispositions development, 3–6
Nature gap, 263
Nature's palette, 124–127
Nature's Theater, 48–49
Nature-based classroom
    adding nature to your classroom, 25–33
    creating an outdoor classroom, 34–39
    creating, x, 19–41
    getting started, 20–24
    licensing, 40–41
    moving entirely outside, 39
Nature-based curricula, x, 107–235
New life and growth, 191–195
Ninja Warrior Adventure Course, 230
Nocturnal and crepuscular animals, 153–156
North American Association for Environmental Education (NAAEE), 86

O

Observation skills, 3–4
Office of Energy Efficiency and Renewable Energy, 9
Ojibwe people, 186
Onadaga people, 186
Oneida people, 186
Open-ended questions, 29
Outdoor Afro, 268
Outdoor classroom
    additions to, 36–37
    basics, 34–35
    creating, 34–38
    over time, 37–39
    seating, 36
    sinks, 36
Outdoor exploration, 22–23, 86–105
    animal tracks, 174
    bird migration, 138
    birds, nests, feathers, and eggs, 205
    Earth Day, 197
    evergreen trees, 151–152
    friendship, 176
    gardening, 202
    harvest time, 146
    hibernation and animal dens, 170
    hiking, 96–105
    insects, 111
    language skills, 87
    leaves, 129
    maple sugaring, 188–189
    maps, 213–214
    mathematical thinking, 87–88
    monarch butterflies, 122
    nature's palette, 126
    new life and growth, 193
    nocturnal and crepuscular animals, 154
    owls, 181
    ponds, 210
    rocks and fossils, 218
    sample schedule, 94–97
    seasons, 88–93

seeds, 133–134
snow and ice, 164–165
spiders and webs, 114–115
squirrels and chipmunks, 140–142
teaching materials, 104
winter adaptations, 161
winter birds, 178
winter solstice, 158
worms and slugs, 118–119
Owls, 180–183

P

Patio heaters, 36
Peace, 77–78, 298
Persian New Year, 192
Phenology, 124–127, 221–224
Photography, 73–74
Photosynthesis, 129
Plants, 31–32
Play. *See* Free play; Nature and play
Playing to learn, 24
Ponds, 207–211
Project Feeder Watch, 206

R

Reggio Emilia schools, 2
Relationship building, 17
Resilience, 3
Risk assessment, 75–77
Robin's Nest Relay Race, 205
Rocks and fossils, 215–220
Rules and routines, 287
Runners and seed counters, 238–240

S

Sample monthly outline, 91–93
Sample schedule, 94–97
School readiness, 11
Science activities. *See* Art and science activities
Science area and discovery table, 32–33
Scientific thinking, 9, 68–69, 292
Seasonal topics and activities, xi, 6–7, 40, 88–93,
107–147, 242–243

Seeds, 131–135
Self-efficacy, 75–77
Self-regulation, 253–255, 266
Self-understanding, 4
Seneca people, 186
Sense of community and place, 59–62, 296–297
Sensory and discovery tables, 26–27, 32–33
animal tracks, 174
bird migration, 139
birds, nests, feathers, and eggs, 206
Earth Day, 197
evergreen trees, 152–153
friendship, 177
gardening, 202
harvest time, 146–147
hibernation and animal dens, 171
insects, 112
leaves, 130
maple sugaring, 191
maps, 214
monarch butterflies, 123
nature's palette, 127
new life and growth, 194
nocturnal and crepuscular animals, 156
owls, 183
ponds, 210–211
rocks and fossils, 220
seeds, 134
snow and ice, 166–167
spiders and webs, 115
squirrels and chipmunks, 142–143
winter adaptations, 162
winter birds, 180
winter solstice, 159
worms and slugs, 119
Sensory experiences, 4, 14–15, 21
Site assessments, 256–258
Skills and dispositions, 3–6
critical-thinking, 4
curiosity, 3
ecological identity, 4
experimentation, 4

fine motor, 6
large motor, 5
observation, 3–4
self-understanding, 4
sensory, 4
Slugs. *See* Worms and slugs
Snack time, 97
Snow and ice, 163–167
Social development, 54, 56–59, 285
Songs to sing
"Grey Squirrell, Grey Squirrel, Shake Your Busy Tail," 140, 142
"Head, Thorax, Abdomen," 111
"The Itsy Bitsy Spider," 115
"We Are All a Part of Nature," 158
Spiders and webs, 113–116
Spiritual development, 12–15, 79–82, 299
Spring, 90, 92–93
adventure play, 230–232
birds, nests, feathers, and eggs, 203–206
Earth Day, 195–198
fairy houses, 232–235
gardening, 198–202
maple sugaring, 186–191
maps, 211–215
mud play, 227–230
nature-based curriculum, 185–235
new life and growth, 191–195
phenology, 221–224
ponds, 207–211
rocks and fossils, 215–220
water play, 225–227
Squirrels and chipmunks, 139–143
STEM learning, 28
Storytelling, 62–65, 220
Stress
calming children, 251–252
COVID-19 pandemic, 273
inquiry-based approaches, 16
reducing, 15
toxic, 266
Summer, 90, 93

T
Tapping, 95
Teachers
training, 238
underpaid, 264–265
Teaching materials, 104
Teaching with intention, x, 43–83
aesthetic development, 73–75
communication and emerging literacy, 62–65
creating an assessment tool, 82–83
curiosity and engagement, 51–53
emotional development, 54–56
environmental connection, 46–49
environmental literacy, 49–51
essential intentions, 46–82
large and fine motor development, 70–72
mathematical thinking, 66–67
peace, 77–78
risk assessment and self–efficacy, 75–77
scientific thinking, 68–69
sense of community and place, 59–62
social development, 56–59
spiritual development, 79–82
why it matters, 43–46
Terrariums, 112
Tucker the Turtle, 54–56

U
U.S. Dept. of Education
Green Ribbon Award, 271

V
Valentine's Day, 175–178
Vermicomposting, 118

W
Washington State Dept. of Children, Youth, and Families, 41
Water play, 225–227
Weaving looms, 115
What's Missing? game, 190, 206
Who Migrates? game, 138
Will It Grow? game, 134

Winter, 6–7, 40, 89, 92
    animal tracks, 172–174
    birds, 178–180
    evergreen trees, 150–153
    friendship, 175–178
    hibernation and animal dens, 168–171
    nature-based curriculum, 149–183
    nocturnal and crepuscular animals, 153–156
    owls, 180–183
    snow and ice, 163–167
    solstice, 156–159
Winter adaptations, 160–162
Winter solstice, 156–159
Wisconsin Dept. of Public Instruction, 83
Wisconsin Model Early Learning Standards (Wisc. Dept. of Public Instruction), 83
Wonder Circles, 152
Wood-burning stoves, 37
Worms and slugs, 116–119, 201

Y

Yale University School of Forestry and Environmental Science, 6